the
NEGR
LEAGUE
Autograph G

the NEGRO LEAGUES

Autograph Guide

BY KEVIN KEATING & MICHAEL KOLLETH

Tuff Stuff Books
Published by Tuff Stuff Publications, 1934 E. Parham Road, Richmond, Virginia 23228.
Tuff Stuff Books and Tuff Stuff Publications are divisions of Landmark Specialty Publications Inc.

To order additional copies of this book, or to request a free catalog, please contact:
Tuff Stuff Books, P.O. Box 1050, Dubuque, Iowa 52004, or call 1-800-334-7165

Library of Congress Cataloging-in-Publication Data
Keating, Kevin
Kolleth, Michael

ISBN: 0-930625-51-X

Library of Congress Catalog Number: 98-87760

Editorial Director: Larry Canale
Editor: Dan Sullivan
Copy Editors/Proofreaders: Tom DeZego and John Harrington
Editorial Assistant: Sean Ryan

Design Director: Tim Roberts
Graphic Designer: Fred Wollenberg

Typefaces: Garamond (primary) and Univers (secondary)

Cover Design: Tim Roberts and Christine Schup

Front Cover Art: Rube Foster photo courtesy of
Chicago Historical Society/*Chicago Daily News*

"Not only in the shading of their skin,

but in the brilliant and dazzling brand

of baseball they play, they are more

colorful than the leaves of autumn."

Chester L. Williams

The Pittsburgh Courier, 1936

Table of Contents

Acknowledgments

The Expert Panel

To guide us in our judgments regarding the value and scarcity of the autographs contained in this book, we convened a panel of eight respected baseball autograph experts. This august group has more than 150 years of combined experience in the sports-autograph hobby, and we are grateful that they so willingly volunteered their valuable time toward the completion of this endeavor. They served strictly in an advisory capacity and are not responsible for any inaccuracies or omissions in the signature analyses.

- Doug Averitt of MVP Autographs
- Bill Corcoran of Bill Corcoran Autographs
- Ron Gordon of Ron Gordon Autographs
- Mike Gutierrez of MVP Autographs
- Mark Jordan of Mark Jordan Inc.
- Pat Quinn of Sport Collectors Ltd.
- James Spence of James Spence III Vintage Autographs
- Wayne Stivers of Mr. Sports Collectibles

Signature Contributors

We would like to thank the following collectors, dealers, and historians for contributing signature samples used in this book: Richard Albersheim, Luis Alevo, Doug Averitt, Don Bell, Don Bodow, Todd Bolton, Lamar Bradley, Dick Clark, Steve Cooper, Bill Corcoran, Phil Dixon, Scott Gaynor, Don Gitersonke, Ron Gordon, John Hickey, Dr. Lawrence Hogan, Tony Holland, Bill Jernick, Sandra Johnson, Mark Jordan, Dan Kowalski, Leland's, Larry Lester, Lee Milazzo, Joseph Mitchell, Ron Oser Enterprises, Steven Raab, Matthew Rejmaniak, Philip Ross, Yuyo Ruiz, James Spence, Jim Stinson and Greg Tucker.

Our special thanks go out to Wayne Stivers. Wayne is an autograph and memorabilia dealer who also boasts one of the world's largest Negro leagues collections. He was kind enough to provide more than 300 signature samples for this project. He also served on our panel of experts and provided much-appreciated guidance with the "Negro Leagues Signature Gallery" chapter.

The Historians

There are six historians whose contributions to this book cannot be overstated. The authors owe a particular debt of gratitude to Larry Lester and Dick Clark. Both men played important roles in rallying support for this project inside the Society for American Baseball Research (SABR) Negro Leagues Committee. Larry kept us on this historical high road by editing some of the information contained in the player biographies as well as proving some outstanding signature samples. The landmark volume edited by Dick and Larry, *The Negro Leagues Book,* was an invaluable research tool and is a fundamental text for all serious collectors and baseball historians. Reviewers have noted that the book is "destined to be a classic." It already is.

We would be remiss in not extending our thanks to four pioneering writers. Their works not only served as sources for some of the biographical and historical information used in this book but also played an important role in introducing the authors, and undoubtedly many of our readers, to the glories of the Negro leagues. They are Phil Dixon, John B. Holway, Robert Peterson, and James Riley. If this book inspires you to take a deeper look into the history of black baseball, we would recommend any of the books written by these fine gentlemen. A partial list appears in Appendix E: Selected Reference Sources.

We would also like to extend our special thanks to Jerry Malloy for helping with biographical information on the great 19th-century players.

Finally, we'd like to extend our thanks and profess our admiration for the skill and dedication of content editor Dan Sullivan. First-time authors are a genuine challenge for any editor. We gave Dan rough stones to work with and he turned them into gems.

Foreword

Looking Forward...
and Thinking Back

By Wilmer Fields

Most ballplayers can probably remember the first time they signed an autograph. They may not remember exactly where or for whom they signed it, but they probably remember the special feeling that went along with it. For me it was in 1939. I was a rookie playing for the Homestead Grays B team, pitching against semipro teams. Being on that ballfield, wearing that Grays uniform and signing that first autograph made me feel good— like a professional ballplayer. And I hope that autograph brought the young man I signed it for a little closer to the game. It's hard to believe that was 60 years ago. Today I still get a few autograph requests a week through the mail. You know, I still feel good about signing, but today I enjoy it for another reason.

Every time I sign a baseball, a photo, or a copy of my autobiography, I like to think that the item I sign will carry with it the story of the Negro leagues long after I'm gone. Maybe it will find its way into the hands of a Little Leaguer who will ask: Who was this man and who did he play for? I hope it fires his or her curiosity about all of the great black ballplayers who paved the way for Jackie Robinson to make it in the major leagues in 1947. Today the age of the average Negro leagues player who took to the field during the heyday of organized black baseball, 1920–50, is 76 years old. Each year there are fewer of us first-

person historians to provide insight and to boost interest in the leagues. So if you ask me whether I mind signing autographs, my answer is no. It's not a burden. It's an opportunity. I think many of the other players feel the same as I do.

From the time organized black baseball began to lose its stars in the late 1940s until the time Satchel Paige made it to Cooperstown in 1971, the accomplishments of the players in our leagues went virtually unrecognized. Even during the days when the leagues were a big business, few outside the black community knew who players like Josh Gibson, Buck Leonard, or Sam Bankhead were. They were stars without a national stage. During the 1970s, things began to change. We saw an increase in interest in black baseball. By the 1990s, many of our players finally received the recognition they deserved as truly outstanding ballplayers and fine individuals. For some, it came too late. They died before they could hear or read their names mentioned in the same sentence as Babe Ruth, Ted Williams, Joe DiMaggio, or Walter Johnson. But history has recorded their deeds and names for posterity. And now, fortunately, Willie Wells, Mule Suttles, Ray Dandridge, and the names of the legion of other stars in the Negro leagues galaxy will be passed down through the generations.

The 250-plus member Negro Leagues Players' Association has two primary goals. We advocate the financial well-being of all former Negro leagues players. We do this by securing and distributing pension money and by making sure that a fair share of any profits made from the merchandise related to the leagues ends up where it belongs—in the pockets of the former players. We also work to ensure that Negro leagues history is remembered, honored, and perpetuated.

Autograph collectors help us on both fronts. By paying signing fees, they help supplement the retirement income of many of our members. And, as discussed before, each item they save is a little piece of history, a teaching tool, and an heirloom.

Like many former players, I'm constantly amazed at the prices some Negro leagues memorabilia and autographs now command. Many of us now wish we had saved a Josh Gibson or Oscar Charleston autograph ourselves, but it just wasn't a priority in those days. People generally didn't collect the autographs of black ballplayers. While it's heartening to see that there is such public demand for our memorabilia, I would encourage all collectors to look beyond the financial value of the items they collect and to concentrate on their historical value. The Negro leagues were an important part of the history of our country and of our great national pastime. Help us keep the legacy alive. Happy Collecting!

Wilmer Fields

Wilmer L. Fields
President,
The Negro Leagues
Baseball Players' Association

Introduction

"You said you would pay $20 for a Josh Gibson autograph," Negro leagues outfielder Jimmie Crutchfield wrote in a letter to a collector in the early 1970s. *"I have autographs of Josh and Satchel Paige and Buck Leonard on one card. Do you think they are valuable? I got them around 1946. Would you care for a photostatic copy?"*

While $20 seems like a paltry sum for an autographed card that would today command in excess of $2,000, back then it was a legitimate offer. Prior to Paige's induction into the Baseball Hall of Fame in 1971 and for a decade thereafter, interest in the Negro leagues was limited to a small but highly dedicated band of baseball and social historians. You would have been hard-pressed to find more than a handful of sports-memorabilia collectors who knew of the remarkable on-field exploits of Bullet Rogan, Bingo DeMoss, or Willie Foster. Still fewer would have thought that items autographed by these men had significant historical and, by extension, monetary value.

Transcending the Sport

Times, priorities, and interests change. In early 1997, Willie Foster autographs were selling for more than $4,000 at auctions and in private sales—world-record prices at the time for non-document signatures of a person who died after World War II. Let's stop for a minute to put that in perspective. Four thousand dollars is more than the combined book value of similar autograph samples of Babe Ruth, Lou Gehrig, Ty Cobb, and Honus Wagner. That's pretty good company.

The demand for Foster's autograph skyrocketed almost exclusively on the strength of his induction into the National Baseball Hall of Fame in 1996. This does not, however, account for the leap in prices and demand for non–Hall of Fame Negro leagues–related autographs and memorabilia. The increase in collector appreciation of these artifacts parallels an increase in public interest in and recognition of the Negro leagues as a social and sporting phenomenon. Much of this has to do with the extraordinary skills of these great players: The heat of a Chino Smith line drive. The brutal arc of a Mule Suttles moon shot. Cannonball Redding's demonic fastball or Ray Dandridge's masterful glove work. But to view black baseball only in this narrow context is to miss its broader significance.

The story of the Negro leagues is the story of a triumph of a culture and the failure of a nation. We were reminded of this fact in 1997 when Americans honored the memory of Jackie Robinson on the 50th anniversary of his major-league debut. One would hope the tributes not only triggered memories of Robinson's talent and personal courage, but also compelled us to remember the thousands of remarkable African-American players who came before. Such men paved the way both for Robinson and for those who followed. In his autobiography, Buck O'Neil underscores the significance of the Negro leagues and Robinson's debut in initiating the civil rights movement: "What people didn't realize, and still don't, was that we got the ball rolling on integration in our whole society. Remember, this was before Brown v. Board of Education. When Branch Rickey signed Jackie, Martin Luther King was a student at Morehouse College. We showed the way it had to be done."

Relics: The Footprints of Culture

This book is a celebration of the accomplishments of black baseball within the social and historical context in which it was played. Our mission is to honor the memory of this important institution and to help perpetuate the accomplishments of those who turned sport into an agent of social change. The humble medium we chose to help showcase these legends is autograph collecting. Films have been made, books written, and museums constructed to keep the memory of the black baseball leagues alive. We believe memorabilia collecting has a legitimate role to play in the ongoing educational process.

In a 1996 radio interview, Ken Burns, director of the documentary *Baseball* and member of the Negro Leagues Baseball Museum's board of directors, noted that the key part of the word "history" is its second half—story. It is through storytelling that cultures and societies pass on their legends, their myths, their glories, and their failings. What better way to tell a story than through an artifact? Memorabilia turns the abstract into the concrete. Such artifacts alter tense, making the past the present. To read about Biz Mackey's genius behind the plate is one thing; to see his battle-scarred catching gear is a wholly different experience. The same can be said of an autograph—be it a handwritten note from Satchel Paige, Oscar Charleston's hasty pencil scrawl on the back of a scorecard, or a photo Wilmer Fields signed just for you at a card show. These items transport us back to a different time and place and provide us with an opportunity to reflect more deeply on the full history of our national pastime.

Reflecting on Forgeries

Unfortunately, one of the issues that autograph collectors find themselves reflecting on these days has little to do with the historical relevance of the items in their collections, but more with the pedigree of the items themselves. Forgeries in the autograph hobby have reached alarming proportions, especially at the high end of the market. Even *60 Minutes* aired a segment on fake autographs in 1996, and a year later the hobby was being lampooned in such comic strips as *Peanuts* and *Dilbert*.

We strongly urge readers not to deceive themselves. The autograph and sports-collectibles hobby is a multibillion-dollar industry. That doesn't mean it still can't be fun, but to consider it only as the former is pure folly. Where there is fast (and big) money to be made in an unregulated environment, fraud and deception are never far behind. Dealers, law-enforcement agencies, and trade publications—despite their efforts—have proved unable to effectively police the hobby. In the absence of a forgery-defense infrastructure, self-education is the collector's strongest firewall against fraud. We hope this book arms collectors with the basic information they need to approach collecting with confidence.

—K.K. and M.K.

16

Ray Dandridge (signature)

Part I
Negro Leagues Baseball
The Game...and the Hobby

While the history of black baseball goes back to before the Civil War, interest in collecting black-baseball autographs and other memorabilia is a far more recent phenomenon. Fortunately, the last several decades have witnessed a groundswell of interest in both the history of the black game *and* its artifacts.

In Part I, we'll examine the historical record of Negro leagues baseball, the rise of collector interest in black-baseball autographs, and the slow but continuing progress in recognizing the stars of the all-black game through their induction into the Baseball Hall of Fame in Cooperstown.

Chapter 1
An Abridged History of the Negro Leagues

The course of black baseball history is not a smooth progression across a timeline of events. It is a rocky road filled with twists and turns: leagues starting up, leagues failing, leagues reconstituting and falling asunder yet again. It can be a confusing journey for those who approach the topic for the first time. This section is designed to give readers a very broad sense of the evolution and major turning points that influenced the development of the Negro leagues. Several good books and websites cover the topic in detail. Many are listed in the "Selected Reference Sources" in Appendix E.

The Genesis

The first black baseball match recorded in newspaper accounts took place in New York, on the Fourth of July 1859. While it is certain that all-black teams existed before this date, the fact that the match was recorded in print is a significant indication that the game was of general public interest. It is known that there were at least four African-American clubs active in New York in 1860.

Although there were no formal league structures in place, in 1867 the Brooklyn Uniques challenged the Philadelphia Excelsiors in what was billed as the first Colored World Baseball Championship. Later that same year, Major Octavius V. Catto, promoter/manager of the Philadelphia Pythians, sent a representative to the newly formed National Association of Base Ball Players to seek the club's acceptance into the fledging organization. Their bid was unanimously rejected and the Association adopted bylaws barring black players and teams from its ranks.

The Formative Years

Despite these regulations, a number of mixed-race, semiprofessional clubs were active during this era. Bud Fowler became the first black professional player when he broke through with an independent club in 1878. Moses Fleetwood Walker became the first black player to join a major-league club when he took the field for Toledo of the American Association in 1884. Despite the star status of many black players involved in major- and minor-league baseball during this era, the white baseball establishment began to draw its color line in earnest by the mid-1880s. By the close of the 19th century, mixed-race semiprofessional and professional teams were effectively extinct.

As the number of integrated teams decreased, the number of all-black squads increased. In 1885, the first black "professional" team, the Cuban Giants, was organized. By 1889 the club was competing successfully in the integrated Mid-States League. In 1886, the first regional black baseball league, the Southern League of Black Base Ballists, formed and folded after a few weeks of play. The following year, Walter S. Brown made an attempt to set up the first national Negro league when he brought together six large city clubs from the East to form the National League of Colored Baseball Clubs. Due to financial difficulties, however, the league withered away after only 13 contests.

Forbidden from playing in the white minors or majors and without an organized league of their own, many early black clubs took to the road in search of worthy opposition with the hope of making a living from the sport. This "barnstorming," as it was known, set a pattern that black ballclubs would follow throughout the history of the Negro leagues. Three more ill-fated attempts at imposing a league structure on black baseball were made during the early years of the 20th century. All of these leagues failed to last beyond one season. They included the National Association of Colored Baseball Clubs of America and Cuba in 1905, the International League of Independent Professional Baseball Clubs (ILIPBC) in 1906, and the National Colored Professional Baseball League of 1908. The ILIPBC was actually an attempt by promoter Nat Strong to enforce a booking monopoly.

An Organized League

In 1920, former star pitcher turned successful club owner, Rube Foster, forged a loose confederation of teams into the first viable all-black professional league: the Negro National League. As blacks migrated to the North in search of jobs at the end of World War I, the league developed a sufficient fan base to sustain itself. In 1923, the rival Eastern Colored League was formed. It was during the Foster era that the first Negro leagues World Series was held in 1924. The two leagues would meet in series play three more times (1925–27) before the Eastern Colored League collapsed early in the 1928 season. By the end of 1931—a year after Foster's death and in the midst of the Depression—both leagues had faltered.

The Negro National League was reconstituted in 1933 and four years later, a new rival, the Negro American League, was established. The advent of these two leagues provided black baseball with an organizational structure paralleling that of the white major leagues. This structure lasted 12 years and represented the heyday of organized black baseball.

During this period, it became common for stars of the Negro leagues to journey south of the border to play organized winter baseball in several of the Latin American leagues. Most players considered the pay and working conditions in these leagues excellent. "Not only do I get more money, but I live like a king," Hall of Fame shortstop Willie Wells said while playing in the Mexican leagues. "We are heroes here, and not just ballplayers." Adding to the allure was the lack of discrimination. "I've found freedom and democracy in [Mexico], something I never found in the United States. I was branded a Negro in the States and had to act accordingly," Wells said.

By the early 1940s the Negro leagues were among the largest black-owned enterprises in the United States, with revenues in excess of $2 million. Most teams operated at a profit. Attendance at the 1943 East-West All-Star Game reached nearly 52,000.

The Post-Integration Era

In 1947, a former Kansas City Monarch, Jackie Robinson, joined the Brooklyn Dodgers. While the event was a turning point in both the history of baseball and America, it also marked the beginning of the end of the Negro leagues. As African-American fans flocked to see the ever-growing contingent of black baseball heroes compete in the major leagues, the turnstiles at Negro leagues parks clicked less frequently. The signing of Robinson marked the beginning of a rush by major league clubs to spirit away (some would say "pirate") black baseball's premier talent. In 1948, the Negro National League folded. While the Negro American League continued to operate, the quality of play ebbed as the years progressed. The league limped gamely along for another decade or so, but finally collapsed at the dawn of the 1960s. The last East-West All-Star Game, a pale shadow of a once immensely important event, was played in 1963. A handful of teams continued to barnstorm into the 1970s. Only the Indianapolis Clowns outlasted these, hobbling into the early 1980s on the strength of their comedy routines.

Defining a Negro Leaguer

A Negro leaguer is someone who played in the Negro leagues, right? Well, that depends on whom you ask. There is an ongoing debate in baseball circles about which ballplayers can lay claim to the title of "true Negro leaguer." There are two distinct and highly polarized camps debating the issue. Depending with which faction you side, in 1998 there were either approximately 70–75 living Negro leaguers or somewhere in the neighborhood of 400. That's a sizable difference and one that requires some explanation.

The first group—we'll call them the "1948ers"—believes that the title applies only to those players who debuted in the organized professional black baseball leagues before 1948. They contend that

Key Dates in Black Baseball History

1867 National Association of Baseball Players votes to exclude any club with black players.

1878 Bud Fowler takes the field as the first black professional (minor-league) player.

1884 Moses Fleetwood Walker becomes the first black to play for a major-league club.

1885 First black "professional" team, the Cuban Giants, is formed. The team enters the integrated Mid-States League in 1889.

1886 The Southern League of Black Base Ballists, forms and folds after a few weeks.

1887 The National League of Colored Baseball Clubs is formed. It folds in less than one month.

1880s (through 1919) Independent black clubs form throughout the Midwest and East.

1905 National Association of Colored Baseball Clubs of America and Cuba forms, fails.

1906 International League of Independent Professional Baseball Clubs forms.

1908 National Colored Professional Baseball League forms and folds before the season.

1920 Rube Foster forms the first viable black professional league, the Negro National League. The Southern Negro League forms and disbands.

1923 The Eastern Colored League is formed. It disbands in 1928.

1929 American Negro League forms and fails.

1931 Following Rube Foster's death, the Negro National League disbands.

1932 The East-West League forms and disbands. The Negro Southern League is formed.

1933 The second Negro National League is formed.

1937 The Negro American League is formed.

1945 Six-team United States League forms under Branch Rickey.

1946 United States League folds.

1947 Jackie Robinson debuts with the Brooklyn Dodgers.

1948 The Negro National League disbands (and with it, the entire formal league structure slowly disintegrates over the next 15 years).

1960 The Negro American League disbands.

1963 The last Black All-Star Game is held.

1971 The Baseball Hall of Fame opens its doors to Negro leagues stars. Satchel Paige is the first inductee.

once Jackie Robinson joined the Brooklyn Dodgers, it wasn't skin color that kept a player out of the major leagues. Lack of ability or, in some cases, age were the only factors keeping players out of the white leagues. While the Negro leagues remained afloat for more than a decade after Robinson's debut, the '48ers contend that the teams, ransacked of their top talent, were of minor-league quality as the 1950s dawned. Those who debuted in the post-Robinson era played minor-league quality black baseball, they contend. Applying these criteria, there were an estimated 70–75 "Negro leaguers" still living in 1998.

Into the 1950s

The second camp—the "post-'48ers"—takes a more liberal view of the subject. It suggests that the color barrier wasn't smashed with Robinson's debut. It simply started to erode—and it eroded slowly. They point to strong evidence that some major-league teams employed strict quotas on the number of African-American players they signed. It wasn't until two years after Robinson retired from baseball, for example, that the Boston Red Sox fielded their first black player. The post-'48ers contend that skin color did indeed block the paths of some major-league hopefuls in the 1950s. To dismiss these players as sub–major-league quality is, the post-'48ers contend, unjustified.

Two organizations that work on behalf of former players, the elder Negro Leagues Baseball Players Association (NLBPA) and Yesterday's Negro Baseball Players, are both avowedly post-'48ers. They consider all players who donned Negro leagues uniforms

until 1960 legitimate claimants to the title and to all of the rights and privileges it implies. The majority of the members of the two organizations debuted after 1948. Wilmer Fields, president of the NLBPA, says that all players are treated the same regardless of the year they debuted.

These are the two poles. As is the case in virtually any debate, there is a middle ground. In this case it is occupied by, among others, Negro leagues legend Buck O'Neil. In an interview in 1997, O'Neil, who played in the Negro leagues before and well after 1948, conceded that any talented black player had the opportunity to make the roster of a white major-league club after Jackie Robinson broke the color barrier. O'Neil did not, however, dismiss the quality of play in the early 1950s but noted that after 1955 the clubs were of minor-league quality.

Does It Matter?

Is this just splitting hairs? Not really. When pension money and shares of Negro leagues product-licensing revenue are at stake, where the line in time is drawn becomes an important issue. It's also important for collectors. When you acquire the autograph of a player who debuted in 1956, is the player a legitimate Negro leaguer or a Double-A–caliber player who just happened to play on an all-black club? What about a 1949 rookie?

One of the primary purposes of this book is to inspire interest in the Negro leagues through collecting. We are cognizant of the fact that many collectors and historians are interested in the leagues from their inception through their demise. In the interest of meeting the needs of all collectors, we have adopted 1960 as the cutoff date for players to be included in this book. It's also important to note that the majority of the autographs we feature in Chapter 9, "Negro Leagues Signature Gallery," are from players who debuted after 1948. This is purely a matter of availability. It's also worth noting that none of the players featured in Chapter 8, "Key Negro Leagues Autographs," debuted after 1948, although some did play into the 1950s.

The True "Major Leagues"

Historians consider eight 20th-century black baseball leagues to have fielded "major league" quality clubs. They are:

Negro National League

Southern Negro League

Eastern Colored League

American Negro League

The East-West League

Negro Southern League

Negro American League

United States League

Many of the exceptional independent professional clubs that graced the diamond prior to the formation of the Negro National League in 1920—the Chicago American Giants, the Indianapolis ABCs, and several others—were quite capable of holding their own against white major-league clubs and are frequently classified as being of major-league caliber.

There are five late–19th-century and early–20th-century organizations that, while short-lived, were formed with the intention of promoting professional Negro baseball. None of these entities survived long enough for historians to determine whether the standard of play was of major- or minor-league caliber. They are:

- The Southern League of Black Base Ballists
- National League of Colored Baseball Clubs
- National Association of Colored Baseball Clubs of America and Cuba
- International League of Independent Professional Baseball Clubs (ILIPBC)
- National Colored Professional Baseball League

Other organized black baseball leagues and the teams playing within them should, for all intents and purposes, be considered minor-league caliber.

Co-champions Negro National League
1935

WALKER
LEONARD

YELLOW CAB
HOBART 1212
SHAH & SHAH
BUTLER-FLYNN PAINTS
BRODT'S HATS
THIS STADIUM BUILT BY GEO. A. FULLER COMPANY
THE WASHINGTON POST
ELITE
10
2
RUSSELL

Chapter 2
Negro Leagues Autograph Collecting

During the years the Negro leagues were a viable entity and some of America's largest African-American business enterprises, the vast majority of autograph requests received by players came from young fans who congregated at the ballparks. Pitching greats Max Manning and Wilmer Fields remember signing scraps of paper and scorecards for young autograph seekers. The requests at the ballpark were steady, but not overwhelming, Manning noted. While Manning, Fields, and others may have been fan-friendly signers, few autographed items from those days have made their way down through the decades. Occasionally a team-signed sheet, autograph book, or ball finds its way into the public domain, but unlike major league clubs, Negro leagues teams did not sign boxes of baseballs for distribution among themselves and their supporters. According to Fields, teams had a hard enough time getting enough balls for games, let alone signings. "It just wasn't a priority for us," he said, adding that it was also rare for players to sign items for each other. "Nobody thought about getting Josh Gibson's autograph. People just didn't collect autographs back then."

The vast majority of the keepsakes that have found their way into the market comes from the estates of former players or executives who saved some memorabilia. While stars in the white major leagues penned their way through mountains of mailed-in autograph requests, their Negro leagues counterparts rarely if ever received postal requests. Manning does not remember ever receiving such a request during his playing days. If some players did, the items they signed don't regularly surface on the market. "I wasn't getting any mail until I was inducted into the Hall of Fame," Buck Leonard said in his 1995 autobiography. "Now I'm bombarded by requests." Fields reports that he receives a steady but not overwhelming stack of requests each week.

1970s: A Niche in Its Infancy

The development of Negro leagues collecting as a recognizable sector within baseball memorabilia was a process rather than an event. The year of Satchel Paige's induction into the Baseball Hall of Fame, 1971, is a useful starting point when discussing the development of the niche. Paige was the first "full-career" Negro leaguer honored in Cooperstown. His induction sparked interest not only in Paige but also more broadly in the Negro leagues. As more Negro leagues players were enshrined in the 1970s, collector interest increased but generally orbited around the players honored in Cooperstown.

Several well-written books about the Negro leagues published in the early part of the decade fueled public and collector interest still further, but black baseball-related items were still not widely sought after. Not only was collector knowledge of the Negro leagues limited, but access to players was impeded by lack of reliable historical records and addresses for postal requests. Some advanced collectors, however, began to make contact with some of the black game's established stars who were not yet Hall of Fame members. Negro leagues collecting pioneer Bill van Buskirk had signings with Willie Wells and Big Bill Drake in the early to mid-1970s. A number of items signed by Turkey Stearnes also bear dates from the mid-1970s.

1980s: Gathering Momentum

The 1980s saw an explosion of interest in baseball collectibles of all kinds. While Negro leagues items still did not command the same premiums as rare major-league material, prices and demand began to edge up slowly. Negro leagues collectors began to widen the circle, seeking out players who were not viable Hall of Fame candidates. At the same time, historical interest in the Negro leagues both as a social and sporting phenomenon continued to gain force. In the late 1970s and early 1980s, corporations such as Ashland Oil and Schlitz Brewing sponsored Negro leagues reunions. By the end of the decade, some dealers were holding public signings with recognized Negro leagues figures and beginning to build small stocks of autographed material. Prices for rare Negro leagues Hall of Fame signatures began to increase substantially.

1990s: The Boom Times

The Negro leagues began to garner wide public attention in the 1990s. With this came the advent of major Negro leagues player reunions and card show autograph-signing sessions. Manning contends that 1990 and '91 were the peak years for autograph requests. He saw a sharp increase in demand in

the aftermath of a well-publicized Negro leagues reunion and an Upper Deck company promotion he did in Baltimore. It is unclear whether the mere availability of players' signatures drove collector demand, or collector demand drove availability. The truth is probably somewhere in between. Negro leagues reunion shows became annual (and in some cases, semiannual) fixtures on the hobby calendar. During this period, a small number of dealers began to specialize in Negro leagues items. Some took to the road to seek out players who were unable to attend reunions.

Demand for rare vintage items increased during this period as collectors began to recognize the importance and scarcity of early black-baseball collectibles. Some players began selling their personal memorabilia or donating it to various public collections. Leonard donated his shoes and cap to the Baseball Hall of Fame and sold his jersey to renowned collector Barry Halper for $2,000. "It's probably worth a lot more now," he noted in 1995. He was right. In 1996, Ziggy Marcell's Kansas City Monarchs jersey sold at auction for $9,000.

In the ugliest chapter in the short history of Negro leagues collecting, some former players were victimized by collectors and dealers who purchased (and, in some cases, reportedly stole) valuable memorabilia at prices far below reasonable—and one could argue, ethical—prices. Items were plundered from Cool Papa Bell's home while he was ill. Authors have failed to return one-of-a-kind photos and keepsakes belonging to Bell, Leonard, Monte Irvin, and others. Some resentment among players over such incidents understandably endures.

In the mid-1990s, the opening of the Negro Leagues Museum in Kansas City sparked further interest, while the Ken Burns documentary *Baseball* brought the history of the black game into the living rooms of millions of Americans. The National Baseball Hall of Fame passed a special provision calling for the induction of up to five more Negro leagues players (one per year maximum) from 1995–1999. These events reinforced the importance of the Negro leagues in the heritage of American sports and assured continued interest in the history of black baseball.

The Future

It is impossible to predict the future collectibility of any item, and Negro leagues autographs and memorabilia are no exception. Both Manning and Fields claim that the number of requests they receive today is down from the peak years of the early 1990s, but the stream is still fairly constant. Leonard says he would like to see former players earn more money as a result of the increase in interest, but he also hopes that ultimately today's interest in the leagues translates into a sustainable historical appreciation of black baseball history. There are those who say the passing of the Negro leagues' last stars—and their most articulate spokespersons—will sharply diminish collector interest in related memorabilia. Equally vocal are those who contend that the social and political significance of the black game is still not yet fully appreciated by the collecting public, so that interest in such items is likely to grow as they are increasingly seen not only as sporting collectibles, but also as important relics of America's past.

Chapter 3
A Matter of Fame: Who Belongs in Cooperstown?

Jackie Robinson broke two color barriers. The story of the first is known to virtually all Americans. The second, though less momentous in its ramifications, is nevertheless significant for baseball historians and students of the game. It happened in the summer of 1962 when Robinson stepped onto the dais at Cooperstown to be inducted into the Baseball Hall Fame. He was the first African-American player so honored and the first Hall of Famer with a Negro leagues bloodline.

It was a few small steps onto the stage for Robinson, but a giant leap for black baseball. Robinson's induction, enhanced by Roy Campanella's seven years later and that of career Negro leaguer Satchel Paige in 1971, marked the culmination of nearly a century's toil to bring black baseball out of the shadows and into the full light of day.

To date, Cooperstown has enshrined 15 players on the basis of their Negro leagues careers. In all likelihood, one more will be inducted by the close of the millennium. In 1999, the special provision allowing for induction of Negro leagues players expires. When it does, the doors to baseball's gallery of immortals effectively swings shut on many of the black game's finest players. This begs a number of questions. Are 16 enough, or are some Hall of Fame–caliber candidates being shut out? Is 1999 a rational or arbitrary deadline? How many Negro leaguers actually deserve the honor?

In 1972, the Hall of Fame established a Special Committee on the Negro Leagues to help determine which players are the most qualified for induction. The Committee presented the Hall of Fame with a list of 25 candidates. To date, the Hall of Fame has not inducted a player whose name is not on this list. While it is impossible to say whether the Hall of Fame still uses this list as a primary reference point, some noted historians suggest that it does.

Most baseball historians and serious students of the game contend that the Negro leagues are woefully under-represented in Cooperstown: 15 or 16 players are simply too few. If you are interested in helping ensure that other legitimate stars are considered for enshrinement, we suggest that you make your opinions known by writing to the Negro Leagues representative on the Hall of Fame Veterans Committee, Buck O'Neil. He can be contacted in care of the Hall of Fame at:

Buck O'Neil
c/o The National Baseball Hall of Fame
The Veterans Committee
P.O. Box 590, 25 Main Street
Cooperstown, NY 13326

Every letter received sends a message to the Veterans Committee that fans want to see all of the worthy legends of the Negro leagues get a fair chance at induction.

Hedging Your Bets

Pick up any hobby publication and you are likely to see an autograph for sale followed by the catch-phrase "future Hall of Famer," or the less presumptuous but still provocative "possible Hall

Negro Leagues Committee: Original Hall of Fame Candidates

(In alphabetical order as originally presented by the Committee)

1) **James "Cool Papa" Bell**

2) Chet Brewer

3) Ray Brown

4) **Oscar Charleston**

5) **Leon Day**

6) **Ray Dandridge**

7) **Martin Dihigo**

8) **Rube Foster**

9) **Willie Foster**

10) **Josh Gibson**

11) Sammy T. Hughes

12) **Monte Irvin**

13) **Judy Johnson**

14) **Buck Leonard**

15) **John Henry Lloyd**

16) Dick Lundy

17) Raleigh "Biz" Mackey

18) **Satchel Paige**

19) Dick "Cannonball" Redding

20) **Wilber "Bullet" Rogan**

21) Louis Santop (Loftin)

22) Norman "Turkey" Stearnes

23) George "Mule" Suttles

24) **Willie Wells**

25) Joseph "Smokey Joe" Williams

(Players shown in bold are current members of the Baseball Hall of Fame)

of Famer." In the past few years we've seen these tags hung on Jimmie Crutchfield, Buck O'Neil, Double Duty Radcliffe, Turkey Stearnes, and Wild Bill Wright, just to name a few. But never on Chet Brewer, Willard Brown, or Hilton Smith. Do these dealers know something the rest of us don't? Of course not. But they are good salesmen. And who knows, they might be right. Unless dealers in question have second sight or are members of the Hall of Fame Veterans Committee, however, your educated guess is as good as theirs.

The wise collector—one who wants to build a fine collection for as little money as possible—looks down the road a few years and asks, "Which players are likely be inducted into the Hall of Fame?" Buying an autograph before a player is inducted makes solid financial sense. While most Negro leagues historians were not surprised when Willie Wells was inducted in 1997, many collectors apparently were. Despite the fact that Wells had been touted as among the strongest Hall of Fame candidates by historians and dealers alike for many years, his induction triggered a mad scramble for his autograph. Prices of Wells-signed 3x5s doubled the week after his induction.

For those of you who don't own a crystal ball, don't despair. What you do have at your disposal is the insight of the country's top Negro leagues historians. The opinions of these individuals, as well as those of former Negro leaguers, are highly regarded by the Veterans Committee when it comes to choosing potential Hall of Fame candidates. While the lists below are merely guesses, hopes, or personal beliefs, they are solidly grounded in historical research. There are no guarantees that any of these players will be named to the Hall of Fame; a few listed below are considered odds-on favorites. In addition to the lists provided below, we recommend a close study of the original candidates list of the Hall of Fame Committee on the Negro Leagues that also appears in this chapter. As noted, the Hall of Fame Veterans Committee has to date never deviated from this original roll.

Historians' Choices

Our first list was developed by **James Riley,** an author and director of research for the Negro Leagues Museum. Riley lists the players by position and ranks them according to abilities.

Catcher: Biz Mackey, Louis Santop

First Base: Ben Taylor, Mule Suttles

Second Base: Bingo DeMoss, Newt Allen, Sammy T. Hughes

Shortstop: Dick Lundy, John Beckwith

Third Base: Jud Wilson, Oliver Marcelle

Outfield: Pete Hill, Cristobal Torriente, Turkey Stearnes, Spot Poles, Wild Bill Wright, Willard Brown

Pitchers: Smokey Joe Williams, Bullet Rogan,* Dick Redding, Hilton Smith, Ray Brown, Bill Byrd.

The next three lists were developed exclusively for this book by leading SABR Negro leagues historians. The fourth and fifth are extracted from the autobiographies of Buck Leonard and Buck O'Neil. It's worth noting that O'Neil is a member of the Hall of Fame Veterans Committee. As such, he votes on inductions.

Dick Clark: Smokey Joe Williams, Bullet Rogan,* Turkey Stearnes, Biz Mackey, Ben Taylor, Chet Brewer, Jud Wilson, Cristobal Torriente, Louis Santop, and Ray Brown. *Ranked in order of merit.*

Dr. Lawrence Hogan: Smokey Joe Williams, Cannonball Redding, Dick Lundy, Biz Mackey, Ben Taylor, Turkey Stearnes, Louis Santop, Wild Bill Wright, Sol White, Mule Suttles, and Bruce Petway. *Ranked in order of merit.*

Larry Lester: Smokey Joe Williams, Biz Mackey, Hilton Smith, Turkey Stearnes, Willard Brown, Mule Suttles, Jud Wilson, and Ben Taylor. Honorable Mentions: Newt Allen, Chet Brewer, and Louis Santop. *First five players are listed in no particular order.*

Buck Leonard: Smokey Joe Williams, Cannonball Redding, and Biz Mackey. *The players are not listed in order or merit. Leonard notes that he didn't see many of the early stars in action and thus his selections are skewed post-1930.*

Buck O'Neil: (Pitchers) Smokey Joe Williams, Hilton Smith, and Cannonball Redding. **(Hitters)** Turkey Stearnes, Mule Suttles, Louis Santop, Biz Mackey, Willard Brown, Ted Strong. *Players are listed in no particular order.*

Unfortunately for collectors, the autographs of most players cited on these lists are quite scarce. Those that are available on the market with some regularity include Newt Allen, Chet Brewer, Willard Brown,

Bullet Rogan was inducted in 1998, shortly after our survey.

Negro Leagues Members of the Baseball Hall of Fame

Player	Induction Year
Cool Papa Bell	1974
Oscar Charleston	1976
Ray Dandridge	1987
Leon Day	1995
Martin Dihigo	1977
Rube Foster	1981
Willie Foster	1996
Josh Gibson	1972
Monte Irvin	1973
Judy Johnson	1975
Buck Leonard	1972
John Henry Lloyd	1977
Satchel Paige	1971
Wilber Rogan	1998
Willie Wells	1997

Hall of Fame Players Who Began in the Negro Leagues

Player	Induction Year
Hank Aaron	1982
Ernie Banks	1977
Roy Campanella	1969
Willie Mays	1979
Jackie Robinson	1962

Negro Leagues Journalists in the Hall of Fame

Writer	Induction Year
Sam Lacy	1998
Wendell Smith	1993

Bill Byrd, Hilton Smith, Turkey Stearnes, and Wild Bill Wright. All of these players are classified as Readily Available or Limited under the "Scarcity Ratings" presented in Chapter 8.

Most Negro leagues Hall of Fame speculation centers around the players. Noteworthy executives and coaches are often overlooked in such discussions. Rube Foster is the only Negro leagues executive whose plaque hangs in Cooperstown. We asked six SABR Negro Leagues Committee members and baseball historians to provide a list of their top five executive candidates for Hall of Fame consideration. Those who received more than one vote are listed here alphabetically:

Ed Bolden	Owner, Hilldale Club
David Malarcher	Third Base/Manager, Chicago American Giants
Effa Manley	Owner, Newark Eagles
Cumberland Posey	Pitcher/Owner, Homestead Grays
C.I. Taylor	Manager, Indianapolis ABCs
J.L. Wilkinson	Owner, Kansas City Monarchs

Part II
Autograph Collecting Basics

Our historical examination now complete, you may know *who* the players you might be interested in collecting are, but perhaps not *how* to go about organizing a suitable collection. Whether you"re collecting Negro leagues autographs or those from any sports-autograph field, there are a significant number of things you need to know.

Chapters 4–7 will focus on collecting goals, forgeries, autograph values and prices, and tips on how to acquire the signatures you're seeking. This core of practical advice should provide useful to any beginner or novice collector.

Helpful information on these topics can also be found in the Appendices at the end of the book, particularly Appendix A: Glossary of Sports Autograph Terms and Appendix B: Guide to Grading Signature Condition.

Chapter 4
Setting Your Collecting Goals

So many nice things to buy, so little money. This is the classic collector's dilemma. It needn't be that way. Setting collecting goals that match your interests and your budget is the key to making autograph collecting an enjoyable and affordable hobby. Here are a few pieces of advice for anyone entering the sports-autograph hobby.

Think Twice About "Investing" in Autographs: Collect what you like without regard for future financial gain. This advice applies in all antiques and collectibles markets—art, stamps, furniture, and even fine wine. There is absolutely no guarantee that an item will appreciate in value. If it does, consider it a bonus. But don't bet your retirement nest egg on it. If the bottom falls out of the memorabilia market, at least you have something that has personal value. While prices for rare sports autographs surged in the 1980s and have continued to appreciate at above the rate of inflation, they are subject to the same price fluctuations inherent in all collectibles markets. For those who decide to roll the proverbial dice and purchase autographs and sports memorabilia as an investment, the best advice holds true in all markets: Buy high-quality items. They are more likely to at least hold their value.

If you decide to view your collection as an investment, you should know about something that market analysts indelicately refer to as "The Greater Fool Principle." In summary, it states that appreciation of any collectible object is solely a function of the owner's ability to find "a greater fool" who is willing to pay more money for it. Eventually, the principle holds, there are no fools left. Whoever is holding the item at the end of the value chain must either decide to keep the object and derive some personal pleasure from it (which is, after all, the whole idea of collecting), or sell it at a loss. One of the reasons baseball-autograph prices have increased so dramatically during the past decade is that the number of "fools" (and we use that word only in its application to the principle) has increased at a breakneck pace. If the number of buyers in the market stabilizes or decreases over time, you need to ask yourself whether investing in autographs is still an attractive proposition.

Find Your Niche: If you get the chance to view an advanced collection put together by a person with an average income, you're likely to find that the collection is fairly "tight." By this, we mean the collector had an objective in mind and has been focused on reaching his goal to the exclusion of most other items. This focus generally does not develop overnight. For most people, it takes several years of trial and error. But this isn't such a bad thing. Determining what is available on the market, what you like and dislike, and how much you can safely afford to spend are steps all beginning collectors inevitably take.

Many books on memorabilia collecting note that the scale and scope of your collection are limited only by your imagination. This sentiment has a nice Disney-esque ring to it but is only partially true in the real world. Bear in mind two fundamental issues that have a direct impact on a collector's ability to meet his or her goals:

1. The availability of the collectible
2. The cost of the collectible

Let's look at a real-world example. John Q. Collector has set himself the lofty goal of putting together a set of autographs of all of the Negro leagues Hall of Famers. He has to consider the practicality of this quest in light of cost and availability. First, availability. John Q. has to establish whether or not autograph samples from each of these players exists. Fortunately for his sake they do. Second, he has to determine whether he has the financial resources to purchase them over time. A quick back-of-the-envelope calculation shows that at current market prices a set of cut signatures from the Hall of Famers would cost more than $20,000. At this point he has to be brutally honest with himself. Can he afford the set? How long would it take to compile? Will they become more expensive in time? Last but not least, he has to factor in "upkeep" costs. If Biz Mackey and Smokey Joe Williams are elected to the Hall of Fame, he'll need to add these autographs to his collection to keep it whole. And they don't grow on trees.

Start Slowly: Focus on low-cost items until you've been in the hobby for a few years. Take time to study the hobby. Buy subscriptions to a few of the major hobby publications and some auction-house catalogs. It takes time to develop a feel for the market and to decide what type of

items you want to collect. Use this time to network and build a foundation of relationships, contacts, and information. Also, get a feel for how auctions work by bidding on inexpensive items.

Set a Budget: Every dealer has a story of a collector who enters the hobby with more cash than self control. After a short period, this collector disappears, never to be heard from again. More often than not it's a case of the collector's want list being larger than his bankroll. Be brutally honest with yourself. Can you justify paying $4,000 for a Willie Foster autograph? Few people honestly can. You can build a fine and enjoyable collection that includes many Hall of Famers and other legitimate stars for hundreds—not thousands—of dollars. We know thrifty collectors who spend less than $50 a month and have built impressive collections over time.

Sometimes collectors justify "overpaying" for an item because they intend to hold it in their collection for a long time. Don't get caught in this trap. Before you buy any piece of memorabilia, it's prudent to ask yourself how quickly could you sell it if you were forced to and how much could you realistically expect to get for it. People fall in love and often out of love with items in their collections. An expensive impulse buy could end up costing you a lot of money.

Network: If you are looking for a hard-to-find item, be proactive. Collector forums abound. Classified ads in hobby publications are relatively inexpensive. Apart from simply locating the item, you often wind up meeting people who share your interest and can help you with your collecting goals. The Internet also offers an unprecedented low-cost means of networking with like-minded collectors.

Every Negro leagues collector knows that the hardest thing to find is an accurate player address list. Swap information with other collectors.

Educate Yourself: Join the Society for American Baseball Research (SABR). It's the best investment a collector can make. Good historians make good collectors. Few people sorting through a stack of old letters at a flea market would take a second look at one written by someone named John W. Jackson or Walter S. Brown. Would you? After you read this book, you probably would. The experts get the best deals. Who are the most likely Hall of Fame candidates? Educated collectors were snapping up Willie Wells autograph samples years before his induction. They knew it was just a matter of time. In 1996 you could have picked up a Wells-signed photo for less than $200. Price one today. Every collector's library should include *The Negro Leagues Book* published by the Society for American Baseball Research, and *The Biographical Encyclopedia of the Negro Leagues* by James Riley.

Build Dealer Relationships: Make small purchases from a variety of dealers to get an idea of whom you like doing business with. Today there are fewer than five dealers who specialize in Negro leagues autographs, but most major dealers get some related stock from time to time. After a

while, you're likely to whittle your list of suppliers down to a fairly small number. Remember, you don't have to be someone's biggest customer to be one of their best. Who are the reputable dealers? Ask around. Everyone has a different opinion. We would certainly recommend any of the members of our expert autograph panel without hesitation.

Know a Sharpie from a Quill Pen: Every autograph collector should also have a basic grounding in the history of paper and pens and a working knowledge of forgery detection. The following books provide broad overviews of these subjects and have something to offer for the beginning and advanced collectors alike:

Great Forgers and Famous Fakes: The Manuscript Forgers of America and How They Duped the Experts. Charles Hamilton. Glenridge Publishing Ltd., Lakewood, CO, second edition, 1996

Detecting Forgery: Forensic Investigation of Documents. Joe Nickell. The University Press of Kentucky, Lexington, KY, 1996

Forging History: The Detection of Fake Letters and Documents. Kenneth W. Renell. University of Oklahoma, Norman, OK, 1994.

As your collection grows in value, preservation becomes an important issue. There are several organizations such as the Manuscript Society and the Universal Autographs Collector's Club that can provide information on these topics.

Seek and Ye May Find: Do you live in Texas? What a coincidence. So did Smokey Joe Williams. He hails from Seguin. Biz Mackey grew up in Kingsbury, just a few miles away. Rube and Willie

Foster were raised in tiny Calvert. Get the picture? Think about how many of your own autographs are in circulation in or near your hometown. They are on letters, receipts, legal documents, checks, and even in high school yearbooks. Collectors living near Kansas City, Chicago, or Pittsburgh know they live in some of the most fertile Negro leagues memorabilia hunting grounds in the country. Some collectors who pursue particularly rare signatures set aside a portion of their collecting budget to "wildcat"—like someone looking for oil. The collector drills (via newspaper ads, diligent research, and personal contacts) in an area where he believes a rare autograph may indeed exist. More often than not, the well comes up dry, but the occasional cry of *Eureka!* can make it worthwhile. Take into account the risk-reward ratio before you embark on this type of activity. The more you know about the life, haunts, and habits of the person for whom you are searching, the higher your success rate will be.

Notes for Negro Leagues Collectors

Collectors seeking vintage Negro leagues autographs must deal with two issues that don't necessarily confront those collecting major leagues autographs:

1. Lack of information on literacy
2. Limitations on types of signed items

Most major league baseball autograph collectors know that Shoeless Joe Jackson was functionally illiterate. While he could sign his name, it was a task for him to do so. His wife ghost-signed the vast majority of the mail requests he received. That's the kind of information autograph collectors need. Unfortunately, we don't have nearly enough of it where the Negro leagues are concerned. Historians have enough trouble locating the birth and death dates of many of the pioneering players. Determining the degree of literacy of these players is all but out of the question. Until the database of signature samples grows considerably, collectors should go with the law of averages and assume that a player was literate and capable of signing until the preponderance of evidence suggests otherwise.

Biographical reference material cites some key players as illiterate. Literacy—or lack thereof—is measured in degrees rather than absolutes. Terris McDuffie was reportedly illiterate, yet he certainly signed his name fluently on a variety of documents and even some photos. We obtained samples of his signature from three different decades. Biz Mackey was thought to have a problem reading and writing, yet we have seen a Mackey handwritten letter and several signed documents. While it's safe to assume that people with literacy problems may not have been prodigious letter writers, it would be a mistake to conclude that their autographs don't exist.

Anyone who decides to collect rare Negro leagues material must realize that some items simply don't exist or are so exceedingly rare as to be virtually unobtainable. Balls signed by the 1927 New York Yankees exist, but good luck finding a ball signed that same year by the Kansas City Monarchs. Most collectors who pursue vintage Negro leagues items over time tend to become less "medium sensitive" than their major-league counterparts. The scarcity of some autographs is such that most collectors would consider themselves lucky to find one on any item, let alone a single-signed baseball or photo.

Remember, Negro leaguers weren't featured on baseball cards or Wheaties boxes. There were no cases of balls placed in the dugout for signing or stacks of photos stored on the bus for autographing on road trips. Single-signed Negro leagues baseballs from when the leagues were a viable operation are extraordinarily difficult to find. Few people back then would have wasted a whole baseball for one autograph when there was room for 20.

Chapter 5
Detecting Forgeries

The adversarial relationship between collectors and forgers is nothing new. It dates back to the days of Socrates. When the construction of large ancient libraries pushed demand for original manuscripts of the philosophical masters beyond the available supply, forgers found an eager and less-than-discriminating market for their wares.

In the 1980s, in a modern-day twist on this age-old issue, the massive influx of collectors into the sports-autograph hobby created a similar imbalance between supply and demand. Enter again the forger, this time with an eye fixed on the rapidly expanding market for the autographs of the masters of the ballpark. In his landmark book on manuscript forgery, Charles Hamilton singled out baseball autographs as a particularly troublesome area for collectors, noting, "The quantity of forged signatures of Baseball Hall of Famers, usually in pencil, is awesome. They are turned out by the hundreds, and gullible collectors snap them up as if they were treasures."

At least one thing has changed since Hamilton penned these words: Forgeries are now turned out in the thousands. On top of this, autograph values have increased and the stakes have grown correspondingly higher. What is a collector to do? Is buying a baseball autograph any less of a gamble than rolling the dice in Las Vegas?

Everything we do in life, from taking a shower to driving a car, involves some degree of risk.

So does buying an autograph. The question is whether that risk can be reduced to an acceptable level. We believe that through education and the application of common sense, such risks can be decreased dramatically. As Hamilton implies, a forger's success is entirely dependent on the gullibility—or inexperience—of the collector. Your goal, as someone interested in building a forgery-free collection, is to replace gullibility with guile.

We can't make you an expert at spotting forgeries overnight, but we can help you to spot some of the more obvious red flags, to recognize the anatomy of a fraudulent sample, and to avoid some of the common traps that ensnare collectors.

It is helpful to put yourself in the shoes of a forger. Ask yourself what hurdles you would confront in trying to get your "product" onto the market. There are three:

1. **Medium Acquisition and Application:** The forger must obtain an item from the appropriate era (baseball, paper sample, etc.) to apply the signature to, the correct ink, and the correct writing instrument.
2. **Autograph Replication:** The forger must be able to convincingly replicate the signature of the "target."
3. **Marketing:** Finally, the forger must find a channel into a market that accepts the product as genuine.

Let's examine the first two areas—the physical problems a forger encounters. Forgery marketing will be addressed more fully later in this chapter in the section titled "The Role of Dealers and Authenticators."

Medium Acquisition and Application

On rare occasions forgery detection is simple. An authenticator can dismiss an item without even considering the validity of the signature when the forger makes mistakes in his choice of writing instruments or the item to which the bogus signature is applied. Here the analysis is non-scientific. In other cases, forgers may leave telltale evidence of their attempts at deception. As in every walk of life, there is a wide gulf in the degree of "professionalism" (if crime is a profession) exhibited by forgers. A highly skilled forger is unlikely to make any of the easy-to-detect errors described here. Poor forgers commonly do.

Use of Improper Writing Instrument: The majority of vintage Negro leagues (pre-1950) autographs would have been written with a fountain pen or pencil, with some post-WWII samples executed in ballpoint. Ballpoint pens became popular in the late 1940s and early 1950s. By the 1960s they had all but replaced the fountain pen. Fiber-tips (a.k.a. felt-tips) debuted in the mid-1960s. So if you're offered a Josh Gibson–signed 8x10 in red felt-tip marker or a Rube Foster ballpoint pen–signed letter, you'll want to steer clear. If an item in question is extremely valuable, there are expensive scientific methods available to determine the age of the ink and to analyze other aspects of the item's physical composition.

Use of Improper or Impossible Media: Satchel Paige signed thousands of baseballs in his lifetime. But if you find his signature on an official 1986 All-Star baseball, think twice. Media mistakes are usually more subtle—like Leon Day–signed Hall of Fame plaques. He died the same year he was inducted—but did he sign any plaques? Also watch out for key signatures to be added to otherwise legitimate items. A Willie Wells signature could spruce up the value of a 1990s Negro leagues reunion ball, but was he at the reunion? In 1997, a cache of "important historical documents" were deemed bogus when it was discovered that an address on one of the documents contained a zip code. The documents were dated before there were such things as zip codes!

Evidence of Tracing: Examine paper samples carefully for the ghosts left by forgers attempting to trace a signature. These may include erasure marks and indentations on the paper. A $5 photographer's magnifying loupe (which should be in every collector's toolbox) can save you hundreds of dollars of heartache. Also beware of signatures on lightweight papers which make easy canvasses for tracers. Always keep an eye out for erasure marks.

Incorrect Penmanship Style: Take a look at the signature of Octavius V. Catto, who is featured in Chapter 9. During his lifetime, the beautifully cursive Spencerian style was in fashion. The decidedly less flamboyant Palmer style—which most players in this book employed—pushed it aside as the 20th century progressed. If the style of writing doesn't match the era, be careful. This isn't a problem you are likely to encounter regularly, but it bears mentioning, particularly where namesakes are concerned. You can be fairly sure that an undated letter written in Spencer-method script by someone named Charles Smith is not the Negro leaguer Charles "Chino" Smith who played in the 1920s.

Authorized Fakes: While not technically forgeries, rubber stamps, secretarial signatures, and ghost-signed material can be passed off as original to unsuspecting collectors. Negro leagues collectors need to be on guard against all of these variants. While autopens weren't commercially available when the Negro leagues were active, there is always the potential that one could be used today to turn out high-quality forgeries. This is not as far-fetched as it may seem. In 1996, one of the country's most reputable sports-memorabilia auction houses pulled a Babe Ruth single-signed baseball from its catalog upon suspicion that it was signed with an autopen. For a detailed discussion of authorized forgeries, see Appendix C: Ghosts & Namesakes.

Another thing about forgery to bear in mind is that you'll probably never see a counterfeit $1 bill. It isn't worth the forger's time to make them. They tend to print twenties and fifties. The same principle holds true with autographs. Forgers generally concentrate on high-value autographs.

It wasn't long ago that forgers concentrated almost exclusively on deceased players whose signatures commanded premium prices—Christy Mathewson, Cap Anson, and other early luminaries. But as the stakes in the sports autograph world have increased, things have changed. With stars such as Ted Williams, Joe DiMaggio, and Michael Jordan charging more than $200 for an autograph, they have become attractive targets for forgers. And because the pens and balls that are commonly used when these players sign are so readily available, the forger has no problem—no material hurdles to leap.

Autograph Replication

Writing samples can vary dramatically depending on the time, place, and environment. It's hard to imagine, for example, that the virtually illegible scrawl that came from Roy Campanella's pen when he hastily signed autographs at the ballpark was the same as the tight, uniform signature on his signed letters and documents. Penmanship evolves and changes over the course of years—or fluctuates over the course of hours or even minutes. Anyone who has ever seen items signed at the beginning of a public autograph session and those at the end can attest to this fact. Despite such variations, and apart from mechanical problems associated with illness or infirmity, certain underlying characteristics of penmanship remain remarkably constant when a population of samples is examined.

The production of a signature is a conscious act resulting from a series of generally unconscious mental processes and patterns. The conscious replication of these patterns to produce a high-quality forgery is an inherently difficult process. All but the most accomplished forgers have a difficult time mimicking and marrying the mental and physical processes necessary to produce a passable fake. Most commit errors. Those listed here are among the most common.

Instrument Pressure: Forged writing often lacks the variability in the pen or pencil pressure that commonly occurs throughout the execution of a natural signature. Also, the pressure applied when a signature is "drawn" by a forger often lacks uniformity—often taking on a lighter or heavier look when compared with a genuine exemplar. Such drawn signatures also tend to feature abrupt stops, starts and hesitations and the consequent "pooling" of ink in uncharacteristic areas. Naturally fluid handwriting begins with tapered strokes resulting from the fact that the pen attains a certain speed before contacting the writing surface. Tapers also consistently occur at natural signature breaks and at the end of a word as the instrument is rapidly pulled away. These characteristics are often missing in forged signatures.

Tremulous Writing: Shaky handwriting is often the product of advanced age or may result from illness or lack of writing skill. It is also a common (albeit often subtle) trait when a forger attempts to replicate someone else's handwriting. Such signature tremors are the result of subtle hesitations that occur when the forger attempts to replicate an unnatural pattern or is concentrating on the act of tracing.

Improper Scale: The natural size of a signature varies due to any number of factors such as the size of the item to which the signature is being applied. But many amateur forgers tend to produce writing that is smaller than what would naturally be expected. Some have theorized that this is an unconscious attempt to hide the imperfection of the forgery. Increasing the size of the forged signature in essence magnifies the inherent irregularities. Scale variations are harder to determine when examining a single signature but become more obvious as the number of words in the writing sample increases.

Improper Signature: Signatures can vary dramatically over an individual's lifetime. Many otherwise well-executed fakes fall asunder because the forger did not account for this variability. For example, there is a considerable difference in the handwriting of a young Willie Foster in the 1920s and that of an elderly Foster in the 1970s.

Character Formation: A good forger is usually adept at replicating the individual letters that comprise a signature. Since character formation is the most obvious aspect of a sample, being as close to the mark as possible is essential to create the illusion of genuineness. Ironically, the formation of individual letters is one of the last areas handwriting experts examine when evaluating a sample, provided it is relatively close to accepted standards. Instead, they initially focus on more subtle yet telltale traits such as transitions, starts, stops, spacing, breaks, and instrument pressure, as these are areas where a forger is more likely to fail.

Feel: You may hear an expert say that an autograph "doesn't feel right." The concept of "feel" is more substantive than it appears. It is the sum total of some or all of the technical flaws described above. A good authenticator can usually be more specific as to the precise nature of the error or errors but oftentimes there is no one glaring fault in the execution. Many forgeries are calligraphic Frankenstein Monsters. They are collections of characteristics patched together to resemble a natural signature, but taken as a whole are decidedly unnatural.

The Double-Edged Book

One of the primary purposes of this book is to educate. Unfortunately, we can not control whom we educate. Authors who have written other books containing samples of rare autographs tell us that this book is likely to serve as a template for forgers. It becomes double-edged: educational for collectors but inspirational for felons. We can only hope that the good ultimately outweighs the bad and that our readers will, after finishing the book, approach any rare autograph with due caution.

The Role of Dealers and Authenticators

Not everyone who acquires an autograph wants to be an autograph expert, nor should one have to be. While most collectors enjoy educating themselves on issues related to their hobby, few have the time, need, resources, or desire to catalog acceptable variations of Bullet Rogan's signature.

Short of this, collectors must rely on the vast, complicated, and interrelated network of dealers, authenticators, and auction houses to help them build their collections. While the baseball auto-graph hobby is generally populated with honest, hard-working professionals, some people—wittingly or unwittingly—do a disservice to collectors and the hobby by selling bad material. While the percentage of forgeries circulating in the hobby has been greatly exaggerated by the media and law-enforcement officials in recent years, collectors cannot afford to be haphazard in sourcing material. The incidence of forgery—especially at the high end of the hobby—remains a serious and costly problem. As noted, getting their "work" into the market is the third, and arguably most difficult, hurdle encountered by forgers.

Short of acquiring an autograph in person, every purchase a collector makes, to a greater or lesser degree, requires a leap of faith. Your objective should be to reduce the uncertainty associated with the items you acquire to as close to "absolute zero" as practically possible. Listed here are a number of points for collectors to consider as they acquire items for their collections—although almost all of this advice boils down to one simple statement: *Deal exclusively with honest, knowledgeable dealers and auction houses.* That said, let's look at some of the specifics.

Auctions and Plausible Deniability: Auctions often represent a cost-effective way for collectors to obtain legitimate autographs at reasonable prices, and such venues continue to increase in popularity. This is particularly true considering anyone can run even a phone auction by taking out an advertisement, setting a deadline, and responding to the calls. But buyer beware! Not all auctions are created equal.

Keep in mind that whenever you purchase an auction item, you are purchasing your material from a third party, the item's consignor. This third-party selling coupled with the fact that auction houses make their money on the volume of their sales makes them potential clearinghouses for all kinds of material, both authentic and fake. Thus, these auctions are targets for would-be forgers—they offer an anonymity that insulates them from the buyer.

Think about it. If you are a forger trying to find a point of entry for your work, where would you go? Few would be brazen enough to attempt to sell their products to a recognized expert. An auction provides not only the opportunity to attain near or full retail price for the forgery, but also plausible deniability for both the forger and the auction house concerning the transaction.

If an item sold at auction is suspected or determined to be fake, the auction house, has only to make the necessary refund and return the item to the forger, who can claim that the item was purchased from yet another source. In this scenario, the only thing lost is the immediate sale. The auction house's reputation, in all probability, is left intact because it makes no claim of expertise. Moreover, it followed through on its obligation to refund dissatisfied customers and will probably get a customer-service award for its willingness to do so. The forger once again possesses his work and is free to begin the process again with another auction house.

It is wise to limit purchases to established auctions that offer a lifetime money-back guarantee of authenticity on their material. As in all of your purchases, you want to limit your sources for material to those who are bona fide experts in the field from which you are purchasing. This expertise is not easily acquired and is typically limited to a handful of individuals. It is not normally associated with auction houses whose success depends on the sale of large volumes of material in multiple fields. Successful and established auction houses recognize this need for quality control and routinely utilize multiple consultants with expertise in specific fields to screen material before listing it for sale.

Letters of Authenticity and Provenance: A letter or certificate of authenticity (LOA or COA) has no magical power. It does not make a fake item real. Most dealers continue to provide them upon request as they seem to provide an increased level of comfort for some buyers. Be aware that LOAs can boomerang. An LOA from a reputable dealer can be a forger's gift certificate. A legitimate paper pedigree accompanying a signed baseball from Ted Williams or Satchel Paige can quite easily be "transplanted" to a ball that someone has created. Presto, instant credibility. There have been instances of vendors selling LOAs at baseball-card shows for as little as $3.

Beware of tall tales. If someone knows the history of an item, listen to what he says. The story might be interesting. It may in fact be true, but never buy an item based on a story. Indeed, most forgeries are characterized by one of or two factors: a remarkable price or a remarkable story. ("My uncle, God rest his soul, who got this Josh Gibson autograph when he was a child, left this to me when he died last month....") Again, a good story does not make a forged item genuine. A genuine item needs no paper or tall tale to support it. It stands on its own.

If It Seems to Good to be True…: In the autograph hobby, like anywhere else, you get what you pay for. While genuine bargains do surface on occasion, be extra cautious when you see, say, a Rube Foster cut signature for $500. To sell a genuine sample at that price is akin to that person writing you a check for $2,000, since a genuine sample can be easily sold for $2,500-plus. Few people would be willing to make such a sale out of the goodness of their hearts.

Who's An Expert?

One of the most vexing and controversial questions facing collectors is whose opinion to trust regarding the authenticity of an item. Hundreds if not thousands of your hard-earned dollars are spent (or not spent) based on the opinions of "experts." In the absence of an official accreditation system, collectors might justifiably ask, "How do we know someone is an expert?" It's an important question and one that is not easily answered.

Certifications do not make anyone an expert. Nor does owning a large collection. Nor does writing a book. "Expert" is a title that is bestowed on an individual by others. Each collector in time determines whose judgments (for that is the essence of expertise) he or she trusts and upon whom they will confer the title. If you are at the beginning of your autograph-collecting learning curve, ask the opinions of your fellow collectors. Read the trade publications regularly. Find out who is respected in the hobby. Note how long someone has been a dealer and/or a collector. Ask around. You'll find that the same names keep surfacing. Feel free to ask someone's specific qualifications, but remember, few people trying to sell you something are going to tell you they are not an expert!

Determine Your Risk Aversion

Those collecting truly rare autographs understand that such items often come with less-than-perfect pedigrees. Every collector will at some time have to decide how great a leap of faith they are willing to take when approaching a particular item. Some autographs are so scarce that no dealer or expert has handled a large enough population to discern and internalize the signer's handwriting traits. Authentication becomes highly problematic. Many times this material comes to the market in the form of a signature cut from a document or autograph and there is no recognized standard for comparison. If you are offered a Chino Smith or Spot Poles signature, you might be able to determine if the pen and paper are of the right era, but after that you face a high degree of uncertainty. No viable database of signatures exists. We advise collectors to steer clear of such items. The risk is simply too high. Wait until there is sufficient information upon which to base a sound decision.

Chapter 6
Autograph Values and Prices

Economic law dictates that supply and demand are the prime determinants of the cost of any item—including an autograph. When demand exceeds supply, prices go up. When supply exceeds demand, prices head south. This makes perfect macroeconomic sense but does little to tell us how dealers arrive at the prices collectors see listed in catalogs and advertisements. To get a better idea of how supply and demand influence price in the autograph hobby, let's back up and ask ourselves two questions as they apply to the world of autograph collecting:

What determines supply?
What determines demand?

Elements of Supply

Fixed or Growing Population: The most important element of supply is the aggregate population of an autograph. This may seem like common sense, but it's an important fundamental to understand because it has such a dramatic impact on price. The aggregate population of an autograph is either growing or declining. There is no middle ground. The sample population is declining if the person is deceased or is physically unable to sign his name. We say declining rather than fixed because we assume that over time (and at varying rates) autographs are intentionally or inadvertently destroyed or removed from hobby circulation. Batches of discovered material that come onto the market may represent a temporary increase in the number of autographs in circulation, but the aggregate population is always moving lower if the person in question is deceased.

The sample population is growing if the person is alive and signing his name to any item or document. A living person may not be actively signing specifically for public resale, but his autograph population increases every time he signs his name.

Medium Specific Population: A player's autograph may be readily available in one form or on one medium but much harder to find on another. A Cool Papa Bell 3x5 is usually priced at less than $50. One of the few Bell-signed personal checks on the market, however, will set you back at least ten times that amount. In a variation of that theme, certain Buck Leonard–signed baseballs are easy to locate, although the ones he signed before his stroke in 1986 are not. While having a stroke would seem to limit one's autograph-signing capabilities, in Leonard's case his stroke coincided with the burgeoning interest in Negro leagues autographs in the 1980s, and many post-1986 signed balls reached the market during the last ten years of his life. While these balls are priced at about $40, Leonard-signed balls from before 1986, when there was relatively little demand for his signature, are much scarcer and go for $300 and up.

Frequency of Circulation: In the autograph hobby, you may hear that a particular item has been "absorbed into collections." This means that the item in question is popular with collectors and does not frequently surface on the market. The item in question may not necessarily be scarce in pure population terms but it is scarce on the market. A good example is the autograph of Hall of Famer Martin Dihigo. He signed many items in his lifetime but they surface infrequently. To a certain extent, the fact that an autograph is widely held and does not frequently circulate in the hobby distorts the market's view of the sample population. The market may perceive the aggregate supply to be much smaller than it actually is. Remember, it's what the market perceives that counts when it comes to pricing.

Elements of Demand

In many ways, demand is a more complex variable than supply in a market for non-essential goods such as autographs. There are many reasons for this, but to simplify matters we can say that demand can fluctuate dramatically based on a very human and sometimes economically irrational factor: emotion. While this also can be said of the broader consumer market, it is especially true in the sports-hobby field. Let's take a look at some of the factors that might influence the demand for a particular autograph.

Event Driven: Demand for a player's autograph will generally rise on the basis of an event such as election to the Hall of Fame. The death of a player may also focus public attention—and thus foster a greater demand for his signature.

Player Popularity: Simply put, the better-known the player, the greater the demand for his auto-

graph, and consequently the higher the price it can command. Some autographs are more salable in certain areas. A shortstop who played for the Detroit Stars would probably sell better in the Motor City than in Salt Lake City.

Speculative Buying: Some collectors play hunches on which players will eventually reach the Hall of Fame. They buy players' autographs now to avoid paying a premium later. Such speculation can drive up prices.

Condition and Relevance: No two autographs are created alike. As a general rule, signatures that are perceived to be in better condition or of superior quality (cards signed on the unlined side of an index card versus the lined side, a pen signature versus pencil signature, and so on) are in higher demand and command premium prices. Also, signatures on items with baseball or personal relevance are of greater interest to collectors than autographs on a neutral medium. A Rube Foster–signed letter pertaining to baseball strategy is obviously more interesting to most collectors than a receipt he signed for groceries and commands a commensurate price.

Document Versus Non-Document Signatures: Given concerns over authenticity, many collectors prefer the safe harbors of signed documents— checks, receipts, wills, pay slips—to cut signatures or signed album pages that otherwise have no inherent, verifiable authentication characteristics.

Macroeconomic Conditions: Autographs are luxury items. They are generally purchased with discretionary income. As such, overall demand in the autograph market is, to a certain degree, subject to economic cycles. The more discretionary income in the pockets of collectors, the greater the demand and vice versa.

Price Variations Between Dealers

Collectors often ask why two reputable dealers with the same item in their inventories may be asking considerably different prices. First of all, it's rare that two dealers have the exact same item. In the autograph world, little details—pen type, date, quality of paper, and so forth—mean a lot. For the sake of discussion, however, let's assume that two dealers have the exact same item yet there is a 25 percent difference in their prices. Why does this happen? Is one dealer greedy? Is the other charitable? Pricing variations can be accounted for by one or both of the following:

- **Cost of Acquisition**
- **Individual Pricing Policy**

There is no Wall Street of autographs. Dealers often have to pay considerably different prices for the same "stock." Let's use a real-life example to demonstrate this point. In 1997, a small batch of genuine Turkey Stearnes autographs came onto the market through a collector for less than $25 apiece. At this unusually low price, they were snapped up very quickly. Let's imagine the fortunate dealer who bought these signatures sells them for $400 each. He is seen as offering the goods at a relatively cheap price despite the fact

that he has earned $375 per sale. Another dealer who paid $600 for a Stearnes signature a few days earlier has the item listed at $750. He stands to gross only $150 yet is seen as pricing his goods at stratospheric levels in comparison. Get the point? The price of an item reflects what the dealer had to pay for it and often what he believes the market will bear. Some dealers would simply balk at paying $600 for a Stearnes signature. Others are willing to pay such prices to fortify their reputations and to make highly desirable items available to their clients.

That leads us neatly into pricing policy. Every business has a unique philosophy when it comes to setting prices. Two dealers may acquire an item at the same price and one may decide to price it at a dramatically different level than that of his competitor. While it is possible to write a doctoral dissertation on the subject of pricing, for our purposes we'll divide autograph-dealer pricing policies into two basic camps:

- **Inventory Availability/Accumulation**
- **Inventory Turnover**

By exploring the rationale employed by exponents of these philosophies, collectors can gain insight into pricing differences between dealers that aren't necessarily a result of differences in purchasing polices. Note that the two camps described here are the polar extremes. Most dealers employ a combination of both or have de facto policies that fall somewhere in between. They regulate inventory size and cash flow by adjusting prices.

A dealer using an inventory availability/accumulation policy will set the price at the maximum threshold he believes the market will bear regardless of the price he paid. Because he is confident that he will eventually sell the item at or near his asking price, he is willing to hold it in inventory (and tie up the cash he has invested in its purchase) until a buyer comes along. His high price makes it economically viable for him to do so. This policy is epitomized by a New York non-sports autograph dealer who in 1997 offered a Jackie Robinson-signed postcard for $4,995. Obviously by charging about 10 times more than the prevailing market price, he can afford to hold onto the piece for a few years—or decades in this particular case.

At the opposite end of the spectrum is the inventory turnover philosophy. Businesses subscribing to this school of thought are interested in getting a fair and relatively immediate return on their investments to free up capital for more purchases. It's not uncommon for a dealer to buy a large collection, mark it up, and sell it to another dealer or collector almost instantaneously.

What does all of this mean to the collector? Understand that pricing is an art, not a science, and that policies vary from dealer to dealer and item to item. There is no right or wrong pricing policy. There are dealers who succeed or fail at both ends of the spectrum.

There is one final factor in pricing that should not be overlooked. Just as you would expect to pay a higher price for the services of a top-notch lawyer or doctor, some dealers command premium prices because of their expertise. Those with reputations for integrity have more loyal customers and can in some cases charge higher prices than a weekend dealer at a flea market. As with all things, you get what you pay for. Which is a better value, a genuine Jackie Robinson autograph for $400 or a fake one for $100?

The Meaning of Value

Much more in the way of professional advice and real-life anecdotes could be presented to help you in evaluating cost versus value in building your collection. But in conclusion, maybe the words of Wilmer Fields in the Foreword of this book might prove the best guide. He asked collectors to look beyond the financial value of the items in their collections and to spend more time thinking about their historical value. That's sound advice. We should all avoid becoming the embodiment of Oscar Wilde's quote about people "who know the cost of everything but the value of nothing." Collecting is about more than keeping score in a ledger book. It's about keeping history alive and vital for future generations.

Chapter 7
Acquiring Autographs by Mail

One of the most common and cost-effective ways to acquire an autograph is through the mail. As many Negro leaguers are not on the baseball card show circuit, postal requests may also be the only way to acquire certain autographs. Many collectors have very high success rates in soliciting signatures by mail. Those who do observe some simple rules of etiquette:

- Always include a self-addressed, stamped envelope (SASE) with adequate return postage.

- Requests should be brief, sincere and handwritten. Do not send form letters.

- Do not include an unreasonable number of items—one or two is the norm.

- Do not expect the player to provide material to sign. Requests such as, "I would appreciate a signed photo if you have one," are unfair financial impositions on the player.

- Enclose a reasonable signing fee with your request.

Some autograph collectors may disagree with, or at least wince at, the final point. While it's true that some players are kind enough to answer mail requests for free, others consider it bad business. And rightly so. They are fully aware that there is a thriving market for baseball autographs and many resent the collector who acquires autographs for free solely to turn a quick profit. "I used to give autographs free, but now I charge," Buck Leonard said in his 1995 autobiography. He noted that many requests were profit-driven. Negro leagues players report that most requests they receive are not accompanied by a signing fee. One player noted that even when fees are included, checks for as little as $5 have been known to bounce. If you're wondering why collectors sometimes get a bad rap, that's one of the reasons. The bottom line: If you fail to include a signing fee, don't be surprised or disappointed if your SASE is returned with a price list or your request is simply unfulfilled.

How Much is Right?

How much should you send with your autograph request to make sure this doesn't happen to you? A good rule of thumb is $5 per signature for non–Hall of Fame players who are not listed in the "Key Negro Leaguers" section in Chapter 8. Those who are listed in this section but are not Hall of Fame players generally charge between $10 and $20 per item. Hall of Fame members such as Hank Aaron, Ernie Banks, and Willie Mays commonly charge $30 or more per signature on a flat item and considerably more for bats and special items. These are broad guidelines. To avoid "overpaying," collectors may wish to send a SASE requesting the player's signing fees.

For many former players, signing is an important supplement to their retirement income. Remember, none of these players had multimillion-dollar contracts or shoe-endorsement deals. We urge you to keep this in mind when you solicit an autograph by mail.

Collectors must also recognize that a player has an absolute right to privacy in his home and in his mailbox. Your autograph request is unsolicited. He is under no obligation to honor or acknowledge it. With this in mind, never send important or valuable items to be signed unless you have received a written commitment from the player to sign it beforehand. Also be patient. Players sign in their free time. The speed of reply will vary greatly depending on the player's personal circumstances.

The Address Issue

One of the major problems facing those hoping to collect Negro leagues autographs has been the lack of a reliable mailing list. In the early 1980s, a few relatively accurate lists began to circulate among collectors. Unfortunately, the majority of lists that exist today are woefully out of date. One list that was made available on the Internet was pulled off-line in late 1997 out of concern for the privacy of some former players. The best way to obtain player addresses is to network with fellow collectors. Some have developed impressive private lists and are happy to share them with other collectors.

Buck O'Neil

Part III
Negro Leagues Autographs

In Part III of our study—the heart of the book—the history and the hobby come together as we present both the stories and the signatures of the actual individuals who make up the historical record of Negro leagues baseball.

Chapter 8, "Key Negro Leagues Autographs," is the main offering. A comprehensive "user's guide" is followed by more than 100 biographies and signature samples from our elite group. Chapter 9, "Negro Leagues Signature Gallery," continues with signature samples of important non-player figures as well as those of hundreds of other rank-and-file players who made up the "roster" of black baseball during some six decades of organized play.

Additional material contained in the Appendices will be of particular interest to readers here. Specifically: Appendix C: Ghosts and Namesakes, which outlines some cautionary advice about confusion among autograph signees and their signatures; and Appendix D: Collectors' Challenge: The Ones That Got Away, which presents important information about significant Negro leaguers whose signatures are still unavailable in today's market.

Chapter 8
Key Negro Leagues Autographs

In this chapter, we focus on the autographs of 110 historically significant Negro leagues players and administrators. This roster is not intended to represent the best or most influential. Opinions vary as to who would or would not be included on such a list. Our goal is to present a collection of important figures that covers all eras and positions and provides collectors with a feel for the rich history and evolution of black baseball.

Autograph values were also considered. We believe that introducing young people to the history of the Negro leagues is important. Autograph collecting is a means of accomplishing this goal. The hobby needn't be expensive to be fun and educational. With this in mind, we included a number of all-star caliber players whose autographs are within the resources of collectors of all ages and income levels.

One hundred and ten is still an extraordinarily narrow cut from the wide swath of black baseball history. Any list of this type must include all Hall of Fame players, as this one does. After that select group, the process becomes more subjective. To guide us in our choices, we consulted a number of outside sources, including:

- The 1952 *Pittsburgh Courier* All-Time Negro Leagues All-Star teams
- The SABR Negro Leagues Committee All-Time All-Star team
- Input from SABR Negro leagues historians and prominent collectors
- Negro leagues "Dream Team" lists prepared by various players
- *Total Baseball*'s list of the 100 greatest players of all time

Readers will note that this chapter does not include star players who debuted in the Negro leagues but made their marks primarily in the major leagues, including Hank Aaron, Ernie Banks, Joe Black, Bob Boyd, Luke Easter, Jim Gilliam, Willie Mays, Minnie Minoso, Don Newcombe, and Hank Thompson. Signature samples from these players are included in Chapter 9, "Negro Leagues Signature Gallery." We do, however, include Dan Bankhead, Willard Brown, Sam Jethroe, and Hall of Famers Roy Campanella and Monte Irvin. These players were established stars in the Negro leagues before they embarked on successful careers in the major leagues. Jackie Robinson and Larry Doby are included for their pioneering efforts as the first African-American players in the respective major leagues.

Also not included are more than two dozen Negro leagues stars who do belong in this chapter. The reason? There simply are, to our knowledge, no irrefutable signature samples available. Please consult Appendix D: Collectors' Challenge: The Ones That Got Away for biographical information and career stats and highlights for such venerable Negro leaguers as Bingo DeMoss, Oliver Marcelle, Jose Mendez, Cannonball Redding, and George Stovey, among others.

How to Use This Guide

The entries in this chapter contain biographical information, playing statistics, and, where possible, photographs of our key Negro leaguers. In addition, we present an assortment of signature samples of each player, a detailed analysis of his signature (when possible), and price/availability guidelines.

Biographies/Career Statistics

Player Names: The names listed in large typeface are those by which the player is commonly known within the collecting community. The player's full legal name appears directly underneath along with the notation a.k.a.—also known as—appearing where applicable.

Career: We list the years the individual was active in baseball as a player, coach, or executive. In some instances this includes the Cuban, Mexican, minor, or major leagues. Years as a scout are generally not included.

Primary Teams: We list the primary one-to-three teams with which the player is most commonly associated. As a general rule, we list a team if the player was on its roster for five years or more. If a player was notoriously nomadic, we note Various Teams and/or Various Leagues.

Biographical Data: We provide the year and place of birth and death where available. In some cases, the information is incomplete or was unavailable. Negro leagues historians will note that a substantial number of the dates listed here differ from previous reference books. These new dates are the result of recent findings from members of the SABR Negro Leagues Committee.

Career Overview: In an attempt to place the contribution of the player or administrator into context, we have included a short career resumé on each. These were written with the beginning collector in mind. *The Negro Leagues Book,* James Riley's *Biographical Encyclopedia of the Negro Baseball Leagues,* John Holway's *Black Baseball Stars,* and Mike Shatzkin's *The Ballplayers* served as primary source materials.

Player Photos: Where possible, we have included an artistic or photographic image of the player. As the Negro leagues were not widely covered by major news organizations nor were the images of black ballplayers used for product endorsements, photographic records are sketchy. Single-player images are even more rare, thus many of the photos shown here were gleaned from team photos. Those images that have survived are often prints several generations removed from the original and hence, characteristically grainy.

Notes on Negro Leagues Statistics

While the Negro leagues were in many ways well organized, keeping statistics was not a priority. As such, today we are left with a shortfall of accurate quantitative information on player performance. Thanks to the ongoing and determined efforts of groups such as the SABR Negro Leagues Committee, more pieces of the complex statistical jigsaw puzzle fall into place every year. But as noted in

The Negro Leagues Book, "This is a mammoth task that is nowhere near complete."

The numbers we provide in this section should be regarded as more qualitative than rigorously quantitative indicators of performance. The quality of the box scores historians have relied upon to recreate the past renders Negro leagues statistical reconstruction as much an art as a science. Many performance indicators considered indispensable today, such as stolen bases, strikeouts, or at-bats, were commonly left out of game reports.

For a period, the Elias bureau showed an interest in gathering the statistics from league games, but its plan fell asunder, as did those of some well-intentioned newspapers that sent reporters to keep the scorebook. One in particular who covered the Grays failed worse than most. Buck Leonard says, "He'd show up in the third inning and ask one of the players on the bench, 'What happened in the first inning?'...and if the guy didn't see what happened on the field, he'd put down, 'singled to center' or 'flied out to center.'... So finally we gave him the nickname 'Singled to Center.' Or he'd come in and say, 'Got a pencil?' What would we be doing with a pencil!... They'd [these reporters] say 'so-and-so doubled to right and so-and-so walked'...and none of it was true!"

The numbers used throughout this book were in many cases gleaned from the Baseball Encyclopedia and are based primarily on the work of the SABR Negro Leagues Committee. We have decided not to pepper the text with the countless qualifications such as "according to available statistics." We ask that the reader to take into account the less-than-perfect nature of the numbers as well as the following points:

- During the 1920s, some Negro leagues teams played as many as 70–90 "official" games per season. This figure does not include barnstorming or exhibition contests. During the 1930s and 1940s, the number of league games played fell dramatically—sometimes to well under 60 league-sanctioned contests. This was a simple matter of economics. There was more money to be made barnstorming. These variations make comparison of career records difficult at best. Players whose careers spanned the 1920s tend to have greater lifetime numbers than those who took to the diamond in the 1930s and 1940s. Case in point: Turkey Stearnes. Stearnes, who played a good portion of his career in the 1920s, is the all-time Negro leagues home run leader. He tallied 181 round trippers in his 18-year, 903-game career. Josh Gibson, a man widely regarded as black baseball's premier power hitter, knocked 146 home runs in 16 seasons despite playing in just over half as many official games, 501. This is because Gibson played in the 1930s and 1940s.

- In the player biographies we often use the caveat "against all levels of competition" when describing a pitcher's record or a hitter's performance. This implies that the pitching or hitting record we refer to is an aggregate of league play, barnstorming games, and exhibitions. Since many

Negro leagues clubs were major-league quality and their non-league opponents were not, figures carrying this caveat tend to be somewhat inflated.

- Much of the available Negro leagues pitching data was derived from linescores or written accounts of games. As a result, earned run averages are not available. Strikeouts and bases on balls are generally understated. It's also worth noting that due to small rosters, complete games were far more commonplace than in the white major leagues.

- The best Negro leaguers may seem to have higher batting averages than the best white major leaguers of similar eras. One of the reasons commonly cited for this variation was the depth of pitching on the Negro leagues squads—or rather the lack thereof. Economics dictated that black clubs carry about 14–18 players per team. It was rare for a club to keep a stable of more than five pitchers. Because hurlers were in short supply, they tended to stay in games much longer than their major-league counterparts, whether or not they were getting knocked around. Also, with such spartan rotations, it's likely that Negro leagues hitters also faced more sore-armed starters. Several Negro leagues players have suggested that lack of pitching depth was about the only thing that set black baseball apart from the white majors. That said, it's worth noting that in games against their white counterparts, the black players hit at about the same clip as they did in the Negro leagues, suggesting that the differential may not have been particularly dramatic.

- Park sizes and conditions are always a variable in baseball, but in the Negro leagues the differences were often enormous. As such, they produced some noteworthy anomalies. In the 1920s, the St. Louis Stars played in a park that Cool Papa Bell said had more garbage than grass. "The fence was about to fall down and so were the bleachers. It didn't seem much better than playing in the fields back in Mississippi." It also featured a Little League–caliber 250-foot left-field fence. At the other end of the spectrum, the Homestead Grays played many of their games in Griffith Stadium, home of the Washington Senators. Imagine Josh Gibson's home run count if he would have played in some cozy park rather than in such cavernous confines.

- The most eagerly awaited event on the Negro leagues calendar was the East-West All-Star Game. Its popularity exceeded that of the Negro leagues World Series. The matchups proved so popular and profitable that two games were played in 1939, 1942, and 1946–48. Keep this in mind when we refer to the number of all-star appearances made by a player. Stars from the late 1940s will generally have more appearances than their counterparts in the preceding decade.

The *Pittsburgh Courier* Poll

One of the better reference points for Negro leagues player performance is a poll conducted by the *Pittsburgh Courier* newspaper in 1952. This influential African-American newspaper asked a panel of black baseball veterans and sportswriters to cast votes for the best Negro leagues players of all time. Based on their input, the paper published a list of five all-star squads and a list of honorable mentions. Most historians agree that those surveyed did an admirable job in rating the game's greats. We believe these results shed a considerable amount of light on a player's value to his team—perhaps even more so than available statistics. Where relevant, we note how a player fared in the poll. We refer to it simply as the *Courier* poll.

Signature Samples

We provide a sample, and in some case multiple samples, of the player's autograph. In an effort to ensure the authenticity of these signatures, every attempt was made to source the standards from signed contracts, personal and endorsed checks, and signed correspondence. As Negro leagues autographs are in many cases exponentially more scarce than those of white major league players of comparable eras, locating document signatures was not always possible. In some cases we feature signatures on 3x5 index cards and other non-document media. These were generally used in those instances where the player in question died after 1970. In such cases there are generally enough samples in the hobby for our autograph panel to authenticate them beyond a reasonable doubt. Any sample that was called in question by any panel member during the review process was eliminated from the book.

We note the source and approximate date or era of the signature and any anomalies or points of interest.

Pittsburgh Courier All-Time All-Star Teams

	First Team	Second Team	Third Team
1B	Buck Leonard	Ben Taylor	Jud Wilson
2B	Jackie Robinson	Bingo DeMoss	Bill Monroe
SS	Pop Lloyd	Willie Wells, Sr.	Dick Lundy
3B	Oliver Marcelle	Judy Johnson	Jud Wilson
LF	Monte Irvin	Pete Hill	Rap Dixon
CF	Oscar Charleston	Cool Papa Bell	Larry Doby
RF	Cristobal Torriente	Chino Smith	Fats Jenkins
C	Josh Gibson	Roy Campanella	Ted Radcliffe
	Biz Mackey	Bruce Petway	Louis Santop
P	Joe Williams	Dave Brown	Slim Jones
	Satchel Paige	Dick Redding	Bill Holland
	Bullet Rogan	Nip Winters	Phil Cockrell
	John Donaldson	Dizzy Dismukes	Webster McDonald
	Bill Foster	Don Newcombe	Bill Byrd
Util.	Martin Dihigo	John Beckwith	Emmett Bowman
	Sam Bankhead	Newt Allen	Dick Wallace
Mgr.	Rube Foster	Cum Posey	Ed Bolden
Coach	Dizzy Dismukes	C.I. Taylor	
	Danny McClellan	Dave Malarcher	

	Fourth Team	Fifth Team
1B	Ed Douglas	George Carr
2B	George Scales	Bunny Downs
SS	Dobie Moore	Pelayo Chacon
3B	Ray Dandridge	Dave Malarcher
LF	Jimmy Lyons	Frank Duncan
CF	Mule Suttles	Turkey Stearnes
RF	Spot Poles	Jelly Gardner
C	Frank Duncan	Doc Wiley
	Bill Perkins	Speck Webster
P	Ted Radcliffe	Stringbean Williams
	Frank Wickware	Ray Brown
	Danny McClellan	Rats Henderson
	Leon Day	Luis Tiant Sr.
	Bill Jackman	Leroy Matlock
Util.	Rev Cannady	Jose Mendez
Mgr.	Vic Harris	

Honorable Mentions: 1B) Leroy Grant, Mule Suttles; **2B)** Nate Harris, Sammy T. Hughes, Frank Warfield, Ray Dandridge, George Wright, Harry Williams; **SS)** Gerard Williams, Bobby Williams, Morton Clark; **3B)** Bill Francis, Jim Taylor; **OF)** Minnie Minoso, Jap Payne, Blaine Hall, Ted Strong, Ted Page, Vic Harris; **P)** Jose Mendez, Lamon Yokely.

Where a sufficient number of samples of a player's autograph exist, we provide an analysis of his signature. We also note where the database of samples is insufficient for a detailed analysis.

In those cases where personal checks signed by the player are circulating in the hobby, we note the estimated number in circulation. The circulation estimates for Hall of Fame players are from James Spence III Autographs, which monitors these figures. Estimates of non–Hall of Fame players were provided by panel members or gleaned from reference material.

Glossary of Terms

The following are terms that are commonly used in the signature analyses contained in this book.

Break or Pen Lift: Point at which the writing instrument is removed from the surface of the signed item.

Figure-8: As the name implies, a character formation resembling the numeral "8."

Open Letter: Incomplete closure of a letter. Used primarily in conjunction with a letter with a rounded appearance.

Horizontal Plane: The highest horizontal point in a signature sample.

Letter Space Variability: The degree to which the space between character formations vary in a given sample.

Character Size Variability: The degree to which the size of the character formations vary in a given sample.

Peak: The highest ascending point in a signature sample.

Seated Sample: Implies a signature written in no particular haste (such as that on an official document) as opposed to a sample signed quickly, such as those signed briskly by an individual processing a multitude of signature requests.

Stylized vs. Traditional Letter: In common philograpical terms, stylized refers to characters that appear "printed" as opposed to traditional letters, which are formed in a "cursive" Palmer-method style.

Instrument Pressure: Refers to the degree of pressure applied to the pen, pencil or other instrument when making an imprint.

Signature Slant

The late autograph expert Charles Hamilton contends that major court cases involving the authenticity of a signature have been won or lost based on the slant of the writing. As such, the angle at which the writer leaves his mark on the writing surface is an import factor to consider when separating philographic fact from fiction. We employed a

Signature Slant Calculation

90 degrees   "l" slant=120 degrees

John Q. Public

variation of the slant analysis methodology used by Hamilton in the analyses conducted for this book. Working from the base of the signature, we plotted the trajectory of the tallest ascending character, usually a "t," "l" or the stems of the letters "b" or "d." Ninety degrees represents a perfectly vertical character line. Numbers greater than 90 degrees indicate a slant to the right, less than 90 degrees a slant to the left. The Hamilton method works remarkably well when there is a baseline for the writer to sign on—such as that on a personal check or contract. The degree of signature slant is fairly consistent under such circumstances. On unlined paper—such as an autograph book or personal letters—the degree of variability increases and thus the margin of error. We measured only the slant of those signatures where the sample base was large enough to render the analysis useful, something collectors should note when evaluating a signature.

Consistent Slant: Implies a standard variation of plus/minus 5 to 10 degrees.

Standard Slant: Implies a standard variation of plus/minus 10 to 15 degrees.

Inconsistent Slant: Implies a standard variation of plus/minus 15 degrees or more.

Scarcity Ratings

We provide subjective ratings reflecting the availability of the player's autograph within the baseball autograph hobby. These ratings are based on input from the autograph panel and several longtime Negro leagues collectors. We do not use the date of a player's death as the sole criterion for classification. While it is certainly a primary factor in the scarcity equation, it is only one of many factors impacting the potential population and availability of an autograph.

Readily Available: An autograph that can be easily located through dealers or at sports collectors conventions. Generally that of a living player or a player deceased after 1990.

Limited: An autograph available on the market but in limited quantities. Generally that of a player deceased between 1980 and 1990. Genuine samples may surface publicly on a monthly/quarterly basis.

Very Limited: An autograph that occasionally surfaces on the market. Generally that of a player deceased between 1970 and 1980. Genuine samples may surface publicly on a semiannual/annual basis.

Scarce: An autograph that rarely surfaces on the market. Usually that of a player deceased between 1960 and 1970. Genuine samples may surface publicly on an annual basis.

Rare: A limited number are known to exist in the hobby. Genuine samples may surface publicly on a one- to five-year basis.

Very Rare: Less than 10 authentic samples are known in the hobby. Samples are rarely offered more than once every five years.

Keep in mind that an autograph deemed "Rare" at the time of publication may in time become more common. Large finds of material do occur.

Price Guidelines

This section offers broad guidelines for the retail price of an item. We do not provide standard book values.

The price ranges published here were derived from advertisements of authentic items sold by reputable dealers in the trade press, and through catalogs and auctions. Prices realized in private sales were also taken into account. Our expert panel of dealers and collectors provided further guidance. We opted to provide broad price guidelines rather than the "average" price indices offered in standard price guides for the following reasons:

1. The Forgery Effect: Calculating the average retail price of an item is a beautifully simple means of establishing the book value of an item. This system works well for baseball cards and other items where forgeries are not epidemic and condition variables are accounted for. Neither of these important factors, however, are usually considered when setting book prices for autographs. As a general rule, bogus autographed material tends to be offered at bargain basement prices. As such, it reduces average prices to unrealistic levels. The more commonly forged the item in question, the greater the gap between the fantasy of the book price and the reality of the marketplace for genuine samples.

While condition is an all-important consideration in the realm of card collecting, it is generally not properly accounted for in setting book values for autographs. As most collectors know, not all cuts or 3x5s are created alike, but when prices are averaged to determine book value they are generally treated the same. Common sense says that an ink-signed government postcard from someone's playing days is worth considerably more than the same autograph on a soiled napkin.

2. The Comparable Player Scenario: If the database of retail price information on a player's autograph is small, some price guides will look to the prevailing market price for a player of similar merit. In the case of deceased players, they may look for a player of similar merit who died the same year or close to it. This system can produce odd results. Is a Willie Foster (d. 1978) autograph comparable in scarcity and value to that of Hall of Famer Heinie Manush, who died in 1977? Some price guides say yes. In 1997, one listed the book value of a Willie Foster–signed 8x10 photo at $200 and a signed baseball at $1,500. No member of our expert panel (which has well over a century of combined autograph-hobby experience) has ever heard of or seen a Foster-signed 8x10 or single-signed ball. The last Foster items to hit the open market—two signed 3x5 index cards—sold at auction for more than $4,000 each. It's hard to imagine premium items such as balls or 8x10 photos selling for substantially less than that.

So are price guides useful at all? Absolutely. If you are looking for a more common item such as a Buck O'Neil–signed baseball or Ray Dandridge–

signed photo, they're usually very close to the mark. But keep in mind that the validity of a book price decreases as the scarcity of an item increases.

Living Players and Those Deceased Post-1970

For living players and those deceased after 1970, we provide broad price guidelines for ink-signed, non-personalized 3x5 index cards that are autographed on the unlined side. The physical condition of the card and the signature will also have an impact on the price. We chose 3x5 cards as the benchmark medium for a number of reasons:

- They are the basic medium on which many collectors acquire autographs through the mail. It has been the collector's choice for this purpose since the 1930s.

- They are a neutral medium with relatively low variability in composition and fewer condition variables than other signed items.

- They are one of the most cost-effective and convenient mediums for collectors to obtain an autograph.

Players Deceased Pre-1970

For players deceased before 1970, the value guidelines apply to cut signatures and/or 3x5 index cards, as described previously. Negro leagues signatures were not widely collected through the mail before the late 1970s, thus the amount of 3x5 cards signed by these players is limited. The size, closeness of cut, suitability for matting, and the overall physical condition of a cut signature will have an impact on its value.

Signed contracts, personal and/or endorsed checks, letters, and other documents command a significant premium over the prices noted for cut signatures and 3x5s. Expect the premium to be even greater if the document in question has significant personal or baseball content.

The guidelines published here are valid only at the time of publication. Large finds of new material, or increases or decreases in demand, inflation, appreciation, and a variety of related factors all contribute significantly to fluctuations in prices.

Value Categories

The price-range line for each entry provides broad value categories reflecting the prevailing retail price of the autographs. Prices will vary among dealers owing to a number of factors, including the price the dealer paid for the signature, regional demand, the condition of the signature, the writing instrument employed, etc. For purposes of this exercise, we assume that the signature in question is in Near-Mint condition.

- Less than $25
- $25–100
- $100–250
- $250–500
- $500–1,000
- $1,000–2,000
- $2,000–4,000
- *Not Established:* Indicates that the number of samples circulating within the hobby is limited to the extent that there is no prevailing market price. It does not imply a value greater than $2,000–4,000. The value may in fact be substantially less.

In cases where the signature was at the extreme high end of a price range, we generally classified it in the next-highest value category, taking into account historical appreciation rates. In some cases we deviate from these standard categories to provide a more precise representation of prevailing prices.

Single-Signed Baseballs

We also provide broad price guidelines for single-signed baseballs that are readily available on the market. These include living players, those deceased after 1990, and Hall of Fame players who died after 1980. Before the 1990s, it was rare for collectors to seek non–Hall of Fame Negro leagues signatures on balls. There are no single-signed baseballs readily circulating within the hobby for approximately 70 percent of the people listed in the "Key Negro Leaguers" section of this chapter that follows.

Signature Reproduction

Ideally all of the signatures featured here would be reproduced at photographic quality from the original documents. Many of the autographs we present, however, are from libraries, museums, or personal collections, so that in most cases only photocopies were available. In some instances, the quality of the sample we received was substandard but the signature was rare enough to justify its reproduction. We did the best we could with what we had.

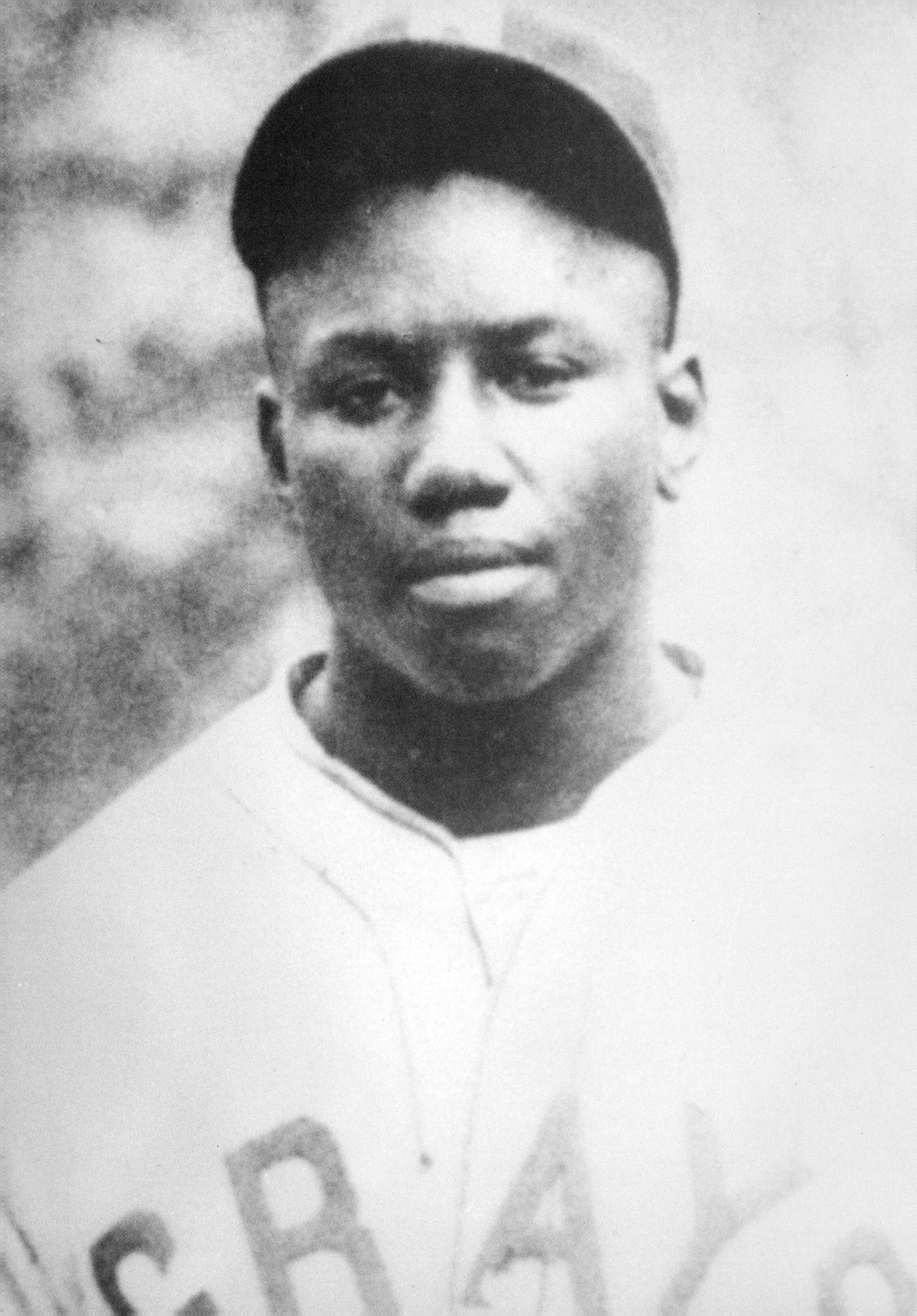

Newt Allen

Newton Henry Allen Sr.

Born: 1901, Austin, TX   **Died:** 1988, Cincinnati, OH

Career: 1922–1947, Kansas City Monarchs, St. Louis Stars

Known for his smooth-as-silk fielding, Allen was the captain of many of the powerhouse Kansas City Monarchs clubs of the 1920s and 1930s. Historians usually cite him among the best all-around second basemen in Negro leagues history. At 5-foot-8, 160 pounds, the scrappy Allen didn't generate much power, but he was a superb contact hitter, a skilled bunter, and a demon on the basepaths. He posted a .298 lifetime average. The four-time all-star spent a year with the St. Louis Stars, where he was paired with Willie Wells to form the best double-play duo in the Negro leagues. Allen was named a second-team utility player in the *Pittsburgh Courier* poll.

Signature Analysis

Allen's signature remained remarkably consistent throughout his life in letter size variability and character formation. He sometimes signed his full name, "Newton," though this was typically shortened to "Newt." Samples from the last few years of his life show typical signs of aging. Standard characteristics of his signature include the following:

- Standard "l" slant of 125 degrees.

- The "N" begins from the left to right, dipping down to form the character's left side. The bottom of this dip establishes the horizontal base for the rest of the signature, notwithstanding the right side of the "N," which is the only portion that dips below this horizontal plane.

- The "N's" upward loop begins its downward slant at a point parallel to the height of the instrument's first point of contact.

- Height of the "N" is matched by the top of the "t," the "A," and both "l's."

- The only breaks are between the "N" and "e," and the first and last name. The end of the "w" has only a subtle dip before beginning the ascender to the "t."

Allen was a popular player and was responsive to requests for his autograph. His signature occasionally surfaces on the market.

Scarcity: Limited   **Price Range:** $100–250

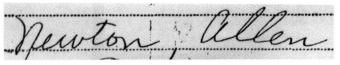

Signature from marriage contract, 1922

Signature from K.C. Monarchs team-signed sheet, 1935

Signature from postal request, post-playing days

Signature from baseball card contract, mid-1980s

Dan Bankhead

Daniel Robert Bankhead

Born: 1920, Empire, AL   **Died:** 1976, Houston, TX

Career: 1940–65, Birmingham Black Barons, Memphis Red Sox; *Major Leagues:* Brooklyn Dodgers

Bankhead is usually remembered as the first African-American to pitch in the major leagues. What's often overlooked is that he earned his way onto the Brooklyn Dodgers' staff by proving himself as a fine Negro leagues hurler. Possessing a blazing fastball and a mystifying screwball, he pitched his way onto three Negro leagues all-star teams. While Bankhead was certainly a good pitcher, some Negro leaguers felt there were far better major-league prospects in their ranks. "He wasn't one of our aces," Buck Leonard said. An arm injury kept him from reaching his full potential with the Brooklyn Dodgers. He was released after four years but carved out a fine career in the Mexican League. He was one of five Bankhead brothers to play in the Negro leagues.

Signature Analysis

Due to the many autograph requests he fulfilled as a Brooklyn Dodger, Bankhead's autograph is easier to locate than most Negro leaguers who died in the 1970s. Signatures signed by Bankhead after his playing days are actually more difficult to locate.

The greatest variable in Bankhead's signature is its overall flamboyance, as is clearly evident in the two samples featured here. Despite the variations incumbent in these different styles, Bankhead's signature exhibits a number of historical consistencies:

- Breaks between "D" and "an"; first name or middle initial when used "R" and "B"; "B" and "ank"; and "k" and "h." He sometimes added other breaks as well.

- Standard "B" stem slant of 140 degrees.

- "B" is the most consistent letter and is comprised of a single stroke that begins in a downward movement before doubling up and to the right before moving into the right formation of its character. It finishes with an unnecessary loop that leads over to the almost imperceptible break preceding the next letter, "a."

Scarcity: Limited   **Price Range:** $25–100

Signature from government postcard, 1950

Signature from note to fan, 1960s

Sam Bankhead

Samuel Howard Bankhead

Born: 1905, Empire, AL   **Died:** 1976, Pittsburgh, PA

Career: 1930–51, Pittsburgh Crawfords, Homestead Grays

The rocket-armed Bankhead was so versatile that he earned all-star berths at five different positions. A punchy hitter with excellent speed on the bases, he posted a lifetime batting average of .285 in Negro leagues play and a .342 mark in exhibition matchups against white major leaguers. The eight-time all-star spent his prime years with the powerhouse Pittsburgh Crawfords and anchored the infield of the 1935 club—the Negro leagues' answer to the 1927 New York Yankees. Bankhead is a first-team utility player in the *Courier* poll. He was the eldest and best of the five Bankhead brothers to play in the Negro leagues.

Signature Analysis

Although he died before the onset of collector interest in the Negro leagues, his accomplishments, combined with the publicity brought to him by his Brooklyn Dodgers sibling, Dan, increased interest in the acquisition of his signature. Samples do occasionally surface. Bankhead was reportedly responsive to mail requests for his autograph. Bankhead's signature shows the following characteristics:

- Breaks consistently exist between "S" and "amuel"; the first and last name; "B" and "ank"; and "k" and "head."

- Intersection that forms top loop of "S" occurs at approximately two-thirds the height of the "S" and at about twice the height of the succeeding lowercase letters.

- "l" ends with an extraneous upward stroke that inadvertently forms a "U."

- Ascender to "d" does not double down to form the loop characteristic in the standard formation of a cursive "d" and simply ends with a single stroke up that curves back to the left.

- Inconsistent "l" slant of 125 degrees.

Scarcity: Limited   **Price Range:** $100–250

Signature from all-star game pay slip, 1944   *Signature from postal request, post-playing days*

David Barnhill

David Barnhill

Born: 1913, Greenville, NC **Died:** 1983, Miami, FL

Career: 1937–53, New York Cubans

Barnhill was a wolf in sheep's clothing. At 5-foot-6, 135 pounds, he was an unlikely power pitcher, but those who stepped up to face him found themselves looking down the barrel of a gun. "He was right up there with Slim Jones and Satchel Paige," said Hall of Famer Buck Leonard. "He threw as hard as anybody. He was one of the best we had in our leagues." Barnhill was one of the great strikeout artists of his era and one of the Negro leagues' top hurlers in the East during the early 1940s. The four-time all-star had a lifetime .686 wining percentage in Negro leagues play and enjoyed an excellent stint in the minor leagues.

Signature Analysis

Barnhill was responsive to requests for his autograph. His signature remained remarkably consistent throughout his life. Standard characteristics of his signature include:

- Consistent break between "D" and "a" in "David."
- Final letters in first and last name, "d" in "David" and "ll" in Barnhill, rival or exceed the height of the capital letters.
- Degree of slant of the final letters is often considerably greater than the earlier portion of the name.
- Standard "B" slant of 95 degrees and standard "ll" and "d" slant of 130 degrees.

Scarcity: Limited   **Price Range:** $100–250

Signature from government postcard, 1950

Signature from financial document, post-playing days

Pepper Bassett

Lloyd P. Bassett

Born: 1909, Baton Rouge, LA   **Died:** 1981, Los Angeles, CA

Career: 1936–54, Birmingham Black Barons, Various Teams

Bassett is remembered in part for a comedy sketch that required him to catch part of the game in a rocking chair. This memory tends to obscure the fact that he ranked among the best all-around receivers of his era. The powerful four-time all-star's best years at the plate came more than a decade apart. In 1937, he hit .395 with the Pittsburgh Crawfords. Eleven years later, he posted a .350 mark with the Birmingham Black Barons. Rocking chair aside, Bassett was a strong all-around fielder. His lifetime batting average was .279.

Signature Analysis

Bassett died before the increased interest in Negro leagues autographs. The number of samples in circulation is limited. Although we can find no reference indicating that "Pepper" was his true legal middle name, he commonly used the first letter "P" as a middle initial when signing autographs. The following consistent elements appear in his autograph:

- Consistent "l" slant of 105 degrees.

- Breaks between the capitals "L" and "B" in the first and last name.

- The "y" connects to the "o" in "Lloyd" at the upper extreme of the "o."

- Slant increases subtly as the last name progresses.

Scarcity: Limited   **Price Range:** $100–250

Signature from the Bill Yancey Collection, 1938/39

Signature from postal request, post-playing days

"Cool Papa" Bell (HOF 1974)

James Thomas Bell

Born: 1903, Starkville, MS   **Died:** 1991, St. Louis, MO

Career: 1922–46, St. Louis Stars, Homestead Grays, Pittsburgh Crawfords

How fast was "Cool Papa"? Olympic gold medal sprinter Jesse Owens used to race players in exhibitions before games, but promoters wouldn't let Bell challenge him. They were convinced that Bell would win. The basepath kleptomaniac is widely regarded as one of the fastest men to ever play the game. Infielders claimed that if Bell hit a grounder that bounced more than once, they had virtually no chance of throwing him out at first. Bell used this warp speed to terrorize Negro leagues catchers and rob opponents of base hits for more than 20 seasons. He is credited with a .337 lifetime batting average. Bell was voted to Negro leagues all-star squads every year from 1933 to 1944 except for the seasons played in Latin America. He was among the most respected players in the history of the Negro leagues and was named a *Courier* poll second-team outfielder.

Signature Analysis

Bell was one of the few Negro leaguers actively collected prior to the onset of wide-spread interest in black baseball. He was an immensely popular and obliging signer. When signing documents, Bell would simply write "James Bell." When fulfilling autograph requests he almost always signed using his full name and nickname until a stroke in the late 1980s left him virtually blind. In spite of his disability and failing health, he continued to sign on a limited basis until he died. His post-stroke examples varied considerably in clarity and formation. Often, he would drop the "James" part of his autograph during this final period of his life, though Bell continued to write his nickname "Cool Papa."

Historical consistencies:

- Bell tended to connect all letters in each segment of his signature, using breaks only between names.

- The top loop of the "J" formed somewhat of a distinctive triangle. Distinct curved movement up on base of "C" that forms a small hook before continuing the instrument movement horizontally to form the first "o."

Pre-stroke characteristics:

- Clear character formation evident in all letters.

- Bell almost always dated the material he signed using numbers and dashes, e.g., "12-12-72."

- Bell used distinct, standard quotes around "Cool Papa." A clear loop is used to form all three "l's."

- The bases of the first "P" and the "B" are both formed similarly with a simple downward stroke that loops back up to the left before moving right. This single stroke continues through the point where the character begins, intersecting that point as it swings to the right before dropping to finish the character's formation. Entire signature written on a singular horizontal plane.

Post-stroke characteristics:

- Quote marks used around "Cool Papa" were written more horizontally like equal (=) signs used here than standard vertical quotation marks.

- "Papa" drops to a new horizontal plane below that of "James Cool."

- The signature is completed along this second distinctive plane. The "l" in "Cool," and "P" and "B" are no longer formed using a loop. Each is instead made using a single line stroke. This single line "l," moreover, is formed adjacent to the second "o" in "Cool" that precedes it, making "Cool" look something like the word "God."

Bell had a habit of signing 3x5 index cards in the extreme corners. This makes finding an easily mattable sample somewhat of a challenge. There are a handful (less than 10) of Bell-signed personal checks circulating in the hobby. Bell-signed baseballs are available on the market. Post-stroke balls range from $150–250. Pre-stroke samples command a significant premium.

Pre-Stroke Samples
Scarcity: Readily Available   **Price Range:** $25–100

Post-Stroke Samples
Scarcity: Readily Available   **Price Range:** Less than $25

Signature from all-star game pay slip, 1944

Signature from personal letter (pre-stroke), 1973

Signature from postal request, 1973

Signature from personal letter, 1990 (post-stroke)

Gene Benson

Eugene Benson

Born: 1913, Philadelphia, PA

Career: 1933–49, Philadelphia Stars

The man they nicknamed "Spider" lived up to the name. Few flies that strayed Benson's way escaped his web. He was one of the finest fielding outfielders in the Negro leagues during the 1930s and 1940s. Benson perfected and popularized the basket catch that Willie Mays later used to thrill major league fans. The four-time all-star was an accomplished bad-ball hitter whose speed helped him compile averages of .367, .339, and .340 during the peak years of his career. He had a lifetime average of .294. He was a member of Satchel Paige's touring all-star squad.

Signature Analysis

Benson has been an obliging signer and a regular on the autograph circuit. Collectors should find his signature an easy and reasonably priced acquisition.

Like most of his counterparts who share his longevity, insufficient autograph samples predating the 1980s exist to conduct a thorough evolutionary analysis. Although he sometimes uses his full name, "Eugene," more recent examples are commonly signed "Gene." These post-1980 examples show the following consistencies:

- Distinct and legible formation of all characters along a horizontal plane.
- Standard "B" stem slant of 130 degrees.

Benson single-signed baseballs are widely available on the market with prices ranging from $25–40 for samples signed during the 1990s.

Scarcity: Readily Available   **Price Range:** Less than $25

Signature from postal request, post-playing days

Signature from public autograph session, 1990s

Ed Bolden

Edward Bolden

Born: 1882, Concordville, PA **Died:** 1950, Darby, PA

Career: 1910–50, Hilldale, Philadelphia Stars

Bolden was a quiet postal clerk with an entrepreneurial flair, a keen intellect, and a passion for baseball. He built the two most prominent Philadelphia-area clubs, the Hilldale club and the Philadelphia Stars, from the ground up. In 1923, he played a key role in the formation of the Eastern Colored League, and his Hilldale Club went on to to capture its first three pennants. Bolden formed the Philadelphia Stars in 1933. During his 40 years in black baseball, Bolden served as an officer in three leagues, his own Eastern Colored League, the Negro National League and the Negro American League. He was cited as the third-team manager in the *Courier* poll.

Signature Analysis

Bolden undoubtedly signed numerous documents in his capacity as a team owner and league official. To date, few of these items have surfaced. Because he died before the onset of collector interest in the Negro leagues, his signature is not easy to locate. Bolden's autograph exhibits the following consistent characteristics:

- "E" begins with a vertical rightward slant that curves back to the left before dropping to form the rest of the letter. Breaks exist between "E" and "d" and again between the first and last name.

- A distinct stroke moves horizontally to the right from the completion of the "o" to form the base of the loop in the "l," giving the "l" a strong resemblance to a cursive "e" or even a "c."

- Standard "l" slant of 140 degrees.

Scarcity: Scarce **Price Range:** $250–500

Signature from Hilldale club document, 1912

Signature from the Bill Yancey Collection, 1938/39

Signature from Negro leagues document, 1945

Chet Brewer

Chester Arthur Brewer

Born: 1907, Leavenworth, KS   **Died:** 1990, Whittier, CA

Career: 1925–48, Kansas City Monarchs, Mexican Leagues, Cleveland Buckeyes

Brewer is one of baseball's most underrated hurlers. The lanky right-hander used the army of pitches at his command (including a devastating emery ball) and marksman-like control to carve out an outstanding 24-year career that included three 30-win seasons against all levels of competition. During his best year, 1929, he fashioned a 17-3 record and reeled off 31 consecutive scoreless innings. His incomplete Negro leagues record is usually cited as 129-79. The three-time all-star was the first African-American to play professional baseball in Mexico. He pitched three no-hitters there in 1939. Brewer spent nearly three decades as a scout and instructor for the Pittsburgh Pirates. He is on the original list of Hall of Fame candidates put forward by the Committee on the Negro Leagues (see Chapter 3).

Signature Analysis

Brewer was a popular and well-respected figure. He remained involved in baseball in various capacities throughout his life and was a good signer. Fewer than 100 Brewer-signed personal checks from the late 1980s are circulating within the hobby. Like most of his counterparts who share his longevity, insufficient autograph samples predating the 1980s exist to conduct a thorough evolutionary analysis.

Though he sometimes used his full name and middle initial—"Chester A."—to sign such documents as checks, he usually responded to autograph requests with the less formal "Chet Brewer." We observed the following consistencies in his signature:

- Breaks exist between "C" and "h," names (including middle initial when used); and "B" and "r." "B" exhibits greatest flamboyance and is formed with two strokes, a simple vertical stroke and a large second stroke that begins left of the first stroke and sometimes encases the vertical stroke altogether.

- Slant was irregular and his last name typically slanted up on a subtle but distinct diagonal plane apart from that formed with the base of his first name.

- Consistent "t" slant of 125 degrees.

Scarcity: Limited   **Price Range:** $25–100

Signature from Panamanian passport, 1945   *Signature from personal check, 1988*

78

Otto Briggs

Otto Briggs

Born: 1891, King Mt., NC   **Died:** 1943, Philadelphia, PA

Career: 1914–34, Hilldale

Briggs was an expert at finding his way to first base. If hitting the ball wasn't an option, then he'd get hit by it. He even wore extra-baggy uniforms to increase the probability. The fleet-footed outfielder was an important weapon in the offensive arsenal of the powerhouse Hilldale clubs of the early 1920s. As lead-off man, he hit .393 in 1923 and followed up with a .342 mark and 54 stolen bases. When Briggs joined Hilldale and was named team captain, he became its first paid player, effectively shifting the club's status from a top-flight amateur aggregation to a professional franchise.

After his career in baseball, Briggs served as circulation manager for his family's newspaper, the *Philadelphia Tribune*. In this endeavor he doubtless signed many documents, but few have surfaced to date. An insufficient database of samples precludes a detailed analysis of his signature.

Scarcity: Scarce   **Price Range:** $250–500

Signature from personal letter, 1941

Barney Brown

Barney Brown

Born: Kimball, WV   **Died:** Unknown

Career: 1935–56, New York Black Yankees, Philadelphia Stars

Brown sported No. 1 on the back of his Philadelphia Stars uniform as an immodest, although not entirely inaccurate, statement of his rank among the Negro National League hurlers of the late 1930s and early 1940s. Many say the screwballer's use of No. 1 was entirely justified. The lefty was named to four Negro leagues all-star teams. He spent a number of his prime years in Mexico, where he was considered one of that country's premier hurlers. He was twice named the Most Valuable Player in the Puerto Rican league, where he led all pitchers in victories in 1941 and 1946. Brown was also good with the bat, and was often used as a pinch hitter.

Signature Analysis

Brown died before the increased interest in the Negro leagues. His signature rarely surfaces in the market. The first sample shown below is from his playing days, while the second is from late in his life and shows typical characteristics of aging. There are some noteworthy consistencies between the samples despite the three-decade separation. These include:

- "B" begins with single downward vertical stroke that loops back up to the left before moving right to form the remainder of the character.

- Breaks exist between both "B's" and their subsequent lowercase succeeding letters, as well as between both names.

- Little or no effort appears to have been made to separate the "w" and "n."

Scarcity: Scarce   **Price Range:** $250–500

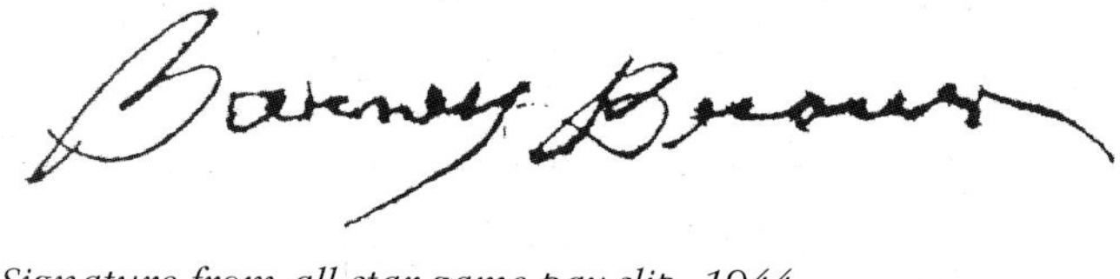

Signature from all-star game pay slip, 1944

(SIGNATURE)

Signature from Hall of Fame player questionnaire, 1974

Larry Brown

Larry Brown

Born: 1905, Pratt City, AL **Died:** 1972, Memphis, TN

Career: 1920–47, Memphis Red Sox

Brown earned the nickname "Iron Man" for catching more than 230 games against all levels of competition in 1930. While his offensive statistics were average at best (he was a .260 lifetime hitter), his skills behind the plate were enough to carry him to seven Negro leagues all-star games. Unsubstantiated legend (and one Brown constantly reinforced) has it that he gunned down Ty Cobb five times in an exhibition game in Cuba. His best season at the plate was 1928, when he notched a .292 average and led the Sox in doubles. Brown was a heady ballplayer and managed the Memphis Red Sox in the 1940s.

Signature Analysis

Collectors should note that there was a major-league player of the same name who played from 1963–74. A sample signature is featured in Appendix C.

Brown's signature, perhaps more so than any other in this book, demonstrates that some of the basic characteristics of one's handwriting remain despite infirmity. The shaky 1970 signature shown below exhibits many of the core characteristics of the clean, fluid signature from his playing days.

Brown's autograph exhibits the following historical consistencies:

- Inconsistent "L" slant of 120 degrees.

- The only clear break in the signature is between the capital "L" and the "a" in his first name.

- Base of capital "B" remains unfinished.

- Formation of the "r" in "Brown" begins inside the bottom half of the capital "B."

Scarcity: Very Limited   **Price Range:** $100–250

Signature from the Bill Yancey Collection, 1938/39

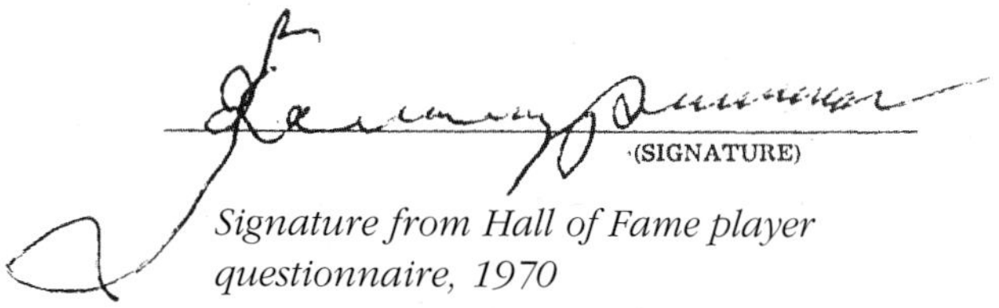

(SIGNATURE)

Signature from Hall of Fame player questionnaire, 1970

Ray Brown

Raymond Brown

Born: 1908, Ashland Grove, OH   **Died:** 1968, Dayton, OH

Career: 1930–48, Homestead Grays

Brown is historically wed to the unstoppable Homestead Grays teams of the 1930s in more ways than one. In addition to being the son-in-law of team owner Cum Posey, he was the team's one-man army on the mound. Equipped with a dazzling array of pitches, Brown once reeled off 28 straight victories during the 1937 and '38 seasons. He pitched a perfect game against the Chicago American Giants in 1945. Brown's 101-30 lifetime mark translates into an incredible .771 winning percentage, the best in Negro leagues history. He was also a strong switch-hitter and was often called on to play the outfield. Brown was named a fifth-team *Courier* poll pitcher and is featured on the original list of Hall of Fame candidates put forward by the Committee on the Negro Leagues (see Chapter 3).

An insufficient database precludes a detailed analysis of his autograph. The featured sample is the only one located in the preparation of this book. Collectors should note that a major leaguer of the same name played for the Chicago Cubs in 1904.

Scarcity: Scarce   **Price Range:** $250–500

Signature from handwritten letter, playing days

Willard Brown

Willard Jessie Brown

Born: 1911, Shreveport, LA   **Died:** 1996, Houston, TX

Career: 1935–56, Kansas City Monarchs; *Major Leagues:* St. Louis Browns

"Home Run" Brown was one of the most potent power hitters of the 1940s, on either side of the border. Blessed with outstanding strength, speed, and a cannon-like arm, he ranks among the most gifted athletes ever to play in the Negro leagues. He made five all-star appearances and is credited with a .352 lifetime batting average in league play. He led the Negro leagues in roundtrippers in 1946. At age 36, he was signed by the floundering St. Louis Browns and earned distinction by becoming the first African American to hit a home run in the American League.

Signature Analysis

Brown's signature is sought after by major league and Negro leagues collectors alike. As such his autograph surfaces regularly. Brown developed Alzheimer's Disease in the late 1980s. Because of this he was not a regular on the autograph circuit.

The limited samples of Brown's signatures from early in his life vary significantly in character formation from those of later years, which show the following characteristics:

- "W" is the largest letter, with the stroke beginning from the left and sweeping to the right before dropping to form the character.

- Common breaks occur between "W" and "ill," "J" and "essie" when middle name is used, and "B" and "rown."

- Middle name or initial is commonly used with bottom loop of "J" triangular in shape and occasionally crossed to form a figure-8. "B" is formed with a single stroke that begins from the base with a simple upward stem before sweeping to the right.

- "o" is connected with a dissecting movement to the right that connects to the "w."

- "n" is wider than it is tall.

- Second "l" tends to be taller than the first (this seems to be a quality attributable to all samples we examined).

- Standard "d" slant of 115 degrees.

Scarcity: Readily Available   **Price Range:** $25–100

Signature from Monarchs team-signed sheet, 1935

Signature from postal request, post-playing days

Signature from American League Blue Book *questionnaire, 1950s*

"Pee Wee" Butts

Thomas Butts

Born: 1919, Sparta, GA **Died:** 1973, Atlanta, GA

Career: 1938–55, Baltimore Elite Giants

A seven-time all-star, Butts was an excellent fielder and above-average hitter who, according to Roy Campanella, was cut from the same cloth as a major leaguer with the same nickname, Pee Wee Reese. "Butts could do everything," Campanella said. "He just didn't get the opportunity to go to the majors." This Pee Wee regularly flirted with the .300 mark, peaking at the plate in 1940 with a Negro National League–leading .391. He was a sparkplug player who compensated for his lack of power with good speed and excellent bat control. He joined Junior Gilliam to form one of the best double-play duos of the 1940s. Butts finished his career with a .280 batting average.

Butts died before the onset of collector interest in the Negro leagues. An insufficient database of samples precludes a detailed analysis of his autograph.

Scarcity: Very Limited   **Price Range:** $100–250

Signature from all-star game pay slip, 1944

Signature from autographed sheet, playing days

Bill Byrd

William Byrd

Born: 1907, Canton, GA   **Died:** 1991, Philadelphia, PA

Career: 1932–50, Baltimore Elite Giants

Spitball or fake spitball? Fast knuckler or slow knuckler? How about a wicked curveball for variety? Byrd's bag of tricks helped propel him into the upper echelon of Negro leagues hurlers of his day. Because his repertoire was so varied, he could effectively control the wear-and-tear on his arm. During two periods in which complete records are available, he is credited with completing 56 of the 85 league games he started. Byrd was a fixture in Negro leagues all-star contests. His eight appearances on the mound tie him with Hall of Famer Leon Day for the all-time lead. He is credited with a 115-72 lifetime record and was named a third-team pitcher in the *Courier* poll.

Signature Analysis

Byrd was generous with his autograph and samples are quite easy to find on the market. Byrd single-signed baseballs sometimes surface on the market with prices around $75 for samples signed during the late 1980s and early 1990s. His signature, which was remarkably consistent throughout his life, exhibits the following characteristics:

- Signature breaks commonly fall between the capital "B's" and the second letters of both his first and last names, and between the "y" and the "r" in his last name.

- He often used the letters "Wm" as shorthand for his formal name, William, when signing official documents.

- "W" is formed from the horizontal base with an upward left-to-right unnecessary stroke before dropping to form the left bottom to the letter; moreover, the bottom formations of the "W" are pointed. "B's" are made with a single stroke that begins at the top left and drops vertically before sweeping back up and over to make the letter's loops.

- Inconsistent "B" slant of 120 degrees.

Scarcity: Limited   **Price Range:** $25–100

Signature from the Bill Yancey Collection, 1938/39

Signature from all-star game pay slip, 1944

Signature from postal request, 1980s

Signature from public autograph session, 1990s

Roy Campanella (HOF 1969)

Roy Campanella

Born: 1921, Philadelphia, PA **Died:** 1993, Woodland Hills, CA

Career: 1938–57, Baltimore Elite Giants; *Major Leagues:* Brooklyn Dodgers

While Campanella carved out his place in Cooperstown based on his play in the majors, he had an outstanding nine-year career in the Negro leagues that began at the age of 15. During that period, he compiled a batting average of .353 and earned a reputation as one of the game's best defensive players. Campy learned the fine art of catching from the master of the mitt, Biz Mackey. He was a four-time Negro leagues all-star. In his 10-year major-league career with the Brooklyn Dodgers he was named National League MVP three times.

Signature Analysis

There are four distinctively different Campanella signatures, as illustrated below. The versions which predate the tragic accident that left him partially paralyzed in late 1957 are the rarest and most desirable.

Pre-Accident Signature: Within this signature population, there are three distinct variations. The first is a tight, uniformly flowing example (Samples A and B). The second, Sample C, is known as the "hurried" variation. The final version, and the rarest of the pre-accident autographs, is a printed signature. Samples A and B show the following consistencies:

- Consistent "ll" slant of 135 degrees.

- Overall slant height length of "R" generally exceeds that of the "C" in proportion to the same difference between the slant height of the "C" to that of the "p."

- Top loop of "R" overhangs "oy," as does top of "C" to "a," and final "l" to "a."

- Only the "y" and "p" extend below the distinct horizontal plane formed by the base of all other letters.

- Breaks are found after "R," between names, after "C," and normally at the "p."

- Note that Campy sometimes completed his "p" before lifting the instrument to complete the "anella." Other times he would break at the base of the "p," forming the letter with its loop as a separate stroke that then continued to complete his name.

- "ll's" are closed or near closed are generally twice the height of other lowercase letters.

- The final "a" ends abruptly at its base.

Sample C, the "hurried" autograph, is distinctively more sloppy than the example just described. It commonly appears on pages of vintage, "in-person" autograph albums, as well as on scorecards and other media normally associated with the acquisition of "in-person" autographs. There are a limited number of "printed" Campanella signatures (Sample D) circulating in the hobby. These signatures usually, but not exclusively, pre-date his Major League playing days and may be encountered on vintage Negro leagues–signed material.

Device-Assisted Signature: Following Campanella's tragic accident he used a device that allowed him to grip a pen well enough to sign autographs. He did a number of public signing sessions using this device and produced understandably shaky and inconsistent autographs. To our knowledge, the minimum fee for these signatures was $150, which would establish a base of value for such items at this figure. The highly variable nature of these autographs will render them a real challenge for authenticators in the future. Collectors generally acquired these to fill holes in their collections. As an example, a collector pursuing a set of all the signed Perez-Steele cards might have been motivated to get Campy's signature to complete the set. An example of this autograph is shown below as Sample E.

Collectors should also note that Campanella's wife ghost–signed many autograph requests on his behalf. Her signature is quite easy to recognize. See Appendix C for a sample and a detailed description.

Pre-Accident Samples
Scarcity: Limited   **Price Range:** $500–1,000

Post-Accident Samples
Scarcity: Limited   **Price Range:** $150–300

Sample A: Signature on letter to Branch Rickey, 1948

Sample B: Signature from player contract, 1953

Sample C: Signature from autograph book (hurried), 1950s

Sample D: Signature on scouting report letter, 1946

Sample E: Device-assisted signature (highly variable), 1991

Octavius V. Catto

Octavius V. Catto

Born: 1840, unknown   **Died:** 1871, Philadelphia, PA

Career: 1860s–71, Philadelphia Pythians

Catto was one of the prominent early organizers of black baseball and was responsible for bringing the race issue to the forefront of the sport. He was the promoter and manager of one of the first great all-black clubs, the Philadelphia Pythians, and played a key role in establishing the city as a major hub of black baseball. After the Pythians claimed the 1867 "Colored World Championship," Catto dispatched a representative to the National Association of Base Ball Players (NABBP) to petition for the acceptance of black clubs into its ranks. The NABBP did the opposite, barring all black clubs and teams with black players. Catto was an early driving force in the African-American civil rights movement. He died at age 31 after being shot by a white man during a voting rights riot.

Signature Analysis
Due to the fact that he died more than 125 years ago and at a young age, Catto's autograph is extraordinarily scarce. We were able to obtain two samples spanning 10 years of his life from museum sources. Catto employed perfect Spencerian-style penmanship. His letters are calligraphic works of art and show a high degree of consistency. We note the following traits from the limited sample population:

- Occasionally substituted initials (O.V.C.) for full name even on personal letters.

- Signature breaks between "C" and "a" in last name and the "t" and the "a" of his first name.

- Occasional break between the "O" and "c" of his first name. Consistent "tt" slant of 120 degrees.

- Consistent use of middle initial "V." Period (.) appears after last name, as was the common practice of the era.

Scarcity: Very Rare   **Price Range:** Not Established

Monogram signature from personal letter, 1860   *Signature from personal letter, 1870*

Oscar Charleston (HOF 1976)

Oscar McKinley Charleston

Born: 1896, Indianapolis, IN   **Died:** 1954, Philadelphia, PA

Career: 1915–54, Indianapolis ABCs, Pittsburgh Crawfords

Brutally strong and cobra-quick, Charleston was black baseball's finest outfielder of the 1910s and 1920s. He is considered by many the best all-around player in the history of the Negro leagues. "He was the greatest player I have ever seen in my eight-and-a-third decades of life," Buck O'Neil said. Early in his career the fleet and fiery Charleston was compared to Ty Cobb. As he grew older, rounder, and more powerful, writers drew analogies to Babe Ruth. His 1921 statistics tell the full story. He posted a .434 batting average and led the circuit in doubles, triples, stolen bases, and home runs. He is credited with a .350 lifetime batting average. Charleston was named a first-team outfielder in the *Courier* poll and is listed on *Total Baseball*'s roll of the Top 100 Players of all time. He was also considered an excellent manager. Charleston took his rightful place in Cooperstown in 1976.

Signature Analysis

There are fewer than five Charleston-endorsed checks circulating within the hobby from his days as manager of the Brooklyn Brown Dodgers. A small cache of receipts and other documents from his playing days in Cuba have also surfaced. Most of these documents have been absorbed into collections and rarely come up for sale.

Charleston is a popular target for forgers. Collectors should approach the purchase of his autograph with a high degree of caution. His signature remained fairly consistent throughout his career showing the following characteristics:

- "O" is closed with an inner loop, resembling an "e," which drops to the letter's base and continues into the "s."

- There are no consistent signature breaks in his first or last name.

- Standard "h" slant of 125 degrees. There is irregular spacing between letters; distance between "r" and "l" is about twice that as between the "l" and "e."

- Top of "C" is one-half to two-thirds the height of the "h."

- Bottom hump of "h" is typically closed and resembles an "i."

Scarcity: Scarce   **Price Range:** $1,000–2,500

Signature from Homestead Grays team-signed sheet, 1931

Signature from the Bill Yancey Collection, 1938/39

Signature from endorsed check, 1945

Signature from handwritten letter, 1940

"Bus" Clarkson

James Buster Clarkson

Born: 1918, Hopkins, SC   **Died:** 1989, Jeannette, PA

Career: 1930–52, Philadelphia Stars; *Major Leagues:* Milwaukee Braves

Satchel Paige thought so much of Clarkson's hitting that he intentionally walked him with the bases loaded. Often overlooked when discussing the great Negro leagues shortstops, Clarkson was a solid fielder, but he earned his money with his bat. He boasted an impressive .319 average over the course of his 14-year Negro leagues career. He was one of the few shortstops in the game who could make a legitimate claim to the cleanup spot in the order. He led the Puerto Rican League in home runs in 1951. In 1952, at age 34, he made a cameo (25 at-bats) appearance for the Milwaukee Braves in the major leagues.

Signature Analysis

Clarkson was unresponsive to mail requests for his autograph. His ranks among the most difficult autographs to find among major or Negro leagues players who died in the late 1980s. The limited number of samples located for this publication show the following consistencies:

- Consistent "l" slant of 115 degrees.
- No breaks except between names.
- "C" begins with an extraneous and sometimes closed downward loop.
- "C," "l," and "k" share the same general height.
- Right edge of "n" rises approximately twice the height of its left edge.

Scarcity: Very Limited   **Price Range:** $100–250

Signature from player contact, 1940s

Signature from Dallas Eagles document, 1953

Pancho Coimbre

Francisco Coimbre (Frank Coimbre)

Born: 1909, Coamo, PR   **Died:** 1989, Ponce, PR

Career: 1926–51, New York Cuban Giants; Puerto Rican League

Roberto Clemente claimed the best all-around Puerto Rican player ever to step on a ballfield was his mentor, Coimbre. Coimbre started his mainland career at age 30, after 12 full seasons in his homeland. He feasted on American pitching, posting .330-plus marks every season and a .361 lifetime average in his seven seasons in the Negro leagues (1940–46). Coimbre made two all-star appearances and both times batted third in the powerful lineups. He was also considered among the top fielders at his position. After his playing days, he worked as a scout for the Pittsburgh Pirates and was instrumental in signing Clemente.

Signature Analysis

Coimbre was a popular figure in Puerto Rican baseball circles, but he remained out of the range of many American autograph collectors. His signature is not widely available considering he died only a decade ago. The following three elements were consistent in the limited sample population we examined:

- Bottom of "C" underlines the "o" which is centered on the "C."
- Right portion of "b" is not defined, making the letter more closely resemble an "l."
- Inconsistent "F" slant of 125 degrees.

Scarcity: Limited   **Price Range:** $100–250

Signature from player contract, 1939

Signature from all-star game pay slip, 1944

Signature from postal document, 1983

Andy Cooper

Andy Cooper

Born: 1896, Waco, TX   **Died:** 1941, Waco, TX

Career: 1920–41, Detroit Stars, Kansas City Monarchs

Cooper was an extraordinarily consistent pitcher who parlayed his mound savvy into a successful managerial career. His 125 league victories place him second to Willie Foster on the Negro leagues all-time win list, and his .674 winning percentage ranks among the best of the 1920s. With Detroit from 1922–27, Cooper fashioned an exceptional 72-25 record. He had similar solid years after moving to the Monarchs where he joined Satchel Paige and Bullet Rogan on Kansas City's powerhouse staff. As a manager, he led the Monarchs to three Negro American League flags. "Cooper was a smart manager and a great, great teacher," pitcher Hilton Smith said. He died at age 45 shortly after his club claimed the 1940 crown.

An insufficient database precludes a detailed analysis of his autograph. The featured sample is the only one located in the preparation of this book.

Scarcity: Very Rare   **Price Range:** Not Established

Signature from K.C. Monarchs team-signed sheet, 1935

William Cornelius

William McKinley Cornelius

Born: 1907, Atlanta, GA   **Died:** 1989, Chicago, IL

Career: 1928–46, Chicago American Giants

The man they called "Sug" (as in Sugar) broke in with a bang, placing third in all-star voting in his freshman year on the strength of his outstanding curveball. During his 19-year career, he made three trips to the midseason classic and started the game twice. His best season was 1936 when he posted a 20-4 mark. He trumped that win total with 22 the following year. "Cool Papa" Bell said Cornelius was as good as any pitcher in the Negro leagues during his prime.

Signature Analysis

Cornelius died just as collector interest in the Negro leagues was on the rise. He was an active and accommodating signer during the short period when his autograph was in demand. Samples do occasionally surface in the hobby. Those from late in his life show the following consistencies:

- Breaks between capital letters "W" and "C" and the lowercase letters that follow.
- The "C" that forms a right angle at its lower left base and resembles more of an "L" in its appearance.
- "e" in last name resembles an undotted "i."
- Standard "ll" slant of 115 degrees and consistent "W" slant of 120 degrees.

Scarcity: Limited   **Price Range:** $25–100

Signature from postal request, 1980s

Sam Crawford

Sam Crawford

No Biographical Information Available

Career: 1910–38, Chicago American Giants, Various Teams

Historian James Riley cites Crawford as one of black baseball's best pitchers of the early 1910s. His deadly duo of pitches—a rip-snortin' fastball and a mesmerizing knuckler—kept hitters off stride for nearly three decades. Evidence of Crawford's prowess is largely anecdotal as statistics and biographical information related to his career are scant. He was, however, known as being particularly effective against the fine Cuban clubs of the day. An intelligent player, Crawford also served as a coach and manager at various stages in his career.

An insufficient database precludes a detailed analysis of his autograph. The featured sample is the only one located in the preparation of this book. Collectors should not confuse this Sam Crawford with the Hall of Fame outfielder of the same name who played during the same era.

Scarcity: Rare   **Price Range:** $250–500

Signature from K.C. Monarchs team-signed sheet, 1935

Jimmie Crutchfield

John William Crutchfield

Born: 1910, Ardmore, MO   **Died:** 1993, Chicago, IL

Career: 1930–45, Pittsburgh Crawfords

Crutchfield was regarded as one of the finest defensive outfielders of his time. The 5-foot-7 sprinter joined "Cool Papa" Bell and Sam Bankhead in the 1936 Crawfords outfield to form a trio that could get to the ball faster than any other in the leagues' history. He was known for occasionally showing off his glove skill by making catches behind his back. Crutchfield, who is frequently compared to Lloyd Waner, is credited with a .270 lifetime average. The four-time all-star was considered an excellent contact hitter and hit-and-run man.

Signature Analysis

Crutchfield was extremely popular with collectors and was a responsive signer. His autograph is widely available within the hobby. Crutchfield single-signed baseballs occasionally surface on the market with prices starting at $100.

Like most of his counterparts who share his longevity, insufficient autograph samples predating the 1980s exist to conduct a thorough evolutionary analysis. Later-life samples exhibit the following characteristics:

- Consistent "t" slant of 120 degrees.

- Written on a well-defined horizontal plane, broken only by the bottoms of "J," "C" (whose ending in an extraneous loop downward makes its appearance almost like that of a cursive "Y"), and "f." "J" is the largest letter, and is sometimes preceded by "Col."

- Breaks are found after "J," between names, and after "C."

- Small "c" resembles his "i's."

- Top of "d" is one-half to two-thirds the height of its preceding "l."

Crutchfield usually signed his first name "Jimmie"; however, samples spelled "Jimmy" do occasionally surface.

Scarcity: Readily Available   **Price Range:** $25–100

Signature from note to a collector, 1970s

Signature (full and nickname) from endorsed check, 1992

Ray Dandridge (HOF 1987)

Raymond E. Dandridge Sr.

Born: 1913, Richmond, VA   **Died:** 1994, Palm Beach, FL

Career: 1933–53, Newark Eagles, Mexican Leagues, Minor Leagues

"I never saw anyone better as a fielder," Hall of Fame pitcher Hoyt Wilhelm said of Dandridge. The knuckle-baller isn't alone in his assessment. Mongoose-quick and rocket-armed, Dandridge was arguably black base-ball's finest hot-corner tender of the 1930s and 1940s. His presence helped solidify the image of the Newark Eagles' "Million Dollar Infield" as one of the finest defensive aggregations in the history of baseball. He also could get it done with the bat, as his .322 lifetime batting average indicates. At 35, he was signed by the New York Giants organization. Despite a .362 average in 1949 and the AAA MVP award the following year, he was never called up to the parent club. Dandridge finally received the recognition he deserved when they displayed his plaque in Cooperstown.

Signature Analysis

Like all Hall of Fame players, Dandridge's autograph is highly sought after by collectors. Fortunately, he was an obliging signer, so collectors should find his autograph to be an easy acquisition. There are more than 100 Dandridge-signed personal checks circulating within the hobby. Single-signed Dandridge baseballs are still widely available, with prices ranging from $50–100 for samples penned during the 1980s and 1990s.

Like most of his counterparts who share his longevity, an insufficient number of autograph samples predating the 1980s exist to conduct a thorough evolutionary analysis. Later-life samples demonstrate that Dandridge varied some aspects of his signature—such as the use of his full first name versus "Ray," a middle initial ("E."), or a "Sr.," as well as some changes in letter formations and overall flow. Even so, the following characteristics remained consistent:

- Standard 'd' slant of 130 degrees.
- Consistent break falls between "D" and "a."
- Only "y" and "g" dip below horizontal plane.
- Small "r" closely resembles a "v."
- As a result of slant and letter proximity, top of "g" falls below shadow of top of "d." Likewise, bottom of "g" falls below the bottom of shadow of "d."

Scarcity: Readily Available   **Price Range:** $25–100

Raymond Dandridge

Signature from pay slip, 1936

Raymond E Dandridge Sr

Signature from personal check, 1983

"Ducky" Davenport

Lloyd Davenport

Born: 1911, New Orleans, LA   **Died:** New Orleans, LA

Career: 1935–49, Various Teams

At 5-foot-4, Davenport was built a lot like "Wee" Willie Keeler. Records show he hit like him as well. A scrappy fleet-footed slap hitter, Davenport earned berths on five all-star teams during his 16-year career. The waddling outfielder valued cash over consistency. He never played for the same team more than two years in a row, but his skills were such that the consistent .300-plus hitter never had trouble finding a job. Teams usually perched Davenport in the top third of the lineup and based him in centerfield to get the most out of his speed. He played a good portion of his career south of the border.

Davenport died before the increase in interest in Negro leagues autographs. He was reportedly responsive to mail requests for his autograph. An insufficient database precludes a detailed analysis of his signature.

Scarcity: Very Limited   **Price Range:** $25–100

Signature from the Bill Yancey Collection, 1938/39

Signature from postal request, 1970s

"Piper" Davis

Lorenzo Davis

Born: 1917, Piper, AL   **Died:** 1997, Birmingham, AL

Career: 1942–58, Birmingham Black Barons, Minor Leagues

A three-time all-star, Davis was a versatile infielder, excellent hitter, and well-respected manager with the Birmingham Black Barons during the 1940s and 1950s. He broke into the Negro leagues with a .368 batting average in 1942. While his batting average roller-coastered throughout the 1940s, he hit full stride from 1947–50 with marks of .360, .353, .378, and .383. Davis was an excellent major-league prospect. Unfortunately, he signed with the Boston Red Sox, a club that did not field an African-American player until 1959—after Jackie Robinson retired. But Davis did carve out a fine career in the Pacific Coast League.

Davis was a popular and obliging signer. He was a regular guest at Negro leagues signings and reunions. His autograph is easily obtainable through dealers. Single-signed Davis balls are readily available on the market from $25–40 for samples signed in the 1990s.

Signature Analysis

Like most of his counterparts who share his longevity, insufficient autograph samples predating the 1980s exist to conduct a thorough evolutionary analysis. We have included a sample signed with a Sharpie as Davis commonly used that type of pen. Davis signature samples from the 1980s and 1990s show the following consistencies:

- Standard "L" slant of 115 degrees. Consistent breaks after "L" in first name, "P" in nickname.

- Nickname "Piper" is commonly in quotations.

- The final "o" in "Lorenzo" is formed directly from the final stroke of the "z."

Scarcity: Readily Available   **Price Range:** $25–100

Signature from public autograph session, 1990s

Signature from Negro leagues reunion, 1990s

Leon Day (HOF 1995)

Leon Day

Born: 1916, Alexandria, VA   **Died:** 1995, Baltimore, MD

Career: 1934–50, Newark Eagles

Intimidating and intense, Day was the dominant Negro National League pitcher of his era. In 1937, with the legendary Newark Eagles' "Million Dollar Infield" at his back, the strikeout artist compiled a 13-0 record against all levels of competition. On the strength of his 90 mph–plus fastball, Day carved out full-season strikeout records in the Negro National League and the Puerto Rican leagues. Plus, he holds the career king-of-the-hill mark in K's for East-West All-Star competitions, and he set the Negro National League record with 18 strikeouts in a game. Day was also a crafty second baseman and an excellent hitter. He has a solid .288 career average. Day's .698 winning percentage is one of the best in Negro leagues history. He was a fourth-team choice in the *Courier* poll.

Day was an active signer during the early 1990s but he died less than two weeks after learning he was voted into the Hall of Fame. As such, he did not have time to saturate the market with autographs. It's worth noting that Hall of Fame postcard plaques are not available before induction ceremonies. Therefore, collectors will not find authentic Day-signed plaques on the market. While he is not a common target for forgers, some fraudulent Day material has surfaced.

There are fewer than 100 Day-signed checks on the market. These all come from the same source: autograph dealer James Spence. In the early 1990s, Spence negotiated an exclusive deal to purchase all of Day's canceled checks. Day, however, had not had a checking account for more than 40 years. It was only after the two made the arrangement that Day opened an account. Thereafter he sold the canceled documents to Spence. Day single-signed baseballs are available on the market ranging from $100–200 for samples signed during the 1990s.

Signature Analysis

Like most of his counterparts who share his longevity, insufficient autograph samples predating the 1980s exist to conduct a thorough evolutionary analysis. Later Day samples varied tremendously in size, shape, slant, and formation. Nevertheless, he maintained a constant instrument pressure as well as the following consistencies:

- Break only between names and after "D."

- Small loops, which were often closed, at stems of "L" and "D."

- Top loop intersects left base of single-stroke "D" at conclusion of character's formation. Bottom loop of "y" comes close to or intersects its descender.

- Inconsistent "L" slant of 125 degrees.

Scarcity: Readily Available   **Price Range:** $25–100

Signature from pay slip, 1936

Signature from Negro Leagues Reunion, 1990

Signature from personal check, 1994

Lou Dials

Oland Cecil Dials

Born: 1904, Hot Springs, AR **Died:** 1994, Modesto, CA

Career: 1925–36, Chicago American Giants

Dials was certainly a good player. The question is: just how good? Of all of the players listed in this section, the information regarding Dials' prowess at the plate is the most widely disputed. According to some reports he won batting titles in 1931 and 1933 and posted a .300-plus lifetime mark. Others show he didn't win either title and his lifetime mark was a decidedly more modest .268. Regardless, Dials was good enough to be considered as one of the first players to break the color line. He and pitcher Chet Brewer were almost signed by a Chicago Cubs farm club in 1943. While the move was ultimately quashed, such attention speaks to his status in the league. Dials was considered an above-average fielder with more than adequate power and speed. He was named to all-star squads in 1936 and 1943 and earned MVP honors while playing in Mexico in 1939.

Signature Analysis

Dials single-signed baseballs are still available on the market but are becoming increasingly difficult to find. Samples have recently been offered for $100-plus.

Like many of his counterparts who share his longevity, insufficient autograph samples predating the 1980s exist to conduct a thorough evolutionary analysis. Samples from later in his life show the following consistencies:

- Standard "D" stem slant of 90 degrees. Break only between names.

- "L" closely resembles an "S" in formation.

- "D" is often the largest letter.

Scarcity: Readily Available   **Price Range:** $25–100

Signature from public autograph session, 1990s

Signature from public autograph session, 1990s

Martin Dihigo (HOF 1977)

Martin Madaleno Dihigo Llaus

Born: 1905, Matanzas, Cuba   **Died:** 1971, Havana, Cuba

Career: 1923–45, Cuban Stars, New York Cubans, Mexican and Cuban Leagues

Hall of Famer Johnny Mize called Dihigo the best player he'd seen in any league. Many contend the spectacular Cuban was the most versatile athlete ever to take to the ballfield. While he entered Cooperstown as a second baseman, in a poll of former Negro leaguers and baseball historians conducted in the 1980s, he received votes as the best third baseman and outfielder in the history of the leagues. If Latin American baseball historians had been polled, Dihigo probably would have received a few votes as a pitcher. The fastballer's lifetime record in all leagues was 218-106, good for a .673 winning percentage. His best season on the mound was in Mexico in 1938. He went 18-2 with a microscopic 0.90 ERA. He was no slouch with the bat, either, topping the Eastern Colored League in home runs in 1935 and repeating the feat nine years later in the Negro National League. Recent estimates place his lifetime batting mark in Cuban and Negro leagues play at .319. He is a member of the Mexican, Cuban, and American baseball halls of fame. Dihigo was enshrined in Cooperstown in 1977.

Martin Dihigo was responsive to autograph requests. As rare as his autograph is, there are probably more Dihigo samples circulating in the hobby than any other pre-1980 deceased Negro leagues Hall of Famer.

Occasionally, his autograph is available on single-signed baseballs. There are a small number of Dihigo signatures on baseballs made from a uniquely processed leather. These balls have no markings and are slightly smaller in circumference than regulation baseballs. In most cases they are signed in ballpoint pen on the panel, as was Dihigo's frequent custom, with the salutation "Sinceremente." These balls are unlike any produced by major U.S. manufacturers, suggesting that they may have been made south of the border.

Signature Analysis

- Both capital letters, "M" and "D," exhibit large, flamboyant loops that begin their formation with relatively horizontal right-to-left strokes.

- There is normally a break between the "M" and the "artin," even though it is sometimes masked by an overlap at the break point. Other breaks typically exist between his first and last names, as well as between "D" and "ihig" and "ihig" and "o," although breaks have also been shown between "i" and "h" and "h" and "i."

- The "D" tends to be the largest letter, generally exhibiting a figure-8–type horizontal loop at its base that also makes its way back to the left, typically resting at the letter's farthest leftward point.

- When not placing his name on a lined surface, Dihigo's tendency was to subtly drop the horizontal plane of his last name below that of his first. Inconsistent "t" slant of 125 degrees.

Signature from insurance document, 1939

Signature from insurance document, 1939

Signature from personal letter, 1945

Signature from note to collector, post-playing days

"Dizzy" Dismukes

William Dismukes

Born: 1890, Birmingham, AL   **Died:** 1961 Campbell, OH

Career: 1913–50, Indianapolis ABCs, St. Louis Stars, Kansas City Monarchs

Dismukes was one of the grand old men of the Negro leagues. He spent nearly 50 years in black base-ball and witnessed firsthand the rise and fall of the Negro leagues. During the first 20 years, he was a highly successful submariner on the powerhouse Indianapolis ABCs clubs of the mid-1910s. The last 20-plus years were spent in various high-profile management roles. Dismukes was a highly respected figure and served as coach and manager and in the front offices of several teams. He was instrumental in the Monarchs' signing of Jackie Robinson and later became one of the first African-American major-league scouts. While today he is best remembered for his work in the front office, his accomplishments on the mound were not overlooked by his peers. He was picked as a first-team coach and second-team pitcher in the *Courier* poll.

Signature Analysis

Dismukes died before collector interest in the Negro leagues increased. An insufficient database precludes a detailed analy-sis of his autograph. Because Dismukes was a longtime executive, it's likely that there are documents he signed in existence, but few have surfaced to date. The limited number of examples located for this book show the following consistencies:

- Consistent "D" stem slant of 90 degrees. Breaks exist between "W" and "m," all names and/or abbreviations, "D" and "ismu," and the "u" and "kes."

- All "D's" are two strokes as are the "k's." Specifically, "D" is made with a simple, short vertical line surrounded by a horizontal horseshoe stroke that, of course, opens to the left.

- The "k" is also composed of a simple vertical stroke that is intersected by a simple downward diagonal stroke that loops at its center before extending down to its right base.

- "W" begins with an extraneous vertical movement up before dropping down to form the letter's left edge. Its right edge comes back far to the left, intersecting the imaginary plane created by extending the letter's center point vertically.

Scarcity: Scarce   **Price Range:** $250–500

Signature from American League Blue Book, *questionnaire, 1953*

Signature from handwritten letter, 1950s

Larry Doby (HOF 1998)

Lawrence Eugene Doby

Born: 1923, Camden, NJ

Career: 1942–59, Newark Eagles; *Major Leagues:* Cleveland Indians

Doby did in the American League what Jackie Robinson did in the National League: he broke its color line. While his debut four months after Robinson's didn't generate nearly as many headlines, Doby faced the same obstacles and met them head-on with masterful play in the field and at the plate. He was named to every AL all-star team from 1949–54 and led the league in home runs in 1952 and 1954. Doby caught the eye of major-league scouts after an outstanding four-year career in the Negro leagues, the final year of which he hit .414. He finished his major-league career with a .286 average. Doby was named the third-team second baseman in the *Courier* poll. Now assistant to the president of the American League, he entered the Hall of Fame in 1998.

Signature Analysis

Doby's baseball-related affairs, including his private and public signings, are handled through a sports management agency. He is an active signer and collectors should be able to locate his signature with relative ease; however, mail requests for his signature are generally unsuccessful. Doby single-signed baseballs are widely available on the market at prices ranging from $25-40 for samples signed during the 1990s.

Doby has been widely collected since his days with the Indians. His signature has remained relatively constant over the decades showing the following consistencies:

- Consistent "L" slant of 135 degrees. "L" tends to be the largest letter. Its base loop extends as the left-most point of the signature is more open and larger than that of its top.

- Consistent breaks only between "L" and "arry," first and last names, and "D" and "oby."

- Occasional hurried samples might find the "D" and "oby" connected. "arry" and "oby" are centered on "L" and "D," respectively. "a" and "o" are consistently and meticulously closed.

- Early version "y's" displayed base loops that have been substituted with single strokes in more recent years. Likewise, earlier "rr's" were less defined than later versions, which currently exhibit full cursive definition.

- "D" is simple and exhibits its single loop to complete its formation. Horizontal extension to right from the "o's" closure dissects its continued downward stroke to the "b."

- Height of "L," "D," and "b" are similar and the highest points of the signature.

Scarcity: Readily Available   **Price Range:** Less than $25

Signature from autograph book, 1948

Signature from government postcard, 1951

Signature from public autograph session, 1990s

Signature from public autograph session, 1998

John Donaldson

John Wesley Donaldson

Born: 1892, Glascow, MO   **Died:** 1970, Chicago, IL

Career: 1913–34, All Nations, Kansas City Monarchs

J.L. Wilkinson, owner of the Kansas City Monarchs, saw a lot of great pitchers in his day. But when asked to name the best of the batch, he'd point to Donaldson. Donaldson was black baseball's first great lefty of the 20th century. Hall of Fame manager John McGraw said he would have been worth $50,000 in the major leagues, an astronomical fee at the time Donaldson played. If that isn't praise enough, John Henry Lloyd called him the best pitcher he had ever faced.

Not only was Donaldson devastating from the mound, but he also was a superb hitter whose speed and bat control often landed him at the top of the order. In 1923, he formed the John Donaldson All-Stars and toured the Midwest playing semipro clubs. After integration, he worked as a scout for the Chicago White Sox. Donaldson was cited as a first-team pitcher in the *Courier* poll. He should not be confused with John Donaldson, who played in the major leagues from 1966–74.

Signature Analysis

Donaldson died prior to the onset of Negro leagues collector interest. An insufficient database precludes a detailed evolutionary analysis of his signature. The limited number of examples uncovered for this publication do, however, exhibit the following consistencies:

- Consistent "D" stem slant of 90 degrees.
- Use of middle initial. Breaks between "J" and "ohn," "D" and "on," "n" and "ald," and "d" and "son."
- Dissection of letter base in the conclusion of the formations of both the capital and lowercase "d's."

Scarcity: Very Limited   **Price Range:** $500–1,000

Notarized signature from marriage contract, 1917

Signature from American League Blue Book *questionnaire, 1953*

"Big Bill" Drake

William P. Drake

Born: 1895, Sedalia, MO   **Died:** 1977, St. Louis, MO

Career: 1915–30, St. Louis Giants, Kansas City Monarchs

Drake didn't have the power to throw the ball past many hitters, but he did have enough control to throw at—and hit—a good number of them. In the process, he earned the reputation as one of the meanest hurlers in the game. "If you got a toehold on me, down you went," Drake said. Consistency, coupled with a maddening array of junk pitches, secured Drake a place among the top 10 Negro leagues pitchers in the all-time victories category. His best season was 1920, when he posted a 20-10 mark and became one of only six pitchers to reach the 20-win plateau in the short Negro leagues seasons. Drake claims to have taught Satchel Paige his famous "Hesitation Pitch."

Signature Analysis

The majority of Drake-signed material in the hobby can be traced to signings he did for a noted collector in 1975. He signed a small batch of photographs and a number of 3x5 index cards. Fortunately, Drake left a solid database of variations. He signed using his initials, "W.P.," his nickname, "Big Bill," and a combination of the two, "W.P. 'Big Bill.'" We were unable to locate a sample from his playing days.

The 1975 samples show the following consistencies:

- Consistent "l" slant of 90 degrees.

- "k" in Drake is formed in two distinct pen strokes and marks the only constant break in his first or last name.

- "D" and "r" connection is at the top of the "D."

- The sharp descent formed by this connection forms an "r" that often resembles a "v."

- A period (.) mark after his first name, "William," is present on some samples.

Scarcity: Limited   **Price Range:** $100–250

Signature from endorsed check, 1975

Signature from private autograph session, 1975

Signature from private autograph session, 1975

Frank Duncan

Frank Duncan Jr.

Born: 1901, Kansas City, MO   **Died:** 1973, Kansas City, MO

Career: 1920–48, Kansas City Monarchs

If you can measure a catcher's value by the success of the staff he handles, then Duncan was one of the game's best. As backstop for the Kansas City Monarchs for more than 20 years, he called games for a Who's Who list of Negro leagues pitchers, including Jose Mendez, John Donaldson, Hilton Smith, Satchel Paige, Bullet Rogan, and Chet Brewer. Duncan was considered a master at handling pitchers, and his arm strength and throwing accuracy were top-tier. If you measure value by success at the plate, then the fiercely competitive Duncan's stock falls slightly because his production figures (including a .246 lifetime batting average) were unexceptional.

Duncan was a highly successful manager who piloted the Monarchs to two pennants. He's often is compared to Hall of Famer Al Lopez, also a strong-fielding catcher who became a successful bench general. He is an honorable mention *Courier* poll catcher.

Collectors should not confuse this Frank Duncan with the outfielder/manager of the same name who played primarily with the Chicago American Giants from 1909–28. Nor should they confuse him with his son, Frank Duncan III, who played in the Negro leagues from 1940–47.

Scarcity: Very Limited   **Price Range:** Not Established

Notarized signatures from marriage contract, 1919

Jose Fernandez

Jose Maria Fernandez Sr.

Born: 1896, Guanabacoa, Cuba   **Died:** 1971, unknown

Career: 1916–50, Cuban Stars, New York Cubans

Over the course of his 35-year Negro leagues career, Fernandez evolved from an excellent defensive catcher into an outstanding manager. While his Negro leagues clubs were never beehives of talent, the shrewd tactician was known for making bad teams look average and turning average clubs into contenders. His finest moment at the helm came in 1947, when he led the New York Cubans to the Negro leagues World Series championship. Historian James Riley cites Fernandez as one of the best catchers in the Negro leagues during the mid-1920s. While the Cuban's batting percentages fluctuated widely, he was considered only an average hitter. He was parked in the lower half of the order during the majority of his years in the leagues. Fernandez compiled a .277 lifetime average in his 23 years in the Cuban leagues. He is the brother of pitcher Rudy Fernandez, and his son, Jose Fernandez Jr. played briefly in the major leagues.

Fernandez died before the increased interest in Negro leagues autographs. The two signatures featured here were the only samples located during the preparation of this book. An insufficient database precludes a detailed analysis of his autograph.

Scarcity: Very Limited   **Price Range:** $100–250

Signature from the Bill Yancey Collection, 1938/39

Signature from Cuban coaching contract, 1949 (Descenders "J" and "z" obscured)

Wilmer Fields

Wilmer Leon Fields

Born: 1922, Manassas, VA

Career: 1940–58, Homestead Grays

Fields used a wicked fastball to carve out his place as one of the premier Negro leagues hurlers of the 1940s. In two seasons before leaving for military service, he posted 13-5 and 15-3 records in league play. Upon his return, he resumed his post as stalwart of the Grays' staff, posting a 72-12 mark against all levels of play from 1946–50. Fields was also an excellent hitter. When the Grays folded, Fields opted to play in leagues both north and south of the border instead of the major leagues because the pay was better. From 1950–58, he accumulated an astounding six MVP awards. Fields is the president of the Negro Leagues Baseball Players' Association.

Signature Analysis

Fields single-signed baseballs are widely available on the market with prices ranging from $25–40 for samples signed during the 1990s. Like most of his counterparts who share his longevity, insufficient autograph samples predating the 1980s exist to conduct a thorough evolutionary analysis. The samples from recent years show the the following consistencies:

- Standard "l" slant of 110 degrees.

- Noticeable breaks after "W," between names, and after "F," with a subtle break after the "l" before "d."

Scarcity: Readily Available   **Price Range:** Less than $25

Signature from endorsed check, 1997

Signature from public autograph session, 1990s

Rube Foster (HOF 1981)

Andrew Foster

Born: 1879, Calvert, TX   **Died:** 1930, Kankakee, IL

Career: 1902–26, Chicago American Giants

A powerful force on the field and in the front office, Foster organized a loose confederation of clubs into a formal structure that became the Negro National League, black baseball's first fully functional conference. He is commonly referred to as the Father of the Negro leagues. Before his move to the front office, Foster was one of the game's most effective pitchers. He is credited with 51 wins against all levels of competition in 1902. Despite his prowess on the mound and important contributions as an executive, many contend that Foster did his best work on the bench. He was an ingenious and daring manager who was adept at judging and nurturing young talent. Mentally exhausted from the labors associated with holding his fledgling league together, Foster was institutionalized in the summer of 1926. He spent the last four years of his life in the Kankakee Asylum in Illinois.

Signature Analysis

Foster's autograph is highly sought after. Due to its scarcity and value, it also is commonly forged. The limited number of Foster examples in circulation show enormous variability—so much that at one time there was speculation that one variation was secretarial. The notarized signatures from Foster's pen showcase these variations. The most dramatic, or at least obvious, of which is the formation of the capital letters "A" and "F." The stylized "A" (Samples A and E) and the non-stylized "A" (Samples B, C, D, and F) in "Andrew," are both acceptable variations.

- One of the most distinguishing characteristics of Foster's handwriting is the unusual formation of the ascending stem of the "d" in "Andrew." Foster's pen carries the stem to the left, then doubles back crossing the stem to begin the proceeding "r." This can cause the "d" to resemble a figure-8.

- Signature breaks are inconsistent but commonly occur between "F" and "o" in "Foster."

- Foster varies the construction of his lower case "e's" between a common cursive "e" and a small stylized capital "e" within an otherwise non-stylized signature.

- Signature slant is inconsistent.

- The angle of the small "t" in Foster varies from 90–130 degrees.

- Nickname, "Rube," used inconsistently.

A small cache of typed letters signed by Foster came onto the market in the 1980s. Most of these are addressed to a Mr. Brasfield (spellings differ) of the Henry Grays Baseball Club and are dated 1915. They are written on official Chicago American Giants letterhead. Most concern arrangements for forthcoming games. Several samples from this find have been offered in 1996 and 1997 at prices ranging from $8,000–12,000. Collectors should note that a player named George "Rube" Foster pitched for the Boston Red Sox from 1913–17.

Scarcity: Rare   **Price Range:** $2,000–4,000

Sample A: Notarized signature from Leland Giants incorporation document, circa 1904–05

Sample B: Notarized signature from Negro leagues incorporation papers, 1925

Sample C: Notarized signature from Negro leagues–related document, 1925

Sample D: Signature from business letter, 1915

Sample E: Signature from business letter, 1915

Sample F: Signature from business letter, 1918

Willie Foster (HOF 1996)

William Hendrick Foster

Born: 1904, Calvert, TX **Died:** 1978, Lorman, MS

Career: 1923–38, Memphis Red Sox, Chicago American Giants

If your brother's name happens to be Rube Foster, you've got a tough act to follow. Willie Foster answered the challenge by becoming a legend in his own right. The lanky hurler's 138 victories put him at the top of the Negro leagues all-time wins category. For a two-year period, 1926–27, Foster may have been the best pitcher in any league. In 1926, the power pitcher had a run of 26 consecutive wins against all levels of competition and an 11-3 record in league play. Foster followed this season with a 32-3 record and a 21-3 league mark. His lifetime winning percentage was an impressive .688. Jocko Conlon compared Foster to Herb Pennock but said that Foster had better control. He is a first-team *Courier* poll pitcher.

Signature Analysis

The scarcity of Foster's autograph is one of the hobby's great mysteries. He died recently (autographically speaking) and, given the positions he held, presumably signed many documents. After retiring from baseball, Foster went into the insurance business in South Carolina and later became dean of men and the baseball coach at his alma mater, Alcorn State College (now Alcorn University) in Mississippi. He was also responsive to mail requests for his autograph, but it seems few collectors had the foresight to seek him out. Although a small number of samples have changed hands privately in the past two years, only four Foster autographs have been offered publicly. Each sold for more than $3,000 as of mid-1998.

Collectors should not confuse this Willie Foster with the Willie B. Foster who played in the Negro leagues in 1950. Willie B. Foster's signature is presented in Chapter 9, "Negro Leagues Signature Gallery." Confusing the two could be a costly mistake.

Foster died prior to the onset of Negro league collector interest. An insufficient database exists for a detailed evolutionary analysis of his signature. We are able to provide one verifiable (notarized, in fact) example of Foster's signature from his playing days. Its similarities to the later versions are limited somewhat to slant (almost vertical) and breaks (between "W" and "illie," first and last names, and "F" and "oster." Later versions exhibit both vertical and a subtle backward slant as well as the following characteristics:

- Final upward movement completing the right portion of the "W" loops back to the left, even to or through the continued imaginary line that would exist by extending vertically the first ascender of its base that otherwise forms the center point of the "W."

- The "F" is the largest letter. It begins with a vertical upward stroke within the vertical plane created by the final letter of the previous name. It is dissected with a near-horizontal stroke and a subtle break is then created before continuing with a simple closed "o."

- Inconsistencies relative to the use of his first name. Signed either "Willie," "Bill" or in some cases, as shown below, "Willie" with the nickname "Bill," in parentheses.

- Standard "t" slant of 90 degrees.

Scarcity: Very Limited   **Price Range:** $2,000–4,000

Willie Foster

Notarized signature from Negro leagues incorporation papers, 1924

Willie Bill Foster

Signature from postal request, post-playing days

Bill Foster

Signature from note to a collector, undated

Josh Gibson (HOF 1972)

Joshua Gibson

Born: 1911, Buena Vista, GA   **Died:** 1947, Pittsburgh, PA

Career: 1929–46, Homestead Grays, Pittsburgh Crawfords

Gibson was arguably the greatest power hitter in baseball history. A recent book analyzing the statistics of baseball's finest sluggers contends that the burly receiver would have averaged 61 home runs a year—11 more per year than Babe Ruth—over the course of a full major-league season. Reports place Gibson's lifetime home-run total at more than 800 against all levels of competition. He achieved this stratospheric statistic despite playing a good portion of his career in famously cavernous Griffith Stadium. His lifetime batting average in 16 seasons of league play was .362. A first-team *Courier* poll catcher, he appears on *Total Baseball*'s list of the top 100 baseball players of all time and was the second Negro leagues player elected to the Baseball Hall of Fame. Gibson's son, Josh Jr., played in the Negro leagues from 1949–50. See Chapter 9 for a sample of his autograph.

Signature Analysis

Gibson was second only to Satchel Paige as a fan favorite. His autograph was actively collected by fans during his playing days. Even though he lived a short life and died long before the onset of collector interest in black baseball, genuine Gibson material does occasionally surface. Due to his popularity and the rarity of his autograph, Gibson is among the most popular targets for forgers. Collectors should use extreme caution when purchasing Gibson-signed material.

Gibson's signature remained remarkably consistent throughout his career. A good portion of early material he signed bears his full first name, Joshua. We were unable to locate any documents signed by Gibson during his final two seasons. Due to his mental and physical state at the time, it's safe to assume that the signatures dating to this period would exhibit certain non-standard characteristics. The signatures examined for this book show the following characteristics:

- "J" is formed with double loops.

- Bottom of first "s" is conspicuously open, while the second "s" is closed.

- "G" is closed almost in a "diamond-like" formation with its upper left corner forming a small loop at approximately half the diagonal distance of the overall letter.

- The letter is finally closed at the left portion of its base with a stroke that doubles back to the right, occasionally opening up to form the left reverse portion of a diagonal figure-8.

- A distinct break between the "G" and the "i" that begins under the shadow of the upper right corner of the "G."

- The "s" likewise begins under the shadow of the "b's" ascender. Standard "b" slant of 130 degrees.

Scarcity: Scarce   **Price Range:** $1,000–2,500

Signature from Homstead Grays team-signed sheet, 1931

Signature from player contract, 1932

Signature from the Bill Yancey Collection, 1938/39

Signature from all-star game pay slip, 1944

George Giles

George Franklin Giles

Born: 1909, Junction City, KS   **Died:** 1992, Topeka, KS

Career: 1927–39, Kansas City Monarchs, St. Louis Stars, Brooklyn Eagles

The man many have called the black Bill Terry was a Gold Glove–caliber first baseman whose speed and uncanny quickness were the basis for his success in the field and at the plate. He forged his reputation with the glove by chasing down would-be bloop singles into short right field. Giles (pronounced with a hard "G") was also a skilled slash hitter and a formidable hit-and-run man—an extremely valuable skill to have when you are batting, behind "Cool Papa" Bell, as he did in St. Louis. That club won Negro National League pennants in 1930 and 1931. In 1935, his best all-around season, Giles hit .365 and earned a place on the all-star team. He compiled a .313 lifetime average.

Signature Analysis

Giles commonly shortened his first name to Geo. when signing autographs. He was a responsive and popular signer. Collectors will find his autograph a fairly easy but somewhat pricey acquisition for a player who died after 1990. Like most of his counterparts who shared his longevity, insufficient autograph samples predating the 1980s exist to conduct a thorough evolutionary analysis. Recent examples show the following consistencies:

• Standard "l" slant of 125 degrees.

• No breaks except between names. "i" is dotted to its right.

• Second "e" begins beneath the shadow of its preceding "l."

Scarcity: Limited   **Price Range:** $25–100

Signature from postal request, 1980s

Signature from postal document, 1977

Joe Greene

James Elbert Greene

Born: 1911, Stone Mountain, GA   **Died:** Stone Mountain, GA

Career: 1932–48, Kansas City Monarchs

Long before Lou Boudreau thought up the Williams Shift to hold the pull-hitting "Splendid Splinter" in check, Negro leagues managers employed the tactic in a desperate attempt to thwart the hard-hitting Greene. The burly receiver was among the finest all-around catchers on the early 1940s. "Josh Gibson and I were the two most powerful hitters as catchers," Greene said, and the numbers back up his claim. He led the Negro National League in home runs in 1940 and 1942 and called the games for the legendary Monarchs' staffs of the era. A consistent .300-plus hitter, Greene was batting fifth in the powerful Monarchs' batting order until his prime was interrupted by call into the military service in 1943. Although fairly immobile behind the plate, he carved out a reputation as a skilled defensive player on the strength of his powerful pegs to second. He was named to two all-star teams.

Greene was responsive to mail requests from collectors and his autograph occasionally surfaces in the hobby. The vast majority of Greene autographs in circulation are from his later years and are signed James "Joe" Greene. An insufficient database precludes a detailed analysis of his autograph. He should not be confused with fellow Negro leaguer Charles "Joe" Green.

Scarcity: Limited   **Price Range:** $25–100

Signature from in-person request, vintage

Signature from postal request, 1980s

119

Gus Greenlee

William Augustus Greenlee

Born: 1895, Marion, NC   **Died:** 1952, Pittsburgh, PA

Career: 1931–45, Pittsburgh Crawfords

Greenlee was the owner of the legendary Pittsburgh Crawfords teams of the 1930s and the driving force behind the formation of the second Negro National League in 1933. He served as president of the League for five years. His championship club of 1935 is considered by historians to be one of the finest teams in baseball history. It featured five future Hall of Famers: Josh Gibson, Satchel Paige, Oscar Charleston, Judy Johnson, and "Cool Papa" Bell. Extrapolate this club's winning percentage over a 162-game season and you end up with 117 wins and 45 losses. Greenlee accumulated considerable wealth and political power in the Pittsburgh community through his many business interests. These ranged from owning the popular Crawford Grill to the decidedly more shady numbers businesses that partially funded the baseball club.

While Greenlee likely signed many documents as a businessman and Negro leagues executive, few have surfaced in the market. An insufficient database precludes a detailed analysis of his autograph. The featured sample is the only one located in the preparation of this book.

Scarcity: Scarce   **Price Range:** $500–1,000

Signature from business letter, 1937

Vic Harris

Elander Victor Harris

Born: 1905, Pensacola, FL **Died:** 1978, San Fernando, CA

Career: 1923–50, Homestead Grays

Who says great players don't make great managers? Harris was certainly both, and he is widely underrated in both capacities. The fiery outfielder carved out a .301 lifetime batting average while playing and managing primarily for the Homestead Grays over a quarter of a century. In the late 1930s, Harris took the helm of the great Grays club. A win-at-any-cost-leader, he piloted the team to an astounding nine consecutive Negro National League pennants from 1937–45. The last three years of the dynasty he was a figurehead manager, as his World War II defense job took precedence over the ballclub. He later moved to the Cleveland Buckeyes, where he guided the club to the flag in 1949. As a player, he earned berths on seven all-star teams. Harris is the fourth-team manager and an honorable mention outfielder in the *Courier* poll.

Signature Analysis

Harris was responsive to mail requests from collectors and his autograph occasionally surfaces in the hobby. The vast majority of Harris autographs in circulation are from his later years. Collectors should not confuse his autograph with that of the major leaguer of the same name. A sample of that Vic Harris signature appears in Appendix C. Harris' signature, which remained fairly consistent throughout his life, shows the following characteristics:

- "V" closely resembles a stemless "U."
- Break falls between the "V" and "i."
- Standard "V" slant at 110 degrees.

Scarcity: Limited   **Price Range:** $25–100

Signature from Homestead Grays team-signed sheet, 1931

Signature from the Bill Yancey Collection, 1938/39

Signature from postal request, 1980s

"Rats" Henderson

Arthur Chancy Henderson

Born: 1897, Richmond, VA **Died:** 1988, East End, VA

Career: 1923–31, Atlantic City Bacharach Giants

Henderson's career was like that of Dizzy Dean—brief but brilliant. He was regarded as one of black baseball's finest young hurlers of the 1920s and one of the best curveball artists in Negro leagues history. Cum Posey picked him for his all-star squad in 1924 and 1925, when he posted league marks of 8-1 and 14-10, respectively. Henderson turned in outstanding seasons from 1924–28 but the overuse and damage from throwing a sidearm curve caused his arm to go lame. He struggled into the 1930s, never regaining his early form. Despite the brevity of his career, his greatness was recognized. He was named a fifth-team *Courier* poll hurler.

Signature Analysis

Like most of his counterparts who share his longevity, insufficient autograph samples predating the 1980s exist to conduct a thorough evolutionary analysis. Henderson lived a long life and cheerfully responded to collectors' requests for his autograph by mail. The vast majority of the Henderson autographs in the hobby were signed when he was in his 80s and thus exhibit characteristic signs of aging and a high degree of variability.

The most striking variable is the overall size of his autograph. Some samples spanned nearly 4 inches of a 5-inch index card. Others (typically later samples) stretched barely over 2 inches. Henderson commonly added career or personal notations to mail autograph requests such as his age at the time of the signing or the teams he played for. Samples from his later years show the following consistencies:

- Standard "t" slant of 105 degrees.
- Breaks between names, "Hen" and "derson," as well as between the first stroke of the "H" and its right side.
- "R" closely resembles a "P" with its simple formation.

Scarcity: Limited   **Price Range:** $100–250

Signature from postal request, 1987   *Signature from postal request, 1980s*

122

Bill Holland

Elvis William Holland

Born: 1901, Indianapolis, IN   **Died:** New York, NY

Career: 1920–41, New York Lincoln Giants, New York Black Yankees

"Cool Papa" Bell ranked this ace of the New York Black Yankees' staff among the top four pitchers in Negro leagues history. Holland complemented his money pitch, the fastball, with a solid curve and a deceptive emery ball. He was at his best—or at least most consistent—during the early seasons of his 22-year career. He posted records of 17-2, 13-12, and 16-13 from 1920–23. Holland's best season, however, was 1930 when he won 29 and lost only two games against all levels of competition. There is limited information available on Holland's life after baseball.

Collectors should not confuse him with the Bill Holland who pitched for the Washington Senators in 1939 or the star black baseball pitcher of the same name who played from 1894–1909. An insufficient database precludes a detailed analysis of his autograph. The featured sample is the only one located during the preparation of this book.

Scarcity: Scarce   **Price Range:** Not established

Signature from the Bill Yancey Collection, 1938/39

Sammy T. Hughes

Samuel Thomas Hughes

Born: 1910, Louisville, KY   **Died:** 1981, Los Angeles, CA

Career: 1931–46, Baltimore Elite Giants

You won't find Hughes listed among the league leaders in many categories, but you will find him listed on the "Dream Teams" of such luminaries as Buck Leonard and Roy Campanella. What those "in the know" saw in Hughes was a thinking-man's player whose value to his teams often transcended the box scores. He was outstanding at second base, a superb contact hitter and a talented base runner. He is considered the premier second baseman in the Negro National League during the 1930s and merited an honorable mention at second base in the *Courier* poll. His lifetime average was an even .300. He is on the original list of Cooperstown candidates put forward by the Hall of Fame Committee on the Negro Leagues (see Chapter 3).

Signature Analysis

Hughes died prior to the onset of Negro league collector interest. Thus, a sufficient database for a detailed evolutionary analysis is not available. Collectors should not confuse Hughes with fellow Negro leaguer Sammy T. Haynes. Hughes' signatures show the following consistencies:

- "S" in later version made in a figure-8 fashion with a hook-intersection completing its base.

- Early samples show a simple cursive "S" formation.

- Breaks exist after "S," between names, after "H," and after "g."

- Hughes liked to use his middle initial, "T.," and its roof was formed with a stroke resembling a check mark. "H" is formed with two strokes.

- The first stroke begins at the top left with a small, extraneous horizontal loop formed to the left before dropping vertically down in completion of the letter's left side.

Scarcity: Limited   **Price Range:** $250–500

Signature from the Bill Yancey Collection, 1938/39

Signature from postal request, 1970s

Signature from Hall of Fame, Negro leagues questionnaire, 1972

Cowan Hyde

Cowan F. Hyde

Born: 1908, Pontotoc, MS

Career: 1927–50, Memphis Red Sox

This rocket-powered outfielder played professional-caliber baseball during four decades. Hyde's best years were spent as the leadoff hitter for the Memphis Red Sox from 1937–49, when he worked his way onto three all-star teams. He was a solid hitter with above-average power. While his averages bobbed around the .275 mark, his base-stealing ability and outstanding range in the outfield set him apart.

Signature Analysis

While not a regular on the signing circuit, Hyde has attended Negro leagues reunion signings. He has maintained good relationships with a number of autograph dealers, so his signature should be a fairly easy acquisition. Hyde single-signed baseballs are widely available on the market with prices ranging from $25–40 for samples signed during the 1990s.

Like most of his counterparts who share his longevity, insufficient autograph samples predating the 1980s exist to conduct a thorough evolutionary analysis. More recent examples show characteristic signs of aging. The recent examples provide the following consistencies:

- Commonly adds his nickname, "Bubba."
- Capital "C" begins with a downward, open circular stroke to the left.
- Signature includes first name followed by nickname in quotes before concluding with the last name.
- Only noticeable break comes between "B" and "u."
- Standard "H" slant of 120 degrees.

Scarcity: Readily Available   **Price Range:** Less than $25

Signature from Negro leagues lithograph, 1990s

Signature from endorsed check, 1997

Cowan F. Hyde

Signature from player questionnaire, 1997

Monte Irvin (HOF 1973)

Monford Merrill Irvin

Born: 1919, Halesburg, AL

Career: 1937–56, Newark Eagles; *Major Leagues:* New York Giants

Irvin spent 11 years with the Newark Eagles before moving to the major-league New York Giants in 1949. His performance in both leagues was Hall of Fame caliber. He won the Negro leagues batting title in 1941 and again in 1946 when he posted a stellar .406 mark. Irvin was also a constant home run threat. He was slated to become the man to break baseball's color line but Branch Rickey ultimately decided to sign Jackie Robinson while Irvin was serving in World War II. His best year in the majors was 1951, when he hit .312 with 24 home runs and a league-high 121 RBI. Irvin was chairman of the Hall of Fame's Special Committee on the Negro Leagues, and until recently served on the Hall of Fame Veterans Committee. He was enshrined at Cooperstown in 1973.

Signature Analysis

As a Hall of Famer, Irvin's autograph is highly sought after. He is a gracious and obliging signer and a regular on the signing circuit. A large number of Irvin-signed personal checks have found their way into the hobby. Irvin single-signed baseballs are widely available on the market with prices ranging from $25–40 for samples signed during the 1990s.

Irvin's signature has remained remarkably consistent throughout his life showing the following consistencies:

- Breaks between "M" and "onte," first and last names, and usually, but not always, "I" and "rvin."

- "M" in later versions contains an additional loop before dropping into the left portion of the letter. "o" begins with a simple vertical drop.

- "I" contains a horizontal half of a figure-8 loop when connecting to the "rvin." This loop is conspicuously absent when a break exists. "i" is formed by a horizontal extension from the "v," which then drops vertically before moving into the formation of the final "n." The "in" thus resembles an "m" more than an "in."

Scarcity: Readily Available   **Price Range:** Less than $25

Signature obtained at ballpark (hurried), 1951

Signature from team-signed sheet, mid-1950s

Signature from personal check, 1986

Signature from endorsd check, 1997

Gentry Jessup

Joseph Gentry Jessup

Born: 1914, Winston-Salem, NC   **Died:** 1998, Springfield, MA

Career: 1940–49, Chicago American Giants

Jessup was a four-time all-star and one of the best Negro leagues pitchers of the 1940s. The fireballing righty was the ace and workhorse of an otherwise lackluster Chicago American Giants staff. His moundsmanship was good enough to earn him a spot on Satchel Paige's all-star barnstorming squad. In his best season, Jessup posted a 14-9 league record and a 2.32 ERA. While remembered mostly for his pitching, Jessup was also an outstanding hitter.

Signature Analysis

Jessup was not a particularly active signer. He ranks among the more difficult Negro leagues autographs to obtain among those who lived well into the 1990s—and he was certainly one of the most difficult among the legitimate stars. He did, however, autograph a number of photos featuring Paige's all-star aggregation. Like most of his counterparts who share his longevity, insufficient autograph samples predating the 1980s exist to conduct a thorough evolutionary analysis. The recent examples show the following consistencies:

- "G" starts with a subtle movement up and to the left before it forms an unnecessary flat loop that descends into its body, the bottom part of which forms another unnecessary loop that travels upward before intersecting the letter's descender to the right. This letter somewhat resembles a capital cursive "Y," and its flamboyance is not repeated.

- Noticeable breaks between "G" and "e" and between "J" and "e."

- Closed loop forming the top half of the "J" is considerably larger than that forming its bottom.

- Standard "t" slant of 115 degrees.

Scarcity: Limited   **Price Range**: $25–100

Signature from endorsed check, 1994   *Signature from endorsed check, 1997*

Sam Jethroe

Samuel Jethroe

Born: 1917, East St. Louis, IL

Career: 1938–54, Cleveland Buckeyes; *Major Leagues:* Milwaukee Braves

Jethroe tore up the basepaths—and the pitching—of the Negro American League for seven years before embarking on a career in the major leagues. In 1944 and 1945 he led his league in batting and stolen bases. Jethroe would remain at or near the top of the stolen base tables throughout his tenure in the Negro leagues. The six-time all-star finished second in the Negro American League's MVP voting in 1943. His lifetime Negro leagues average is an impressive .340. He moved into the major leagues system in 1948 and earned Rookie of the Year honors with the Milwaukee Braves in 1950.

Signature Analysis

Jethroe was once a difficult autograph to obtain by mail, but in recent years his response rate has improved. He is a frequent guest at card-show signings. Jethroe-signed baseballs are widely available on the market with prices ranging from $25–40 for samples signed during the 1990s. As Jethroe was widely collected as a major leaguer, vintage material sometimes surfaces on the market. His signature, though at times showing considerable variations in letter formation and slant, shows the following consistencies:

- Inconsistent "t" slant of 115 degrees.

- Breaks between capital and lowercase letters and names.

- "S" is formed with a single stroke that originates from its base far below the signature's horizontal plane with a vertical upward stroke. This stroke then drops sharply from its peak to form two loops, the top of which is often so tight as to show no area, giving the appearance of a "B."

- "am" remain the most consistent and legible letters. "J" is formed using a single, large loop at its top.

- A vertically descending and curved stroke precedes the formation of the "e," which when combined almost gives the letter the appearance of a cursive "u."

- The "roe" is generally written without a visible appearance of an "o." Moreover, the "r" lacks definition, giving this letter combination more the look of cursive "ie" (with an undotted "i").

Scarcity: Readily Available   **Price Range:** Less than $25

Signed player profile document, 1997   *Signature from endorsed check, 1995*

"Heavy" Johnson

Oscar Johnson

Born: 1896, Atchison, KS   **Died:** 1966, Cleveland, OH

Career: 1922–33, Kansas City Monarchs, Memphis Red Sox

He may have run like he had feet made of lead, but the man they nicknamed "Heavy" had a bat of gold. The Cecil Fielder body double launched 60 balls into the bleachers against all levels of competition in 1924 and was considered one of the great power threats of the early days of organized Negro leagues baseball. Johnson was not, however, an all-or-nothing hitter. His discipline at the plate is reflected in his lifetime Negro leagues average, which is listed by various sources as ranging from .337 to .363. During his first four seasons, the behemoth slugger never hit below .345. In 1924, he journeyed into the stratosphere with a .411 average in 81 league games.

An insufficient database precludes a detailed analysis of his autograph. The featured sample is the only one located in the preparation of this book.

Scarcity: Scarce   **Price Range:** $250–500

Signature from note to American League Blue Book editor, 1950s

Judy Johnson (HOF 1975)

William Julius Johnson

Born: 1899, Snow Hill, MD   **Died:** 1989, Wilmington, DE

Career: 1918–37, Hilldale, Homestead Grays, Pittsburgh Crawfords

Johnson was arguably the finest all-around third baseman in the Negro leagues during the 1920s and 1930s. Not only was he a threat at the plate, as his lifetime .300-plus batting average indicates, but his play at the hot corner also was strictly Gold Glove–caliber. He enjoyed his finest years with the bat with Hilldale, carving out averages of .391, .369, and .392 during the team's pennant "three-peat," 1923–25. In his final season with the club, 1929, he went on a rampage, hitting .401. When Hilldale folded, he moved on to anchor third for two more dynasties: the Homestead Grays of the early 1930s and the venerable Pittsburgh Crawfords of the middle years of the decade. He was regarded as black baseball's answer to Pie Traynor. Johnson was a thoughtful and intelligent man who was among the most well-respected players of his time. After his playing days, he scouted for three major-league clubs and served on the original Hall of Fame Committee on the Negro Leagues.

Signature Analysis

Because he lived long after his election to the Hall of Fame and was such an obliging signer, Johnson-signed material is plentiful. Items signed during his playing days are rare. Autographs (especially those on baseballs) from the last four or five years of his life show some evidence of his deteriorating health and may prove somewhat more difficult to authenticate. Johnson single-signed baseballs are available on the market, with prices ranging from $200–300 for samples signed during the 1980s. Johnson often signed balls on the side panel (especially in the last few years of his life); nonetheless, sweet-spot signatures are available.

Johnson normally signed "Judy Johnson," though he occasionally added either "Wm." or "William." The examples shown here, though all originating after his induction, serve well in an evolutionary analysis of his signature from later years and show the following characteristics:

- Standard "d" slant of 110 degrees.

- "o" extends and is connected to the loop of its proceeding "h."

- Considerable character size variability.

- Light pen pressure.

Example A: "J's" are more vertical than remaining signature. No breaks except between names.

Example B: Distinct breaks between "J's" and their proceeding lowercase letters. "u" begins with a simple vertical downward stroke.

Example C: "J's" are constructed with two strokes. "u" is formed with an additional connecting stroke that originates from its left side, below the signature's horizontal plane.

Scarcity: Readily Available   **Price Range:** $25–100

Sample A: Signature from postal request, 1974

Sample B: Signature from postal request, 1976

Sample C: Signature from personal letter, 1978

Sample D: Signature from personal check, 1987

Henry Kimbro

Henry Allen Kimbro

Born: 1912, Nashville, TN

Career: 1936–50, Baltimore Elite Giants

If you've seen Marquis Grissom play, you have a good idea of the type of player Kimbro was. That's what Kimbro says anyway. He's probably being modest. Kimbro was one of the Negro leagues' most talented all-around players of the 1940s. The nine-time all-star was a potent offensive threat. In 1944, he batted .329, finished second in the league to Josh Gibson in home runs and led his league in stolen bases. He is credited with a .320 lifetime average and was consistently among the league leaders in key offensive categories. Kimbro also was regarded as a strong defensive player.

Signature Analysis

Kimbro occasionally attends card-show signings, although not with the frequency of some other Negro leagues players. Kimbro single-signed baseballs are widely available on the market with prices ranging from $25–40 for samples signed during the 1990s.

Kimbro was a consistent signer throughout his career and thus there is a good database against which to plot the evolution of his signature. His signature varies dramatically from sample to sample. His character formation shows few historical consistencies except for a distinct rightward slant. Collectors should note the following tendencies:

- Breaks are common between the capital "H" and "e" in his first name.

- It is not unusual for Kimbro to sign his first name with only the initial "H."

- The capital "K" in Kimbro is the most distinctive character in his autograph. It is formed in two distinct strokes. The first strongly resembles a cursive "S." The second stroke, which tends to look like an "h" or a stylized "l," begins at the middle or lower half of the initial stroke.

- Standard "K" stem slant of 140 degrees.

Scarcity: Readily Available   **Price Range:** Less than $25

Signature from all-star game pay slip, 1944 ("H" obscured)

Henry Allen Kimbro

Signature from player profile document, 1997

Signature from public autograph session, 1994

Sam Lacy (HOF 1998)

Samuel Lacy

Born: 1903, Mystic, CT

Career: Journalist, *Baltimore Afro-American News*

Lacy is the Dean of Negro leagues writers. In 1998, at age 95, he is still typing away at the *Baltimore Afro-American News*, the same newspaper that carried his eloquent coverage of the leagues in their heyday. Lacy and Wendell Smith are widely considered to be the most influential Negro leagues heralds for their crusading efforts to promote integration. Lacy was a central figure in organizing and promoting the Committee on Baseball Integration in 1945. He was also a member of the Hall of Fame's original Committee on the Negro Leagues that helped select the most qualified candidates for induction. In 1989, Lacy won a lifetime achievement award from *Sports Illustrated* for his reporting. He is also a member of the Black Athletes Hall of Fame. In 1998, he received the prestigious J.G. Taylor Spink Award from the Baseball Writers' Association of America at the Baseball Hall of Fame.

Signature Analysis

The signatures of Negro leagues sportswriters were not widely collected, and journalists aren't often sought out as autograph guests at card shows. Lacy signatures are not in broad circulation within the hobby. The 1997 samples featured here were written when Lacy was 94 and show the following consistencies:

- Breaks tend to fall after the "S," between names, and after the "L."
- He tends to place a short underline mark approximately below the "m" in his first name.
- Consistent "L" stem slant of 100 degrees.

Scarcity: Limited   **Price Range:** $25–100

Signature from book questionnaire, 1997   *Signature from postal request, 1997*

Signature from in-person meeting, 1990

Frank Leland

Frank C. Leland

No Biographical Information Available

Career: 1887–1912, Chicago Unions, Chicago Union Giants, Leland Giants, Chicago Giants

Before Rube Foster ruled the roost, Leland was the impresario of Chicago-based black baseball. He played a formative role in establishing the Windy City as the hub of the organized black game at the turn of the century. In 1901, he combined the Chicago Unions and the Columbia Giants to form the Chicago Union Giants, who metamorphosed into the highly successful Leland Giants in 1905. On the strength of Foster's arm and Pete Hill's bat, the club reeled off 48 straight wins in its inaugural season and is considered to be among the finest teams of the first decade of the century. It was under Leland that Foster developed into a marquee pitcher and also honed his considerable business acumen. In a classic case of the student becoming the teacher's master, Foster went on to unseat Leland as Chicago's most influential baseball magnate. The team, which he managed, won 48 straight games in its first year of play and was among the finest clubs—black or white—of the first decade. In 1909, the Giants played three closely contested games against the World Champion Chicago Cubs. A team Leland later formed, the Chicago Giants, was an original member of the Negro National League.

While the date of Leland's death has not been determined, he certainly died before the increase in interest in Negro leagues autographs. The samples featured here are the only ones located during the preparation of this book. A limited database precludes a detailed analysis of his autograph.

Scarcity: Rare   **Price Range:** Not Established

Notarized signature from Leland Giants incorporation document, circa 1904–05

Notarized signature from Chicago Giants incorporation document, circa 1909–10

Buck Leonard (HOF 1972)

Walter Fenner Leonard

Born: 1907, Rocky Mount, NC   **Died:** 1997, Rocky Mount, NC

Career: 1933–50, Homestead Grays

Leonard played Lou Gehrig to Josh Gibson's Babe Ruth in the Homestead Grays' great power tandem of the late 1930s and early 1940s. Gehrig would probably have been flattered by the comparison. Few players in the history of the Negro leagues commanded the respect on and off the field that Leonard did. He was a solid fielder and a .328 lifetime hitter, and his screaming line-drive home runs kept window repairers busy across the country. Leonard was widely considered to be black baseball's finest clutch hitter. Available records show a .433 playoff average and a .320 mark in World Series action. During an eight-year period in his prime, Leonard averaged 34 home runs a year against all levels of competition. He took his rightful place among baseball's immortals when he was inducted into the Hall of Fame in 1972.

Signature Analysis

On April 6, 1986, Leonard suffered a stroke that partially paralyzed his right side. He subsequently taught himself to sign with his left hand, hence the discrepancy between pre- and post-1986 Leonard signature samples. Collectors are advised to seek out pre-stroke signature samples, as post-stroke samples may ultimately prove more difficult to authenticate.

In early 1997, Leonard stopped signing autographs due to poor health. He passed away on Thanksgiving day that same year. Leonard was an extremely popular player and very generous with his autograph after his Hall of Fame induction. His signature should be an easy acquisition.

Leonard single-signed baseballs are widely available on the market with prices ranging from $35–50 for post-stroke samples. Pre-stroke balls are difficult to locate and command a significant premium. More than 100 Leonard personal checks are circulating within the hobby.

Prior to his stroke, Leonard often signed his full name, "Walter Buck Leonard" (though he occasionally dropped the "Walter"), when responding to autograph requests. After his stroke, Leonard found the chore of writing left-handed arduous and restrictive. His wife thus added personalizations to requests obtained through the mail and Leonard limited his signature to simply "Buck Leonard."

Pre-stroke characteristics:

- Standard "d" slant of 115 degrees.

- Breaks between capital and lowercase letters, as well as names.

- Center peak of "W" is highest vertical point of the signature.

- "B" is large, bold, and uniquely constructed, using one stroke that originates from the character's lower left side with an up and rightward diagonal movement.

- "k" is a two-stroke construction. The "k's" arm is literally a "v" that is tangentially attached to the "k's" ascender.

- "L" has two large loops. "e" begins with a stroke from the signature's base that decidedly intersects the "L's" base.

Post-stroke characteristics:

- Consistent "d" slant of 95 degrees.

- Breaks normally limited to between names and between "L" and "eonard."

- The "B" occasionally uses a double-back stroke as its left edge.

- Characters are shaky, yet deliberate and well-defined. They maintain the same general structural appearance as the pre-stroke version. Specifically, the "k" is the same two-stroke construction; the "L" also has two large loops; and the "e" begins with a stroke from the signature's base that decidedly intersects the "L's" base.

Pre-Stroke Samples
Scarcity: Readily Available   **Price Range:** $25–100

Post-Stroke Samples
Scarcity: Readily Available   **Price Range:** Less than $25

Pre-Stroke Samples

Sample A: Signature from the Bill Yancey Collection, 1938/39

Sample B: Signature from postal request, 1972

Sample C: Signature from personal check, 1981

Post-Stroke Sample

Sample D: Signature from endorsed check, 1994

John Henry Lloyd (HOF 1977)

John Henry Lloyd

Born: 1884, Palatka, FL   **Died:** 1965, Atlantic City, NJ

Career: 1906–32, New York Lincoln Giants, Atlantic City Bacharach Giants, Various Teams

When Honus Wagner says it's a privilege to be compared to you, that's quite a compliment. But when Babe Ruth calls you the greatest ballplayer of all time, there's not much left to say. Lloyd is widely regarded as the finest Negro leagues player of the 1910s and 1920s and one of the greatest of all time. "Pop" was peerless in the field and fearsome with a bat. The nomadic Lloyd, who played "where the money was," regularly posted batting averages in excess of .350. In 1928, he broke the sound barrier with a .564 mark—and that's not a typographical error. His Negro leagues statistics show a .353 lifetime mark in 24 seasons of play. "You put Wagner and Lloyd in a bag and whichever one you pulled out you couldn't go wrong," Connie Mack said. The Hall of Famer appears on *Total Baseball*'s list of the top 100 players of all time.

Signature Analysis

Lloyd died long before the onset of collector interest in black baseball. As a result, his autograph ranks among the most difficult of all Hall of Famers to acquire. This is despite the fact that he was reportedly responsive to those collectors who had the foresight to seek out his signature by mail. His signature shows the following characteristics:

- Standard "l" slant of 125 degrees.

- Breaks exist in the early sample between capital and lowercase letters, as well as between names and abbreviations.

- In later samples, Lloyd connects the "J" and "o" as well as the "L" and "l."

- He tended to write out his full middle name with a break between the "H" and "enry."

- "J" is typically the largest letter.

- In later samples, the proceeding "o" is centered at where the "J's" two loops merge. In the examined samples, the arm of the "h" appears together with the "n" to form what appears to be the letter "m." When isolated and examined in this context, the "hn" closely resembles a cursive "lm." "H" in "Henry" is comprised of two strokes.

- "L" in "Lloyd" is formed with two loops. It appears slightly flamboyant in the early samples, though it is the same design in the later versions, where it simply connects to the subsequent letter "l."

Scarcity: Scarce   **Price Range:** $1,000–2,000

Signature from the Bill Yancey Collection, 1938/39   *Signature from note to a fan, 1963*

Signature from a personal letter, undated

Lester Lockett

Lester Lockett

Born: 1912, Princeton, IN

Career: 1938–50, Birmingham Black Barons, Baltimore Elite Giants

A fine all-around player, Lockett ranked among the top hitters in the Negro leagues during the mid-1940s and showed occasional flashes of power. He took the batting championship in 1943 with a .408 mark and compiled a .333 lifetime mark. Lockett, whose style of play has been compared to that of major-league hit-man Bill Madlock, appeared in all-star contests in 1943, 1945, and 1948. Fleet afoot and a capable and versatile fielder, Lockett was at home parked at the hot corner or roving in the outfield. "He was a heck of a player," Buck Leonard remembered. "He could do everything."

Signature Analysis

Lockett is extremely active on the autograph circuit. He has been a constant presence at Negro reunions and Chicago-area shows for the past five years. His autograph ranks among the easiest of all Negro leaguers to acquire. Lockett single-signed baseballs are widely available on the market with prices ranging from $25–40. Like most of his counterparts who share his longevity, insufficient autograph samples predating the 1980s exist to conduct a thorough evolutionary analysis. Samples acquired post-1980 show the following consistencies:

- Breaks between the capital "L" and "e" in his first name and "k" and "e" in his surname.
- The "k" in Lockett rivals or exceeds the capital "L" in height.
- The "tt" ending of his surname structurally resembles a capital "M."
- Standard "tt" slant of 115 degrees.

Scarcity: Readily Available   **Price Range:** Less than $25

Signature from Negro leagues reunion signing, 1997

Signature from public autograph session, 1990s

Dick Lundy

Richard Lundy

Born: 1898, Jacksonville, FL   **Died:** 1965, Jacksonville, FL

Career: 1918–37, Atlantic City Bacharach Giants

When baseball historians talk about the "Big Three" Negro leagues shortstops, they are referring to John Henry Lloyd, Willie Wells, and Lundy. While the first two have found their way to Cooperstown, Lundy is considered by some to be a good bet to complete the trifecta. When Lloyd took over as manager of the Bacharach Giants, he moved himself—possibly the finest shortstop ever—to second base to make way for the young "King Richard." Lundy was a sure-handed, cannon-armed fielder who hit with power from both sides of the plate. He finished his 19-year career with a .324 Negro leagues average and .344 in exhibitions against white major-league competition. He is the *Courier* poll's third-team shortstop. Lundy is on the original list of Hall of Fame candidates put forward by the Committee on the Negro Leagues (see Chapter 3).

An insufficient database precludes a detailed analysis of his autograph. The featured sample is the only one located in the preparation of this book.

Scarcity: Scarce   **Price Range:** Not established

Signature from business letter, 1939

"Biz" Mackey

J. Raleigh Mackey

Born: 1897, Kingsbury, TX   **Died:** 1965, Los Angeles, CA

Career: 1920–47, Hilldale, Baltimore Elite Giants, Newark Eagles

Cum Posey, who owned the Homestead Grays and coached Josh Gibson, said that Mackey—not Gibson—was the best all-around catcher in black baseball history. Roy Campanella, who learned the craft of catching under Mackey's aegis, took the compliment one step further saying that the jocular, cannon-armed receiver was the best he'd seen in any league—black or white. As a handler of pitchers, Mackey was peerless. His snap release and laser-beam pegs to second are the stuff of legends. Mackey was almost as fearsome at the plate as he was behind it. The power-hitting four-time all-star retired with a .322 batting average. Mackey was an intelligent man and a keen student of the game. These traits served him well when he entered the managerial ranks in the later stages of his career. He led the Newark Eagles to a championship in 1946. Mackey and Gibson were named first-team catchers in the *Courier* poll. He is on the original list of Hall of Fame candidates put forward by the Committee on the Negro Leagues (see Chapter 3).

Signature Analysis

Though famously amiable, Mackey was not a prolific signer. While some source material suggests that he was "barely literate," a letter written in his own hand suggests that his writing skills may have improved considerably over the years. His autograph remains on the want list of many advanced Negro leagues collectors. Samples of his signature rarely surface in the hobby.

The following consistent elements appear in the limited sample population examined in preparation for this book:

- Writing style is extremely deliberate.

- "R" is a simple double-stroke formation.

- The "M" begins with a reverse horizontal loop to the left before dropping vertically to form the rest of the character. This loop is the only touch of flamboyance to an otherwise spartan signature.

- There is a noticeable uniform spacing between all letters.

- All descenders, on the "J" (when used), "g," and "y," extend beyond the leftward edge of the portion of their character that is written along the horizontal plane.

- Breaks fall after "R," between names, and after "M." Note that one example appears also to have an exhibited break in the "k" while the other example's "k" is fluid.

- Consistent "l" slant of 110 degrees.

Several anomalies occurred within the limited sample population we examined. Oddly and conspicuously in one handwritten letter example (see below), he ends his last name with the letters "ky." In other samples "key" is used.

Examined but not reproduced in this book is a Mackey signature on an early 1950s team-signed baseball, which he signed using his nickname. In this instance he spelled it "Bizz" (two "zz's" instead of the commonly cited "Biz"). There are not enough Mackey autographs in circulation to determine whether this is a preference or an anomaly, but this double-z variant spelling also appears in some Negro leagues sports columns and all-star programs.

Signature from player contract, 1940s

Signature from personal letter, undated

Signature (nickname "Mack") from team-signed sheet, undated

Dave Malarcher

David Julius Malarcher

Born: 1894, Whitehall, LA   **Died:** 1982, Chicago, IL

Career: 1916–34, Chicago American Giants

"Gentleman Dave" was an exceptional practitioner of "inside ball" as both a player and manager. His .267 lifetime mark provides a false picture of his effectiveness at the plate. He was a notoriously hard out, quick on the base paths, and an expert bunter. He is also widely cited among the top fielding third baseman in Negro leagues history. Malarcher was a disciplined student of the game who went on to manage after finishing his playing career. He was regarded as one of the Negro National League's finest managers. He credited Rube Foster for teaching him strategy. Malarcher was named a second-team coach and a fifth-team third baseman in the *Courier* poll. When his baseball career ended, he became a successful real estate agent and an accomplished poet.

Signature Analysis

Malarcher was an obliging signer and responsive to mail requests. Like most of his counterparts who lived into the 1980s, most of the existing autographs of him are from this later period in his life. These exhibit the following traits:

- Common breaks occur between capital and lowercase letters; names and initials; and "al" and "archer."
- Consistent "l" slant of 115 degrees.
- "D" is divided into four areas.
- "d" dips below the horizontal plane created by its preceding letters.
- "J" dips below the lowest point of the "d." Its bottom point is the lowest vertical point of the signature.
- The initial backward horizontal stroke of the "M" intersects the letter's stems.
- The "h" possesses a pointed arm that gives an appearance of a cursive "li."

Scarcity: Limited   **Price Range:** $200–400

Signature from Hall of Fame player questionnaire, 1972

Signature from postal request, 1970s

Effa Manley

Effa Manley (Maiden Name: Brooks)

Born: 1897, PA **Died:** 1981, Los Angeles, CA

Career: 1935–48, Newark Eagles

Manley played a greater role in the Negro leagues than any other woman. As part-owner of the Eagles with her husband, Abe, she took a hands-on role in all aspects of the team's operations. Following her husband's death, she took control of the club as president and general manager through 1948. On occasion, Manley donated the Eagles' gate receipts to civil rights causes, including the anti-lynching campaign. Hers was the strongest voice calling for major-league teams to adequately compensate Negro leagues clubs for pirating star players. Her club was particularly hard hit.

Signature Analysis

Manley signed many documents in her capacity as a team officer. Many papers from her years with the Eagles were donated to the Newark Public Library. Her signature most commonly turns up in the hobby in the form of inscribed copies of a book she co-authored, *Black Baseball Before Integration*. These books, signed or unsigned, are difficult to locate.

Manley commonly signed for her husband on official Eagles documents. We located three Newark Eagles contracts—those of George Suttles, Willie Wells, and Monte Irvin—that Effa signed on behalf of both management and the player (perhaps as reference copies for the club). Collectors should note this practice when examining Eagles documents.

The majority of Effa Manley signatures located in the preparation of this book are from the 1940s and 1950s. Few samples from later in her life have surfaced. Manley's signature was remarkably consistent throughout this period, showing the following characteristics:

- No consistent breaks between any of the letters in her first or second name.

- Collectors should note that this fluidity carried over into the signatures she ghost-signed for players or other executives.

- The first "f" in her name intersects the descending portion of the capital "E."

- The "E" in her first name is slightly elevated from the base of the signature.

- Consistent "l" slant of 125 degrees.

Scarcity: Very Limited   **Price Range:** $250–500

Signature from player contract, 1940

Signature from inscribed book, undated

Max Manning

Maxwell Manning

Born: 1918, Rome, GA

Career: 1938–49, Newark Eagles

At 6-foot-4, Manning was an imposing figure on the mound. He used all of that leverage to his advantage, becoming one of the most formidable pitchers of the late 1940s. From 1946–48, he amassed a 35-10 record in league play that included a perfect 10-0 season in 1946. That performance landed Manning on the all-star team and catapulted the Newark Eagles into the Negro leagues National Championship. That glorious year, he was second in the league in strikeouts to his Hall of Fame teammate Leon Day and was named Champion Pitcher—the Negro leagues' equivalent of the Cy Young Award. He had follow-up seasons of 15-6 and 10-4. Manning is credited with a 68-32 lifetime mark, good for a whopping .680 winning percentage. He was also a popular and successful pitcher in Cuba and Latin America.

Signature Analysis

Manning is a popular figure and remains active in many Negro leagues–related activities. His signature is widely available through autograph dealers. Manning single-signed baseballs are widely available on the market with prices ranging from $25–40 for samples signed during the 1990s.

Like most of his counterparts who share his longevity, insufficient autograph samples predating the 1980s exist to conduct a thorough evolutionary analysis. Though he sometimes uses his full name, Maxwell, more recent examples are commonly signed "Max." Manning's autograph is remarkably consistent in every respect:

- "M" begins with an extraneous double-back stroke that moves approximately 45 degrees downward to the horizontal.
- It then drops below the horizontal, curving to the right and up to complete the stroke. Both "a's" are centered on the "M" and rest above the hook created at the conclusion of each "M."
- Breaks fall after each "M" and between names.
- Consistent "M" slant of 120 degrees.

Scarcity: Readily Available   **Price Range:** Less than $25

Maxwell Manning

Maxwell Manning

Signature from player questionnaire, 1997

Max Manning

Signature from public autograph session, 1990s

Luis Marquez

Luis Angel Marquez

Born: 1925, Aguadilla, PR **Died:** 1988, Aguadilla, PR

Career: 1945–57, Homestead Grays, Minor Leagues; *Major Leagues:* Various Teams

Marquez played only four years in the Negro leagues before the color barrier started to break down—but they were an unpleasant four years for Negro leagues pitchers. In his sophomore season, Marquez led the Negro National League with a torrid .417 mark and notched 29 stolen bases. He earned all-star berths in 1946 and 1947 and finished his black baseball career with a .371 lifetime average. He was instrumental in the Grays' drive to win the 1948 Negro National League crown, the last in the history of the league. Marquez moved into the major-league system in 1951.

Signature Analysis

Marquez was an obliging signer. During his lifetime, his autograph was sought out by Negro leagues, major-league, and Puerto Rican collectors alike. His signature, while by no means easy to locate, does occasionally surface on the market. Like most of his counterparts who share his longevity, insufficient autograph samples predating the 1980s exist to conduct a thorough and evolutionary analysis. Recent samples show the following consistencies:

- Standard "L" slant of 85 degrees.

- "L" in "Luis" underscores or dissects the remainder of the first name.

- Consistent breaks exist between "L" and "u," "M" and "ar," "ar" and "q," "q" and "u."

- Marquez consistently included his middle initial, a separate and capital "A."

- The final letter, "z," is often formed like the numeral "3."

Scarcity: Limited   **Price Range:** $25–100

Signature from postal request, 1980s

Signature from postal request, 1980s

145

Horacio Martinez

Horacio Martinez (Milito Martinez)

Born: 1915, Santo Domingo   **Died:** 1992

Career: 1935–47 New York Cubans, Cuban Stars

Martinez was selected to the East-West All-Star game four times almost entirely on the strength of his fielding skills. He was widely regarded as the best gloveman among the Negro leagues shortstops of the 1940s. He had a rifle arm, outstanding range, and flawless mechanics. Martinez was a distinctly less dangerous presence in the batter's box. He consistently turned in averages under .250. He was a fast runner and was considered a good bunter and hit-and-run man.

Signature Analysis

Because he lived in Santo Domingo after his career, Martinez did not attend public signings or Negro leagues reunions. Few collectors sought out his autograph. Expect significant differences between his signature from his playing days and the years shortly before his death, as Martinez reportedly suffered from Parkinson's Disease toward the end of his life.

There are, unfortunately, far more inconsistencies in the samples we located for publication in this book than there are consistencies for analysis. Dealers all report dramatic variations in Martinez-signed material, making authentication problematic. That said, the following characteristics remain constant in early samples:

- Standard "t" slant of 125 degrees.
- Descending stem of "a" is integral to the formation of "r" in last name.
- The "H" begins with a simple left-to-right horizontal stroke that takes a sharp vertical turn down to form the letter's left edge.
- The "in" closely resemble a cursive "w."

Scarcity: Limited   **Price Range:** $25–100

Signature from all-star game pay slip, 1944

Jugador

HORACIO MARTINEZ (Coach)

Signature from coaching contract, 1966

"Lefty" Mathis

Verdell Mathis

Born: 1914, Crawfordsville, AK   **Died:** 1998, Memphis, TN

Career: 1940–55, Memphis Red Sox

The 1945 *Negro Baseball Pictorial Yearbook* cited the wiry, hard-throwing Mathis as "the most overpowering pitcher now active." He is one of the most underrated Negro leagues players of the 1940s—a consequence of playing for a perennial cellar-dwelling southern team throughout his career. A heady competitor who mixed his pitches well, Mathis started and won the all-star games for the West in both 1943 and 1944. He held his opponents scoreless in his three appearances in the summer classic. He personally racked up half of the Memphis Red Sox' wins in 1945 when he went 10-11. Mathis had an excellent curveball and one of the best pickoff moves in the leagues. He toured with Satchel Paige's All-Stars.

Signature Analysis

Mathis attended Negro leagues reunions but he was not a regular on the autograph circuit. His signature is widely available through Negro leagues dealers. Mathis single-signed baseballs are available on the market with prices ranging from $25–40 for samples signed during the 1990s.

Like most of his counterparts who share his longevity, insufficient autograph samples predating the 1980s exist to conduct a thorough evolutionary analysis. He sometimes included his nickname, "Lefty." Mathis' signature was remarkably consistent and recent examples with and without his nickname show the following consistencies:

- Consistent "d" slant of 115 degrees.

- Breaks exist between all capital and lowercase letters, as well as between all names.

- Ascenders are formed with loops.

- "V" resembles a "U" and its right-edge stroke is taller than its left.

- "t's" are crossed with strokes exhibiting a subtle left-to-right downward slant.

Scarcity: Readily Available   **Price Range:** Less than $25

Signature from endorsed check, 1992

Signature from public autograph session, 1990s

Webster McDonald

Webster McDonald

Born: 1900, Wilmington, DE **Died:** 1982, Philadelphia, PA

Career: 1918–40, Philadelphia Stars, Chicago American Giants

A crafty submarine-baller with superb control, McDonald had so many pitches at his disposal that he was nicknamed "56 Varieties." His best seasons were 1926 and 1927 when he posted 11-3 and 10-5 records, respectively. McDonald's documented 86-42 lifetime record ranks him among the top 10 winningest pitchers in the history of the Negro leagues. He had a 14-4 mark in exhibition contests against major-league competition and apparently made quite an impression en route to that record. "I'd give half my team for a player like you," Connie Mack told McDonald after a particularly strong outing. A highly respected and intelligent competitor, McDonald helped Ed Bolden organize the Philadelphia Stars. He served as a player/manager of the club. McDonald was named a third-team pitcher in the *Courier* poll.

Signature Analysis

Like most of his counterparts who lived into the 1980s, most of the existing autographs of him are from this later period in his life. The samples reviewed while researching this book show the following consistencies:

- Standard "t" slant of 100 degrees.

- Breaks between "W" and "ebster," first name and "M," "M" and "c," "c" and "D," "D" and "onald."

- "c" more closely resembles a printed "e."

- "ebster" and "onald" are written on a subtle upward slant.

Scarcity: Limited   **Price Range:** $100–250

Signature from postal request, 1973

Signature from postal request, 1982

Terris McDuffie

Terris McDuffie

Born: 1902, Mobile, AL   **Died:** 1968, New York, NY

Career: 1930–45, Newark Eagles, Homestead Grays

He was called—or rather called himself—"Terris The Great." Well, Terris "The Really Good" is probably a more accurate moniker for the flamboyant right-hander. McDuffie had a vast repertoire of pitches and mixed them effectively to keep hitters off balance. His forte was his stamina. In 1927, while he was playing with the Newark Eagles, he started 27 games and finished them all. In 1941, he posted a 27-5 record with the pennant-winning Homestead Grays. McDuffie was the consummate showman on and off the field, and an excellent drawing card for the many teams on which he played.

Although a popular player in his day, McDuffie seems to have signed few items. Some reports indicate that he was functionally illiterate. This may in part account for the dearth of samples. He also died before the onset of collector interest in the Negro leagues. An insufficient database precludes a detailed analysis of his autograph.

Scarcity: Scarce   **Price Range:** $250–500

Signature from pay slip, 1936

Signature from the Bill Yancey Collection, 1938/39

Buck O'Neil

John Jordan O'Neil

Born: 1911, Carabelle, FL

Career: 1937–55, Kansas City Monarchs; *Major Leagues:* Chicago Cubs (coach)

O'Neil is such an articulate and popular spokesman for the Negro leagues that his accomplishments on the field are sometimes overlooked. He was a fine player and an excellent manager. O'Neil's .353 batting average was enough to capture the Negro American League batting crown in 1946. While he did not produce such sterling numbers on a consistent basis, O'Neil was a solid hitter and an exceptional fielder. His lifetime batting average is .292. As a manager, he led the Monarchs to five pennants and skippered four all-star squads. O'Neil was the first black coach in the major leagues. He serves on the Baseball Hall of Fame Veterans Committee and is the chairman of the Negro Leagues Museum in Kansas City.

Signature Analysis

O'Neil is a fan favorite and an obliging signer. As the *de facto* Ambassador of the Negro leagues, he is a frequent and highly sought autograph guest at card shows. Collectors should find his signature easy to acquire. O'Neil single-signed baseballs are widely available on the market with prices ranging from $25–40 for samples signed during the 1990s. O'Neil is considered by some to be a legitimate Hall of Fame candidate based on his outstanding service to the game on and off the field. However, he is not eligible while he serves on the Veterans Committee.

As a result of his service as a Cubs' coach, O'Neil material predating the 1980s is available. O'Neil once commonly signed "John 'Buck' O'Neil," though he now more frequently uses simply "Buck O'Neil." Notwithstanding this fact and a few added "shakes" that are normal for one of his advanced age, an analysis of earlier examples to those of today vary insignificantly:

- Breaks exist between "J" and "ohn," and "O" and "Neil."
- Standard "h" slant of 120 degrees.
- "J" is typically the largest letter.
- "O" stroke extends beyond its closure point into its center, often dividing the inside into two areas.
- The "N's" right top edge falls noticeably below that of its left edge.

Scarcity: Readily Available   **Price Range:** Less than $25

Signature from public autograph session, 1980s   *Signature from endorsed check, 1994*

Ted Page

Theodore Roosevelt Page

Born: 1903, Glascow, KY   **Died:** 1984, Pittsburgh, PA

Career: 1923–37, Pittsburgh Crawfords

Known for his intimidating, spikes-high style, Page is credited with a .335 lifetime batting average in Negro leagues play and a .429 mark against major-league competition. He combined power and speed so well that he was at home at the top or in the heart of the lineup throughout his career. In his prime he was a fine glove man with terrific range but a mid-career knee injury cost him a step or two in the outfield and on the base paths. Fellow outfield great Clint Thomas said that Page was the best right-fielder he had ever seen. "He made playing the outfield one of the fine arts," Thomas said. Page was cited as an honorable mention outfielder in the *Courier* poll. After retiring from baseball, Page turned his considerable athletic skills to another sport—bowling. He owned an alley and wrote a newspaper column on the sport.

Signature Analysis

Page was an active signer and responsive to mail requests for his autograph. His autograph was once widely available through dealers but is becoming more scarce as samples are absorbed into collections. Like most of his counterparts who shared his longevity, insufficient autograph samples predating the 1980s exist to conduct a thorough evolutionary analysis. Those shown below show the following consistencies:

- Inconsistent "d" slant of 100 degrees.

- Breaks between all letters.

- Though letters sometimes overlapped, they were in essence all printed individually.

- The "T" and "P" rivaled each other for largest size and prominence.

- The "T" was formed with a simple vertical downward stoke and a near tangential horizontal stroke at its roof that sometimes extended to become the top loop of the "P."

- "e" and "d" commonly sit below the right roof of the "T," as does the "a" beneath the "P's" loop.

The flamboyant connection of the capitals "T" and "P" as shown in the first sample below is a common variation. The sample on the right—although decidedly less dramatic—is also authentic.

Scarcity: Limited   **Price Range:** $50–100

Signature from postal request,
post-playing days

Signature from postal request, 1980s

Satchel Paige (HOF 1971)

Leroy Robert Paige (Born: Page)

Born: 1906, Mobile, AL   **Died:** 1982, Kansas City, MO

Career: 1926–50, Pittsburgh Crawfords, Kansas City Monarchs, Various Teams and Leagues

Far and away the most popular and celebrated player in the history of the Negro leagues, the charismatic pitcher/philosopher dominated the Negro leagues landscape for more than two decades before finishing his storied professional career in the white major leagues. Even after stripping folklore from fact (a considerable feat when writing about Paige), he still comes away as one of the finest pitchers in the history of baseball. Paige combined a dazzling array of innovative pitches with a screaming fastball and pinpoint control to lay siege to Negro- and major-leagues lineups alike. Joe DiMaggio and Dizzy Dean called the lanky, enigmatic hurler the best pitcher they had ever seen. Paige, a first-team *Courier* poll pitcher, was the first Negro leagues player elected to the Hall of Fame. He appears on *Total Baseball*'s list of the top 100 players of all time.

Signature Analysis

Due to his extreme popularity, Paige received autograph requests throughout his entire adult life. "Paige never complains about autographing anything fans poke before him," *Chicago Defender* sports editor Frank Young noted in 1943. As a willing signer, Paige left behind a large population of samples for analysis. His signature went through several major evolutionary stages. Even within these stages variations abound. The authentication of his autograph is further complicated by the fact that Paige employed a ghostwriter to answer his mail during the years after his induction into the Hall of Fame when demand for his signature skyrocketed. Fortunately for collectors, none of the ghosts were particularly adept at mimicking his signature. See Appendix C for samples of ghost-signed Paige material. While Paige's autograph is not particularly rare, its value and variability make it an inviting target for forgers.

Paige single-signed baseballs are available on the market with prices starting at about $750 depending on vintage and condition variables. Collectors will often see Paige-signed business cards for sale. He signed hundreds, if not thousands, of these as an officer of the minor-league Springfield Redbirds.

Playing Days Samples Versus Later Versions
A great deal of discussion centers around the spelling of "Satchell" with two "l's." Though it is not clear when he dropped one of the "l's" in his first name, it appears to be an alteration he made sometime after his days in the Negro leagues. Some samples from his playing days, however, feature only one "l." There are documented samples of the "ll" variation into the 1950s. Note that many Paige ghost-signed items from the 1970s and 1980s feature two "l's." As a result, collectors should be careful when assessing "ll" samples received through the mail during that period.

• "S" tends to be the largest and most prominent letter in early version.

• "P" becomes more prominent in later samples.

• "S" flattens in later samples.

• Downward stroke to the "g" does not loop in later samples, instead forming a "v" as it extends from its bottom directly up to the right as it begins the "e."

• Name is sometimes underlined.

Historical Consistencies

- The capital "L" in his first name closely resembles a printed "S" and begins with a stroke to the right before doubling back up and to the left to form a closed, horizontal loop at the letter's top.

- "Leroy" shows the greatest consistency throughout Paige's lifetime, displaying little or no evolutionary change; however, Paige seldom wrote his first name, reserving it primarily for official documents.

- There are three primary evolutionary consistencies, including the simple formation of the "P" with a downward stroke that doubles back up to form the letter with a single loop, and a noticeable break between the "P" and the "a" and the open top loop of the "g."

- Early samples show consistent "ll" slant of 115 degrees.

- Later samples show inconsistent "l" slant of 120 degrees.

Scarcity: Limited   **Price** Range: $100–250

Signature from team-signed sheet, 1935

*Signature from letter to Effa Manley,
circa 1930s–40s*

(Jugador)

Signature from player contract, 1939

Signature from appearance contract, 1972

Signature from postal request, 1970s

153

Lennie Pearson

Leonard Curtis Pearson

Born: 1918, Akron, OH **Died:** 1984, Newark, NJ

Career: 1937–50, Newark Eagles

In the midst of a slump early in his career, Pearson sought advice on hitting the curveball from his team-mate "Mule" Suttles. Suttles was apparently a superb teacher. Pearson's work with the lumber helped him earn him spots on five East-West All-Star squads and a .316 lifetime average. He was the captain and an important offensive force on the legendary 1946 Newark Eagles club. As a player, Pearson was comparable to major leaguer Tony Perez. Both were average fielders who usually hit in the neighborhood of .300, and demonstrated above-average power and decent speed on the bases during the early years of their careers. He played in Cuba during the winters, where he won three RBI crowns.

Signature Analysis

Pearson reportedly signed his first name as "Lennox" on occasion. A few such samples have been seen on Cuban team-signed balls. It is uncertain how frequently he used this variation. Pearson died just prior to the onset of Negro leagues collector interest. An insufficient database precludes a comprehensive analysis of his autograph.

Scarcity: Limited   **Price Range:** $100–250

Signature from player contract, 1940s

Signature from loan agreement, 1939

Bill Perkins

William George Perkins

Born: Georgia   **Died:** Unknown

Career: 1928–48, Pittsburgh Crawfords, Philadelphia Stars

While best remembered as Satchel Paige's favorite catcher, Perkins was a bona fide star in his own right. His peak years at the plate were 1932 and 1933 when the burly power hitter produced marks of .332 and .360 for the Pittsburgh Crawfords. Though slow afoot and not particularly mobile behind the plate, the four-time all-star's strong, accurate arm made him a defensive star. He gave would-be base stealers fair warning of his skill by scrawling "Thou Shall Not Steal" on his chest protector. He posted a .287 lifetime batting average and was named a fourth-team catcher in the *Courier* poll. Perkins was reportedly killed in a restaurant but the circumstances surrounding his death remain a mystery.

Perkins died before the increased interest in Negro leagues autographs. An insufficient database precludes a detailed analysis of his autograph. The featured sample is the only one located in the preparation of this book.

Scarcity: Scarce   **Price Range:** Not established

Signature from player contract, 1939

155

Alex Pompez

Alejandro Pompez

Born: 1890, Havana, Cuba   **Died:** 1974, New York, NY

Career: 1916–50, Cuban Stars, New York Cubans

A man of "varied" interests, Pompez (pronounced Pompei) was among the most influential owners and promoters in the history of black baseball. He played a key role in organizing the first Negro leagues World Series in 1924 and served as vice-president of the Negro National League. He eventually worked as a major-league scout when his Cuban Giants became a New York Giants farm team. Pompez funded his clubs with money earned from the numbers racket. "[The numbers] was his main concern," Buck Leonard said. He played cat-and-mouse with the law throughout the 1930s. He served on the Hall of Fame Special Committee on the Negro Leagues in the 1970s.

Signature Analysis

Pompez died prior to the onset of Negro league collector interest. An insufficient database precludes a detailed analysis of his autograph. As a longtime owner, Pomez signed many documents over the years and samples occasionally surface. The samples located for this publication were signed long before his death (later samples may have different characteristics) and show the following consistencies:

- Consistent "l" slant of 100 degrees.

- Breaks between first and last names, "P" and "omp," and second "p" and "ez."

- Formation of "x" is a single horizontal stroke that intersects the extension of the previous letter, "e."

- "The top loop of the first "P" is left open. "m" more closely resembles a cursive "u" and leads into the second "p," which looks more like an "l" or an uncrossed "t."

- "z" closely resembles the number "3."

Scarcity: Very Limited   **Price Range:** $250–500

Signature from the Bill Yancey Collection, 1938/39

Signature from loan agreement, 1946

Signature from Cuban Giants letter, undated

Cum Posey

Cumberland Willis Posey Jr.

Born: 1880, Homestead, PA   **Died:** 1946, Pittsburgh, PA

Career: 1911–46, Homestead Grays

When historians discuss Negro leagues executives who should be in the Hall of Fame, Posey is usually near the top of the list. He was a solid ballplayer in the early 1910s but is best known as the father of the powerhouse Homestead Grays. Over the years, he built a club of semipro steelworkers into a Negro leagues juggernaut. During the heyday of black baseball, the talent-rich Grays defined the word dynasty. His club captured an amazing nine consecutive Negro National League pennants from 1937–45. Posey was known to have a keen eye for talent and a knack for luring players away from other teams to tighten his stranglehold on the league flag. His brother, Seward Hayes Posey (known as See), was a Grays officer. A sample of his signature can be found in the "Executive Box" section of Chapter 9.

Signature Analysis

In his capacity with the Grays and as a Negro National League official, Posey signed many official documents. His autograph surfaces on the market with greater regularity than most other key Negro leagues officials. In 1997, the rubber stamp that Posey used as a league official was offered at auction. It's not clear to what extent he used this apparatus in lieu of his actual signature. Samples located in the preparation of this book show the following consistencies:

- Consistent breaks between names and/or abbreviations, as well as the "P" and "osey."

- "C" begins with a vertical, downward internal loop.

- "P" is a simple, single, almost oval stroke and is the largest letter.

Scarcity: Scarce   **Price Range:** $500–1,000

Signature from endorsed check, 1930

Signature from player contract, 1932

Signature from handwritten note, undated

Alexander Radcliff

Alexander Radcliff

Born: 1905, Mobile, AL   **Died:** 1983, Chicago, IL

Career: 1932–46, Chicago American Giants

Ah, the perils of having a high-profile brother. You never get the credit you deserve. And the younger brother of "Double Duty" Radcliffe deserved plenty. Some consider him the finest all-around third base-man in the history of the Negro American League. While able with the glove, he was at his best in the batter's box, consistently producing .300-plus averages. Not only was he adept at getting on base, he also made regular slow trots around them. He is credited with leading the Negro American League in home runs in 1944 and 1945. Radcliff could have taken out a long-term lease on the hot corner all-star post. He was named to the team 13 times during his 14-year career and complied a .291 lifetime average.

Signature Analysis

While sources indicate a variety of spellings of both his first and last name, he was quite consistent in the use of Alex or Alexander (with an "x" not a "c"). The most inconsistent letter formation is the capital "R" in his last name. We observed no less than four distinct forms.

While his brother spells the family name "Radcliffe," for some reason Alex eschewed this spelling and dropped the final "e." This is consistent throughout his playing days and during his retirement. Signature breaks fall inconsistently throughout the samples we reviewed. The following characteristics remain constant in his autograph:

- Consistent "l" slant of 110 degrees.

- Letters tend to flow on a subtle upward slant.

- Letter-size variability and letter-space relativity are comparable.

Scarcity: Limited   **Price Range:** $100–250

Signature from the Bill Yancey Collection, 1938/39   *Signature from postal request, late 1970s*

Signature from postal request, early 1980s

"Double Duty" Radcliffe

Theodore Roosevelt Radcliffe

Born: 1902, Mobile, AL

Career: 1928–51, Chicago American Giants, Memphis Red Sox

Radcliffe earned his nickname by pitching one half of a double-header and catching the other. Over the course of his nomadic 23-year career, he proved highly—and apparently equally—skilled at both ends of the battery. He appeared in six all-star games—three as a pitcher and three as a catcher. During his prime, he consistently batted in the neighborhood of .300 and was regarded as an excellent handler of pitchers. Radcliffe was the Negro American League's MVP in 1943. He was involved in black baseball in various capacities for more than 50 years. He was selected on the third and fourth teams of the *Courier* poll as a catcher and pitcher, respectively. Sources list his lifetime batting average at .280.

Signature Analysis

Radcliffe is a gregarious and popular signer. He is a favorite at public signings around the country. Like most of his counterparts who share his longevity, insufficient autograph samples predating the 1980s exist to conduct a thorough evolutionary analysis.

He commonly uses the variations "Ted Radcliffe," "Double Duty," "Double Duty Radcliffe" or even "Ted 'Double Duty' Radcliffe." Like his brother Alex, "Double Duty" occasionally fails to form the letter "e" at the end of his last name. Unlike his brother, however, this appears to be an occasional variation in character formation and not a conscious exclusion of the vowel. Though he tends to employ signature breaks in varied locations, the following characteristics have remained consistent:

- Standard "ff" slant of 115 degrees.

- "T" is formed with two simple perpendicular strokes that do not touch and is the largest letter in the signature.

- "D's" are single-stroke formation, which are normally left open at their tops.

- "R" closely resembles a "P" with an otherwise continuous extension to connect to the following letter "a."

Scarcity: Readily Available   **Price Range:** Less than $25

Signature from Homestead Grays team-signed sheet, 1931

Signature from endorsed check, 1993

Signature from public autograph session, 1994

Branch Rickey (HOF 1967)

Wesley Branch Rickey

Born: 1881, Lucasville, OH   **Died:** 1965, Columbia, MO

Career: 1913–65; *Major Leagues:* St. Louis Cardinals, Brooklyn Dodgers

With one stroke of his pen, Rickey set into motion the integration of the major leagues and the consequent destruction of the Negro leagues. His decision to sign Jackie Robinson helped push the issue of race and civil rights to the forefront of America's post–World War II domestic agenda. While his place in history will forever be linked with Robinson's, even before the historic signing Rickey was widely regarded as the finest general manager in the history of the major leagues. A fiery motivator and shrewd judge of talent, he is credited with devising baseball's farm system and building the Cardinals and Dodgers into dynasties. He also founded a black baseball league, the United States League, and a team, the Brooklyn Brown Dodgers, in 1945. The league was designed as a revenue generator and a staging platform for African-American stars that Rickey wanted to bring into the majors.

Signature Analysis

The most consistent element in Rickey's signature is chronic inconsistency. Even samples signed literally moments apart (such as player transfers signed *en masse*) show significant variations. Though authentication of his signature is challenging, pen pressure was always great and all signature flow was rapid at the very least. In fact, Rickey wrote his name with a rapidity one might compare to that stereotypically associated with a doctor's signature. This quickness most certainly contributes to the number of variations; however, there are other consistencies:

- Though breaks vary, "Bran" is dependably connected.

- Letter-size variability consists of lowercase letters of the same height, with the exception of the ascender to the "h" which is generally about twice as high as that of the remaining lowercase letters; moreover, capital letters are three to four times the height of their lowercase counterparts.

- Variable slant of most letters. Bottom of "B" and descender to "y" are the only portions of the signature that extend below the general horizontal plane formed by the other letters.

- Top of "R" tends to be the highest point of his signature.

Rickey secretary-signed documents are not uncommon. Most, however, are initialed by the secretary, as was common practice.

Rickey is widely collected as a Hall of Fame executive. He was responsive to requests for his autograph and also signed many documents over the course of his career that surface regularly in the hobby. There are a small number (fewer than 35) of Rickey-signed personal checks on the market.

Scarcity: Limited   **Price Range:** $250–500

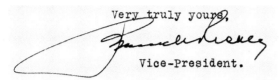

Signature from front-office correspondence, 1928

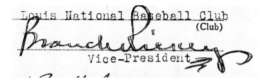

Signature from player contract, 1938

Signature from personal letter, 1949

Signature from personal check, 1964

Jackie Robinson (HOF 1962)

Jack Roosevelt Robinson

Born: 1919, Cairo, GA   **Died:** 1972, Stamford, CT

Career: 1945–57, Kansas City Monarchs; *Major Leagues:* Brooklyn Dodgers

It is impossible to overstate the impact of Jackie Robinson's major-league debut on baseball history, and by association, American history. He is one of the few ballplayers whose accomplishments on the diamond transcend the sport. His life, career, and accomplishments are well-documented. Robinson's Negro leagues stint was brief but had great impact upon the game. During his one year in Kansas City, the superb all-around athlete showed prowess at the plate, hitting for average (.387) and with considerable power. He was signed by the Brooklyn Dodgers organization in the winter of 1945. Robinson had an outstanding major-league career that led to his induction into the Baseball Hall of Fame. He was the first African-American enshrined in Cooperstown.

Signature Analysis

Robinson was an obliging signer throughout his life and normally signed with "Jackie," reserving "Jack" or "Jack R." for documents such as checks. Robinson was one of the few baseball players commonly collected on single-signed baseballs long before they became the medium of choice throughout the hobby. He rarely signed these on the sweet spot. He preferred to adorn empty baseballs parallel to the top part of a panel adjacent to the sweet spot, normally adding his favorite salutation, "Best Wishes." Robinson single-signed baseballs are available on the market with prices ranging from $1,500-4,000 or more depending on condition variables.

Over the years, the Robinson family has released approximately 1,200 Robinson-signed checks onto the market. They recently stated that there are no more in their possession. Some of the checks come with letters of authenticity from his wife, Rachel. Most dated from the early 1950s are signed "Jackie Robinson," while those from later years are usually signed "Jack R. Robinson." The checks debuted on the market in the $300–350 range and in 1997 were selling for $450-plus. Collectors should note that there was another major-league player named Jack Robinson who was active in the 1940s.

Though Robinson's signature varied considerably in details, it is commonly found in one of three styles. The first is the earlier, tight, "sit-down" version, shown here in the signed letter sample from his playing days. This is typical of Robinson's unhurried mail response samples from that era and exhibits a flow and distinct, individual character formation somewhat altered in more hurried, in-person examples and later versions.

The hurried and/or later samples—such as those collected through the mail—exhibit varied signature breaks and less consistent overall flow. We feature a sample obtained through the mail, Sample D, to illustrate this point. They are more choppy, slightly less defined, and arguably not as "neat" as the "sit-down" examples. Despite the variations, the following characteristics remain consistent:

- Standard "b" slant of 125 degrees.

- Breaks vary.

- Early samples may or may not have one between the "J" and "ackie."

- Samples may or may not have a break between the "R" and "obinson." Later samples consistently, though not always, demonstrate a break between the "s" and "on."

- "J" is the largest letter. "k," "R" and "b" are similar in height.

• The "R" is made with a double-back stroke that begins at its top.

Collectors should be aware of a third style commonly received by those who requested his autograph by mail late in Robinson's life. These are ghostwritten samples. These examples, though limited in number, occasionally surface. They are commonly passed as genuine for two reasons. First, legitimate collectors who thought they were getting the real thing acquired them blindly through the mail in good faith. Thus, when they enter the market, they come from legitimate collections with corresponding provenance. See Appendix C for a sample. Second, they do not vary drastically from genuine Robinson autographs. The differences have often been attributed to his failing health. The telltale difference of this version is the "R." Unlike genuine samples, this "R" does not contain a double-back single stroke. It is a simple, single stroke that begins at its base and moves upward before moving to the formation of the top loop of its formation.

Scarcity: Limited   **Price Range:** $250–500

Sample A: Signature from personal letter, 1949

Sample B: Signature from personal check, 1962

Sample C: Signature from personal check, 1965

Sample D: Signature from postal request, 1960s

Neal Robinson

Cornelius Randall Robinson

Born: 1908, Grand Rapids, MI **Died:** Unknown

Career: 1934–50, Memphis Red Sox

Robinson hit a ball so far out of Cincinnati's West End Park that they actually renamed the diamond "Neil Robinson Park." An eight-time all-star, Robinson was one of the Negro American League's most feared power hitters of the late 1930s and 1940s. His best season at the plate was arguably 1939 when he launched more than 50 home runs into the bleachers against all levels of competition. He captured the league home-run crown that year and repeated the feat the following season. Historian James Riley notes that the right-handed outfielder's fence-busting came at the cost of an abnormally high strikeout ratio. Despite this weakness, he recorded a .303 lifetime average. Robinson was at his best in the all-star contests, where he compiled an aggregate .476 average and a Ruthian .810 slugging percentage. He was considered an average fielder and had good speed on the bases.

Most biographical references note the spelling of Robinson's first name as "Neil," short for Cornelius. It appears, however, that Robinson himself favored the variant "Neal." This variation appeared on the three Robinson-signed items reviewed in preparation for this book. Two of the signatures were on team-signed baseballs. These were faded and unreproducable. An insufficient database precludes a detailed analysis of his autograph.

Scarcity: Very Limited   **Price Range:** Not established

Signature from the Bill Yancey Collection, 1938/39

"Bullet" Rogan (HOF 1998)

Wilber Rogan

Born: 1889, Oklahoma City, OK   **Died:** 1967, Kansas City, MO

Career: 1917–38, Kansas City Monarchs

"Bullet" Rogan was the greatest two-way player in the history of the Negro leagues. He joins Babe Ruth as the only moundsman to play major-league–caliber baseball who could legitimately lay claim to the cleanup spot. A workhorse pitcher, he won more than 10 games (the Negro leagues equivalent to winning 20-plus) every year from 1921–28. Many of Rogan's contemporaries consider him a better pitcher than his media-darling teammate, Satchel Paige. The hard-throwing, crafty hurler's .715 winning percentage is one of the highest recorded in black baseball history. From 1923–25 his arm and bat fueled Kansas City's drive toward three consecutive crowns. During those years, he twice batted .412, once .366, and posted records of 12-9, 16-5, and 12-2 on the mound. He is listed on the *Courier*'s first-team pitching staff. He was elected to the Hall of Fame in 1998.

Signature Analysis:

The majority of the small population of Rogan documents samples located to date feature his formal name "Wilbur Rogan." The use of the nickname "Bullet," seems reserved for less formal documents but also appears on the address portion of his passport, which dates from his playing days, so it's clear that he commonly used this moniker. Rogan was a popular and highly respected player. He managed the Monarchs in the latter years of his career and continued his association with the Negro American League after his playing days working as an umpire from 1938–46. (Collectors should note that Rogan's son shares his first anme but uses the variant spelling, Wilbur.)

As is the case with most Negro leagues star who died prior to 1975, Rogan was not widely collected. No government post-cards, 3x5s, or single-signed baseballs have surfaced on the market to date and no Rogan material has been offered for sale publicly since his induction. Today his is considered among the most difficult Hall of Fame autographs to locate. The population of signatures examined for this study exhibit the following characteristics:

- Consistent breaks between the first and second letters of his Christian name and his surname and "B" and "u" in nickname "Bullet."

- Inconsistent break between "g" and "a" in Rogan.

- Loop in formation of "g" in Rogan is typically unclosed.

- Inconsistent "l" slant of 125 degrees in nickname "Bullet" and "Wilber."

- "o" in "Rogan" typically begins off of the signature base line.

Scarcity: Rare   **Price Range:** Not established

Signature from K.C. Monarchs team-signed sheet, 1935

Signature from United States passport, 1930s

Signature from mortgage document, 1960

Louis Santop

Louis Santop Loftin

Born: 1890, Tyler, TX   **Died:** 1942, Philadelphia, PA

Career: 1909–26, New York Lincoln Giants, Brooklyn Royal Giants, Hilldale

Santop was black baseball's greatest power hitter of the early 20th century and one of its finest defensive catchers. The cannon-armed receiver was so strong that he could throw a ball from home plate over the center field fence in most parks. When he wasn't throwing balls over the fence, he was busy hitting them there by the bushel. Jocular and bear-like, Santop was among the most popular players of his day. "'Top' was our greatest star and the best drawing card we ever had," said Hilldale Club owner Ed Bolden. His popularity was based on prowess. Journalist Red Smith cited him as one of the great hitters of all time. Sketchy records show a lifetime batting average of .406 in league play. Santop was cited as the third-team catcher in the *Courier* poll and is listed on the original roster of Hall of Fame candidates put forward by the Committee on the Negro Leagues (see Chapter 3).

Signature Analysis

Santop was reportedly a voracious memorabilia collector. His apartment reportedly was a veritable museum of bats, photos, clippings, and other items from his playing days. Story has it that his collection was willed to his friend Bill Yancey, himself a former player, who is thought to have donated it to the Hall of Fame.

Sources note that Santop suffered from severe arthritis in the years preceding his death. His hands were so racked by the disease, one historian noted, that he hard a hard time rolling his cigarettes. With this in mind, there is likely to be a significant variation between samples from early and late in his life.

Santop died before the increased interest in the Negro leagues. An insufficient database precludes a detailed analysis of his autograph. The sample shown here is the only one located during the preparation of this book.

Scarcity: Very Rare   **Price Range:** Not established

Signature from the Bill Yancey Collection, 1938/39

George Scales

George Walter Scales

Born: 1900, Talladega, AL   **Died:** 1976, Los Angeles, CA

Career: 1921–52, Homestead Grays, Baltimore Elite Giants

Buck Leonard called Scales the best curveball hitter he'd ever seen. There are those who say that Scales is second only to Martin Dihigo as the best-hitting second baseman in black baseball history. A .309 lifetime hitter with solid power, Scales cracked the .400 mark twice early in his 25-year playing career. As his nickname "Tubby" implies, he wasn't exactly Lou Brock on the base paths, but he was quick, agile, and clever enough to hold his own on defense. As coach of the Baltimore Elite Giants, he taught future major-league star Junior Gilliam the finer points of fielding. He was named the fifth-team second baseman in the *Courier* poll.

Signature Analysis

Scales died before there was significant collector interest in black baseball, yet he was responsive to collector requests for his signature and samples periodically surface. His signature shows the following consistencies:

- First name is commonly abbreviated "Geo."
- Consistent break between the "S" and "c" in his last name.
- Standard "l" slant of 120 degrees.
- "l" in his last name is only slightly taller than the "e" and "s."

Scarcity: Limited   **Price Range:** $100–250

Signature from Homestead Grays team-signed sheet, 1931

Signature from the Bill Yancey Collection, 1938/39

Signature from postal request, 1970s

Dick Seay

Richard William Seay

Born: 1904, West New York, NJ   **Died:** 1981, Jersey City, NJ

Career: 1925–47, New York Black Yankees, Newark Eagles

Seay was to the Negro leagues what Bill Mazeroski was to the major leagues: arguably its finest-fielding second baseman. He was a central part of the legendary Newark Eagles' "Million Dollar Infield." If Seay had been half as good with the lumber as with the leather, he would have gone down as one of the all-time greats. While the three-time all-star flirted with .300 on a few occasions during his 22-year career, averages in the low .200s (and even into the .190s) were more the norm. Seay posted an anemic .206 lifetime mark but redeemed himself somewhat with his excellent bunting and hit-and-run expertise. He was at his best in exhibitions against major league clubs, where he hit .310.

Seay died before the increased interest in Negro leagues autographs. An insufficient database precludes a detailed analysis of his autograph.

Scarcity: Limited   **Price Range:** $100–250

Signature from player contract, 1940s

Hilton Smith

Hilton Lee Smith

Born: 1912, Giddings, TX   **Died:** 1983, Kansas City, MO

Career: 1932–48, Kansas City Monarchs

Many consider Smith to be the best all-around pitcher in the Negro leagues during the late 1930s and early 1940s. Bob Feller considered him better than Satchel Paige. Smith won 20 or more games against all levels of competition in each of his 12 seasons with the Monarchs. His best season was 1941 when he posted a perfect 10-0 league mark. The curveball artist pitched in seven consecutive all-star games. Smith was also a strong hitter and a fine fielder who was often used in the outfield or at first base. Smith's name does not appear on the Hall of Fame Negro Leagues Committee's original candidates list; he is, however commonly touted by historians as a legitimate candidate for a plaque in Cooperstown.

Signature Analysis

Smith was an obliging signer. He was responsive to mail requests for his autograph and he did a limited number of public signings in his later years. As a scout for the Chicago Cubs organization, he was more accessible than many former players and samples of his autograph surface regularly.

Like most of his counterparts who shared his longevity, insufficient autograph samples predating the 1980s exist to conduct a thorough evolutionary analysis. From the limited number of early samples located, however, it appears that Smith's signature was remarkably consistent through the decades. It exhibits the following characteristics:

- Standard "l" at 125 degrees.

- Breaks exist between "H" and "ilton" and first and last names.

- Left point of the first "t's" roof commonly touches the preceding "l" as does the right point of the second "t's" roof touch the "h" that follows it.

- "S" is connected to "m" with a continued horizontal stroke.

Scarcity: Limited   **Price Range:** $250–500

Signature from the Bill Yancey Collection, 1938/39

Signature from public autograph session, 1980s

Wendell Smith (HOF 1993)

Wendell Smith

Born: 1914, Detroit, MI   **Died:** 1972, Chicago, IL

Career: 1937–72, Journalist: *Pittsburgh Courier*, WGN Television

With its circulation of 300,000, no newspaper was more influential in Negro leagues circles than the *Pittsburgh Courier*, and no single journalist was more influential in promoting the integration of baseball than its sports editor, Wendell Smith. Through the pages of the *Courier*, and in personal meetings with major-league club owners, he crusaded tirelessly for the integration of the game. Smith was highly influential in Branch Rickey's decision to sign Jackie Robinson. He was also a member of the Hall of Fame's original Committee on the Negro Leagues that helped select the most qualified candidates for induction. Smith was President of the Chicago Press Club at the time of his death. In 1993, the Baseball Writers' Association of America posthumously awarded Smith its J.G. Taylor Spink Award, enshrining him in the writers' wing of the Baseball Hall of Fame.

Signature Analysis

The signatures of Negro leagues sportswriters were not widely collected and therefore there are few Smith signatures circulating within the hobby. Smith was a celebrity in the Chicago area as a television journalist with WGN. He signed some autographs in this capacity. An insufficient database precludes a detailed analysis of his autograph. The limited samples located in preparation of this book show the following consistencies:

- Inconsistent "ll" slant of 95 degrees.

- Breaks between "W" and "en," "en" and "dell, as well as between names.

- The "W" is more closed and formal in early versions. It becomes more open and simple in later samples.

- The base of the "S" drops below the signature's horizontal plane.

Scarcity: Very Limited   **Price Range:** $100–250

Signature from personal letter, 1937   *In-person signature, 1969*

"Turkey" Stearnes

Norman Thomas Stearnes

Born: 1901, Nashville, TN   **Died:** 1979, Detroit, MI

Career: 1923–41, Detroit Stars, Chicago American Giants

"If they don't put him in the Hall of Fame," "Cool Papa" Bell said of Stearnes, "they shouldn't put anybody in." Stearnes' name rests atop the Negro leagues all-time home run list. He tied or led his league in round-trippers seven times from 1923–32, more than any other player in Negro leagues history. "Double Duty" Radcliffe considered him one of the best defensive outfielders in Negro leagues history. He is credited with a .353 lifetime batting average and a .351 mark in games against white major leaguers. Stearnes, who once compared his style of play to that of Carl Yastrzemski, is on the original list of Hall of Fame candidates put forward by the Committee on the Negro Leagues (see Chapter 3).

Signature Analysis

Stearnes was responsive to mail requests for his signature. He ranks among the more active Negro leagues signers of the 1970s. Regardless, his signature is by no means common. Since Stearnes is usually touted as a strong Hall of Fame candidate, many collectors are holding his autograph in their collections.

The majority of the 3x5 samples we examined are inscribed with the date he joined the Detroit Stars (1923) and/or the names of the teams he played for (usually the Chicago American Giants). While he commonly signed "Turkey" Stearnes, he occasionally used his full legal name as shown below.

Stearnes was inconsistent in his formation of the letter "T." We observed no less than three distinct variations of the conso-nant when used as the opening letter of a word. As the formation of a first letter in a name (in this case "Turkey") is usually quite consistent, this is an important point for collectors and authenticators to note. In the cases where he signed with his middle inital, "T," he commonly formed the letter in a non-cursive style.

Most samples we located in preparation of this book are post-1970. These show the following characteristics:

- Nickname "Turkey" occasionally begins with a lowercase "t."

- Breaks may or may not exist between capital and lowercase letters.

- Breaks may or may not show up elsewhere, such as between the "m" and "an."

- Inconsistent "t" slant of 115 degrees.

- The "S" is the largest and most distinctive letter. It is formed from its base with an upward stroke that doubles back down to its center where it employs half of a horizontal figure-8 before dropping to its base where it forms another, but larger, horizontal half figure-8. If one examines only the bottom portion of the "S," beginning with the first horizontal half figure-8, what remains closely resembles a capital, cursive "I."

- A less subtle consistency that does not reproduce is instrument pressure. Stearnes applied only slight pressure when signing with a ballpoint pen. As such, many 3x5 samples have a less-than-bold presentation quality.

Scarcity: Limited   **Price Range:** $500–1,000

Signature from the Bill Yancey Collection, 1938/39

leted copies of the notice set forth above.

(CUSTOMER'S SIGNATURE)

Signature from receipt, 1973

Signature from postal request, 1970s

Signature from postal request, 1970s

"Country Jake" Stephens

Paul Eugene Stephens (Stevens)

Born: 1900, Pleasureville, PA **Died:** 1981, York, PA

Career: 1921–37, Hilldale

Stephens got his tryout with the Hilldale Club by sending owner Ed Bolden a glowing "anonymous" scouting report on himself. This foot in the door was all he needed. *Courier* sportswriter Chester Williams called the crafty Stephens "the Rabbit Maranville of colored baseball." The two were indeed cut from the same cloth in size, skill, and temperament. The pugnacious 5-foot-7 Stephens was popular with fans, an outstanding fielder, and a devil on the base paths. Although a light hitter, he had excellent bat control and was considered a first-class hit-and-run man. A sparkplug player, Stephens' value to his teams transcended the box scores. The 17-year veteran played on championship teams with four different clubs.

Signature Analysis

Stephens died before the onset of collector interest in the Negro leagues. Still, some forward-thinking collectors acquired his autograph by mail and samples do surface on occasion. Like most of his counterparts who shared his longevity, insufficient autograph samples predating the 1980s exist to conduct a thorough evolutionary analysis.

According to biographical information, the legal spelling of the shortstop's last name is "Stephens." But as noted in most reference works, he also employed the variant "Stevens," which he apparently preferred when signing autographs. He also consistently combined his legal forename, "Paul," and his nickname, "Country Jake," to form the variant "Paul Jake Stephens." His signature exhibits the following characteristics:

- The "a" in "Paul" commonly touches or breaches the far right loop of the initial "P."

- Inconsistent "l" slant of 100 degrees.

- Consistently small breaks between three component words in his signature.

- First and last letters of words commonly touch or overlap.

- Sentiment "Compliments of" commonly appears above the signature.

Scarcity: Limited   **Price Range:** $100–250

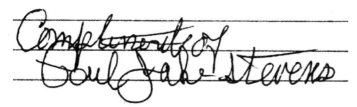

Signature from postal request, 1977

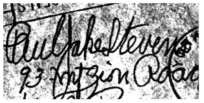

Signature from postal request, 1978

Ed Stone

Ed Stone

Born: 1909, Black Cat, DE   **Died:** 1983, New York, NY

Career: 1931–50, Atlantic City Bacharach Giants, Newark Eagles

Stone was a durable, smooth-swinging outfielder who was at his best with the formidable Newark Eagles teams of the late 1930s. Although not known as a pure power hitter, in 1938 and 1939 he occupied the club's cleanup spot. In this post he hit between legends Willie Wells and Mule Suttles. The two-time all-star's best seasons at the plate were 1937 and 1939 when he recorded averages of .334 and .363, respectively. Historian James Riley notes that the left-handed hitter had an excellent eye at the plate and drew more than his fair share of walks. He was considered a good glove and a strong arm in right field.

Stone died before the increase in interest in Negro leagues autographs. It appears that few collectors had the foresight to pursue his signature. The two samples shown here were the only two located in preparation of this book. An insufficient database of samples precludes a detailed analysis of his autograph.

Scarcity: Very Limited   **Price Range:** Not established

Signature from all-star game pay slip, 1944

Signature from the Bill Yancey Collection, 1938/39

Ted Strong

Ted R. Strong

Born: 1917, South Bend, IN   **Died:** 1951, Chicago, IL

Career: 1937–48, Kansas City Monarchs

One of the finest all-around outfielders of the 1940s, the switch-hitting Strong was a five-time all-star who batted in the top third of the Monarchs batting order during their halcyon days of the 1940s. He led the league in home runs and RBI in 1946 and demonstrated Gold Glove–caliber fielding throughout his career. Strong was a gifted athlete who in the off-season captained the Western touring unit of the original Harlem Globetrotters basketball team. He was cited as an honorable mention outfielder in the *Courier* poll.

Strong died at a relatively young age, well before increased collector interest in the Negro leagues. The signature shown here is the only sample found in research conducted for this book. An insufficient data-base of sample precludes a detailed analysis of his autograph.

Scarcity: Very Rare   **Price Range:** Not established

Signature from the Bill Yancey Collection, 1938/39

"Mule" Suttles

George Suttles

Born: 1900, Brockton, LA   **Died:** 1966, Newark, NJ

Career: 1918–44, St. Louis Stars, Newark Eagles

Physics dictates that when a fast-moving pitch is hit by a powerful man using a bat as thick as the New York City telephone book, the ball is going for a long ride. And that's what Suttles excelled at: launching the ball into orbit. Judy Johnson dubbed him the "Jimmie Foxx of Negro baseball." The "Mule" led the Negro leagues in home runs three times during his career and is second to Turkey Stearnes on the Negro leagues' all-time round-tripper list. Although he struck out frequently and was a liability on the basepaths, the five-time all-star managed an impressive .329 lifetime batting average and a .374 mark in exhibitions against white clubs. Suttles is listed as a fourth-team outfielder and an honorable mention first baseman in the *Courier* poll. He is on the original list of Hall of Fame candidates put forward by the Committee on the Negro Leagues (see Chapter 3).

Signature Analysis

Suttles died before the onset of Negro leagues collector interest. Few examples of his signature in any form have surfaced. We located two document signatures that show the following consistencies:

- "G" closely resembles a cursive "Y." It is a single stroke, clearly open at the base, and it closes with a small loop at its bottom. "o" is formed with a top, horizontal loop that moves to the right to form the next letter, "r." "eorge" and "uttles" are written on a subtle upward slant as they move away from "G" and "S," respectively. "ttl" are spaced equidistantly and closely resemble a single "W" or "M."

- "e" and "s" are written in a peculiar way that gives their appearance that of a "v."

- The "s" is that signature's smallest letter, coming to less than one-half the height of the "e."

- The base of the "s," moreover, is well above the signature's horizontal plane and is finished with a horizontal extension to the right.

- The arm of the "tt's" extend through the "l," joining all three letters.

- Breaks fall after "G" and between names.

- Consistent "l" slant of 120 degrees.

Scarcity: Very Rare   **Price Range:** Not established

Signature from pay slip, 1936

Signature from player contract, 1940s

Ben Taylor

Benjamin Harrison Taylor

Born: 1888, Anderson, SC   **Died:** 1953, Baltimore, MD

Career: 1910–40, Indianapolis ABCs

Taylor was the black baseball's finest all-around first baseman during the early decades of the 20th century. The Gold Glove–caliber fielder produced a robust .324 lifetime batting average. He cracked the .300 barrier in all but three of his 17 seasons as a full-time player. Taylor was also an outstanding pitcher in his formative years. In 1909 he notched a 22-3 mark against all levels of competition, and trumped that performance with a sterling 30-1 mark two years later. But his skill at the plate was such that his move from the mound—*à la* Babe Ruth—was inevitable. He was a highly regarded manager and worked as an umpire after retiring. Taylor was named the second-team first baseman in the *Courier* poll. He is the brother of Negro leaguers C.I. Taylor, John "Steel Arm" Taylor, and "Candy Jim" Taylor.

Collectors should note that Taylor's left arm was amputated in the later years of his life. It is uncertain whether or not he signed with his left hand. Obviously a change of hand would have dramatically altered his signature. Collectors should note that there were two major-league players named Ben Taylor. One played in 1912 and the other from 1951–53.

Taylor died before the increased interest in Negro leagues autographs. An insufficient database precludes a detailed analysis of his autograph. The featured sample is the only one located in the preparation of this book.

Scarcity: Very Rare   **Price Range:** Not established

Signature from letter to Hilldale Club, 1932

"Candy Jim" Taylor

James Allen Taylor

Born: 1884, Anderson SC **Died:** 1948, Chicago, IL

Career: 1904–48, St. Louis Stars, Chicago American Giants

"Candy Jim" lived the history of the Negro leagues. As a player, manager, and league official, he saw the birth of organized black baseball, and died a year after integration began. While he was a strong-hitting third baseman in his day, he is probably best remembered as a manager. His best years at the plate came between 1923 and 1927 when he was a playing manager with the St. Louis Stars. During that period, he broke the .300 barrier three times, including a torrid .389 mark in 1927. He served as vice-chairman of the Negro National League and was named an honorable mention third baseman in the *Courier* poll. He is the brother of Negro leaguers Ben, C.I., and John "Steel Arm" Taylor.

Taylor died before the increased interest in Negro leagues autographs. An insufficient database precludes a detailed analysis of his autograph.

Scarcity: Rare   **Price Range:** Not established

Signature from the Bill Yancey Collection, 1938/39

C.I. Taylor

Charles Ishum Taylor

Born: 1875, SC   **Died:** 1922, Indianapolis, IN

Career: 1904–22, Indianapolis ABCs

Black baseball had two majestic managerial figures against whom all others were measured. They were Rube Foster and Taylor. An outstanding teacher and master strategist, Taylor was considered a class act by all who played for or against him. After attending Clark College and serving in the Spanish-American War, Taylor began his 19-year coaching career in 1904 as a playing manager. He is best know as the architect of the powerful ABCs club that beat Rube Foster's Chicago American Giants for the 1916 Western Championship crown. He was the first vice-president of the Negro National League and was cited as a second-team coach in the *Courier* poll. Taylor died at the young age of 47. He is the brother of Negro leaguers Ben, John "Steel Arm," and "Candy Jim" Taylor.

Taylor died before the increased interest in Negro leagues autographs. An insufficient database precludes a detailed analysis of his autograph.

Scarcity: Very Rare   **Price Range:** Not established

Signature from letter to Cincinnati Reds, 1920

Clint Thomas

Clinton Cyrus Thomas

Born: 1896, Greenup, KY **Died:** Unknown

Career: 1920–38, Hilldale, New York Black Yankees

Thomas and modern-era major leaguer Andre Dawson share more than the nickname "Hawk." They were cut from the same cloth as ballplayers. Thomas was one of the finest all-around outfielders of his era. Fleet-footed and powerful, he excelled at the plate, on the bases, and in the outfield. After batting .342 with the Detroit Stars in 1922, Thomas moved to the Hilldale club where he hit full stride with a .373 average, 23 home runs, and 56 stolen bases. He followed that season with two years at .350-plus. Thomas' lifetime average in league play was .305, and he is credited with 376 home runs against all levels of competition. He was also a star in Cuba during the winter season, where he once hit a home run off a young pitcher named Fidel Castro.

Signature Analysis

Thomas was an active signer in the 1980s and his autograph surfaces regularly on a variety of items. An insufficient database of early signatures precludes a detailed evolutionary analysis of his autograph. Autographs signed after 1980, however, show the following consistencies:

- Standard "l" slant of 100 degrees.
- Breaks after capital letters of first and last name "C" descends below the horizontal plane of the signature.
- "i" is dotted to the extreme right of the character.

Scarcity: Limited   **Price Range:** $25–100

Signature from official document, playing days

Signature from postal request, 1982

182

Luis Tiant

Luis Eleuterio Tiant Sr.

Born: 1906, Havana, Cuba   **Died:** 1977, Havana, Cuba

Career: 1930–44, Cuban Stars, New York Cubans

Tiant's pickoff move was so deceptive that he once struck out a man while throwing to first base. Whether fact or fiction, the story underlines the fact that deceit was central to Tiant's success. The lefty's herky-jerky motion combined with his bag of junk pitches, a solid fastball, and pinpoint accuracy made him one of the most successful pitchers of his day. At one point in his career, he was called the Cuban Carl Hubbell. Tiant was a two-time all-star and a fifth-team Courier poll pitcher. He is the father of the great major hurler of the same name.

Tiant died before the increased interest in Negro leagues autographs. An insufficient database precludes a detailed analysis of his autograph. The featured sample is the only one located in the preparation of this book.

Scarcity: Very Limited   **Price Range:** Not established

Signature from the Bill Yancey Collection, 1938/39

Quincy Trouppe

Quincy Trouppe (Troupe)

Born: 1912, Dublin, GA   **Died:** 1993, Creve Coeur, MO

Career: 1930–53, Kansas City Monarchs, Mexican Leagues; *Major Leagues:* Cleveland Indians

A strong defensive receiver with good power, the switch-hitting Trouppe played ball virtually year-round for 20 years—an amazing feat for anyone, let alone a catcher. When he wasn't behind the plate in a Negro leagues game, he could probably be found on a lineup card somewhere in Canada, Mexico, or the minor leagues. He also spent a brief period with the Cleveland Indians when he was 40 years old. Trouppe consistently hit over .300 in the Negro leagues and earned berths in five East-West All-Star games. He became a successful manager, leading the Cleveland Buckeyes to Negro American League championships in 1945 and 1947.

Signature Analysis

Trouppe was a prolific signer. He was collected as both a Negro and major leaguer. His autograph surfaces on the market regularly. It does, however, command a premium price considering his relatively recent death. Trouppe single-signed baseballs are available on the market on a limited basis. Recent samples have sold for $100–150.

Collectors will note that early Trouppe signatures feature only one "p" in the last name. Trouppe told a noted Negro leagues historian that the "one p" variation is his given name. He added a second "p" while playing South of the border and over time decided to retain the extra consonant. His autograph shows the following historical consistencies:

- Early samples features a break between the "Q" and "uincy," both names, and "T" and "roupe." Later samples show an additional break between the "uin" and "cy," as well as "u" and "p," "p" and "p," and "p" and "e."

- The "Q" in early versions of his signature is a single-stroke oval that begins at the top and doubles through itself, finishing with a movement that concludes with an intersection at its base.

- Later examples are also single strokes but more closely resemble a slanted number "2."

- "T's" were consistently two strokes that do not touch; "p's" vary from one to two strokes. "e's" are generally traditional in early versions and stylized in later samples.

- Standard "T" slant of 130 degrees.

Scarcity: Limited   **Price Range:** $25–100

Signature from Monarchs team-signed sheet, 1935
(Note single "p" variation)

Signature from postal request, 1970

Signature from American League Blue Book *questionnaire, 1953*

Moses Fleetwood Walker

Moses Fleetwood Walker

Born: 1857, Mount Pleasant, OH   **Died:** 1924, Steubenville, OH

Career: 1883–89, Minor Leagues, Major Leagues

A central figure in the history of the national pastime, Walker was the first African-American to play major-league baseball. In 1884, he joined the Toledo Blue Stockings of the Northwestern League for 42 games and hit a respectable .263—23 points above the league average. It was Cap Anson's reaction to the presence of Walker and pitcher George Stovey in an International League match that helped create a color line in baseball that would not be broken for more than a half century. His brother, Welday Walker, was the second black major-league player. After leaving baseball in 1889, Walker, an Oberlin College graduate, became an influential editor and writer. He was justifiably bitter about his treatment by the white baseball establishment and became a leading proponent of the back-to-Africa movement. Walker owned a successful movie theater in his native Ohio.

Signature Analysis

Despite the fact that Walker was a prolific writer, his signature rarely (if ever) surfaces in the hobby. The samples shown below are the first that any of the members of our expert panel had seen. As a player whose historical significance transcends the game, most of his papers are held by museums and libraries.

Though they differ in the use of initials versus his full name, the samples shows below exhibit the following consistencies:

- Standard "k" slant of 100 degrees.
- Notwithstanding the break between the "F" and "leetwood," breaks are found only between names and/or abbreviations.
- The "F" is made with three strokes and it comes close to but does not intersect its stem.
- The three top points of the "W" can almost be connected in a descending line.
- Character-size variability is remarkably constant.

Scarcity: Very Rare   **Price Range:** Not established

Signature from business letter, 1920

Signature from college biography questionnaire, 1922

Willie Wells (HOF 1997)

William James Wells Sr.

Born: 1905, Austin, TX   **Died:** 1989, Austin, TX

Career: 1924–49, St. Louis Stars, Newark Eagles

In his prime, Wells was arguably the best shortstop in baseball—in any league, in any country. The fleet, 5-foot-8, 160-pound mid-fielder was an unlikely power package who once led the Negro leagues with 27 home runs in 88 games. He compiled a lifetime average of .328 that included batting titles in 1929 and 1930. Wells is the Negro leagues all-time doubles leader and ranks fifth in both triples and home runs. He anchored the Newark Eagles' legendary "Million Dollar Infield" and later coached the club to a championship. Wells was also a fan favorite in Mexico where he played in the winter league. In many ways he enjoyed playing there more than in the United States. He was named the second-team shortstop in the *Courier* poll. His son, Willie Jr., played in the Negro leagues from 1945–50.

Signature Analysis

Like most of his counterparts who shared his longevity, autograph samples predating the 1980s are quite rare and thus an evolutionary analysis is problematic. His signature shows a considerable degree of variability, including:

- "W's" were sometimes formed with rounder edges like those found on the bottoms of "U's"; other times they were sharper and more geometric in design.

- "ll's" were sometimes made with open loops while at other times they were constructed with loops closed. "i's" were sometimes dotted; sometimes slashed; and sometimes left with no punctuation at all.

- "Sr.," in its randomness, seems to appear more often than not, especially in later samples.

Traits commonly exhibited in the analyzed sample population include:

- Character-size variability.

- Breaks between "W" and "illie," first and last names, as well as last name and Sr. (when used), and "W" and "ells."

- Inconsistent slant of 110 degrees "ll" in the name "Willie."

Note that Wells was purportedly partially blinded by a stroke. Post-stroke examples exhibit his first name written on an angle of approximately 135 degrees before signature completion with a horizontally written last name (see 1989 index card sample shown on facing page). Other consistencies that are more subtle and tough to reproduce—but visible on originals—are instrument pressure and flow.

Scarcity: Limited   **Price Range:** $250–500

William Wells

Signature from pay slip, 1936

W. Wells S.S.

Signature from the Bill Yancey Collection, 1938/39

Willie Wells 8c

Signature from endorsed check, 1972

mink in sport
Willie Wells sr

Signature from personal letter, 1972

Willie Wells

Signature from postal request, 1989

J. L. Wilkinson

James Leslie Wilkinson

Born: 1878, Perry, IA   **Died:** 1964, Kansas City, MO

Career: 1909–48, All Nations, Kansas City Monarchs

Wilkinson was the founder, owner, and architect of the Kansas City Monarchs. He built the club into one of the Negro leagues' greatest and most consistently profitable franchises. Under his leadership, the Kansas City franchise won 10 pennants and two of the four Negro leagues championships they competed for. Wilkinson helped bring night baseball to the Negro leagues five years before it became popular in the major leagues. He was well liked and respected by his players. Before forming the Monarchs, Wilkinson organized the successful mixed-race All Nations team.

Signature Analysis

Though Wilkinson died decades before the onset of Negro leagues collector interest, he did sign many documents and contracts during his life, some of which have surfaced on the market. Two such examples shown below show the following remarkable consistencies in spite of having been signed 15 years apart:

- Breaks are found between initials and after "W."

- The left side of his "W" begins with an extraneous loop that closely resembles that of the top half of his "J."

- The letter finishes with a horizontal slant to the right which ends at a point commensurate with the height of the "i" that follows.

- Standard "L" slant of 115 degrees.

Scarcity: Scarce   **Price Range:** $250–500

Notarized signature from Negro leagues document, 1925

Bobby Williams

Robert Lawns Williams

Born: 1895, New Orleans, LA   **Died:** 1978, Chicago, IL

Career: 1918–34, Chicago American Giants, Various Teams

A scrappy Pete Rose–like hustler, Williams was heralded as a worthy successor to John Henry Lloyd in the infield of the powerhouse Chicago American Giants clubs of the 1920s. While he may have approached Lloyd's gift with the glove and was probably a faster runner, he couldn't match his predecessor's success in the batter's box. Few could. Williams was, however, a fine bunter and an expert base stealer. As such, he was a perfect fit for Rube Foster's brand of "inside ball." Williams estimated his lifetime bating average at .267. He is an honorable mention *Courier* poll shortstop.

Signature Analysis

Williams died before there was significant collector interest in the Negro leagues. An insufficient database precludes a detailed analysis of his autograph. We note the following consistencies from the limited number of samples examined:

- Standard "ll" slant of 120 degrees.

- Breaks between the capital letters of the first and last name.

- Nickname enclosed in parentheses. "i" dotted to extreme right of the character.

Scarcity: Very Limited   **Price Range:** $100–250

Signature from postal request, 1970s

Signature from postal request, 1970s

Chester Williams

Arthur Williams

Born: Unknown   **Died:** 1952, Lake Charles, LA

Career: 1930–43, Pittsburgh Crawfords, Homestead Grays

The sure-handed, rifle-armed Williams was to the indomitable Pittsburgh Crawfords of the mid-1930s what Dave Concepcion was to Cincinnati's Big Red Machine of the mid-1970s. The four-time all-star hit for power and average, but it was his quickness and Gold Glove–caliber fielding at either short or second that set him apart. Williams was a consistent .300 hitter with excellent bat control. During one winter in Mexico, he fanned only nine times in 74 games. His high-water mark at the plate came in 1936 when he registered a .381 average with the Crawfords—a team that would eventually send five players to the Hall of Fame. He was shot to death in a bar on Christmas Day, 1952.

Limited biographical information exists on Williams. The autograph featured here was the only sample located during the preparation of this book. An insufficient database precludes a detailed analysis of his autograph.

Scarcity: Scarce   **Price Range:** Not established

Signature from the Bill Yancey Collection, 1938/39

Harry Williams

Harry Williams

Born: Pittsburgh, PA   (No Other Biographical Data Available)

Career: 1931–46, Various Teams

Above all else, Williams was versatile. He could play any position—and nearly did—and he could play it anywhere—and nearly did. His vagabond tendencies drove him to suit up for 10 different teams in three different baseball leagues during his superb 15-year career. A fine hitter with average power and good speed, Williams ravaged Negro leagues pitching in 1938, hitting .403. While he never again approached that mark, his skill at the plate usually landed him a slot near the top of the batting order throughout his career. Sources cite Williams as one of the finest bunters of the era. He was named an honorable mention second baseman in the *Courier* poll.

Limited biographical information exists on Williams. An insufficient database precludes a detailed analysis of his autograph.

Scarcity: Scarce   **Price Range:** Not established

Signature from pay slip, 1936

Signature from all-star game pay slip, 1944

"Smokey Joe" Williams

Joseph Williams

Born: 1886, Seguin, TX   **Died:** 1946, New York, NY

Career: 1905–32, New York Lincoln Giants, Homestead Grays

The *Pittsburgh Courier*'s 1952 poll placed "Smokey Joe" ahead of Satchel Paige as the greatest Negro leagues pitcher of all time. Williams' fastball and control were often compared to that of Walter Johnson, whom Williams defeated 1-0 in their only matchup. In 1912, he compiled a 41-3 record against all levels of competition. Ty Cobb considered the 6-foot-5 Williams a certain 30-game winner in the major leagues. His lifetime record against major-league competition was 20-7 and he suffered the majority of those losses after he was 40, going 7-1 at age 44. Legend has it that in 1917 he struck out 20 and no-hit the New York Giants, but lost 1-0 on an error. Williams was said to have thrown 40 no-hitters against all levels of competition over the course of his career.

Signature Analysis

Little is known about his life before or after his baseball career. He is listed on the Hall of Fame's Negro Leagues Committee's original candidates list. Williams is considered a leading contender for a place in the Hall of Fame. As such, his autograph has been actively sought by Hall of Fame and Negro leagues collectors for years. It remains among the most difficult of all potential Hall of Fame candidates to locate.

In light of Williams' importance to collectors, we worked with museums and relevant historical societies to locate an irrefutable Williams-signed document for use as a standard. The search has been going on for two years and has been unsuccessful to date. The samples shown below are from well-known private collections. They are the only examples the members of our autograph panel have seen. While these may in fact be genuine, given the estimated value of Williams' autograph and the lack of a viable standard, we caution readers against using them as the basis for a purchasing decision or for authentication purposes. We can not attest to the authenticity of these samples and feature them here for educational purposes only. Collectors are advised to use extreme caution when purchasing a Williams autograph.

Scarcity: Very Rare   **Price Range:** Not established

Signature from Homestead Grays team-signed sheet, 1931

Signature cut from document or autograph book, date unknown

Artie Wilson

Arthur Lee Wilson

Born: 1920, Springville, AL

Career: 1944–62, Birmingham Black Barons, Minor and Major Leagues

Wilson is regarded as the Negro leagues' premier shortstop of the 1940s. His peers called him the Octopus, "because he seemed to have eight arms," Monte Irvin said. But Wilson also inflicted devastation with his bat. He goes down in history as the last Negro leaguer to hit over .400 in league play. He captured back-to-back batting titles in 1947 and 1948, notching marks of .370 and .402 in those seasons. His lifetime mark is a sterling .371. Wilson earned eight all-star berths in his five-year Negro leagues career (there were two games a year, 1946–48). After leaving the Negro leagues in 1949, he led the Pacific Coast League with a .348 average and grabbed the stolen base title.

Signature Analysis

Wilson single-signed baseballs are available on the market but are not particularly easy to locate. Prices range from $25–40 for samples signed during the 1990s.

Like most of his counterparts who shared his longevity, insufficient autograph samples predating the 1980s exist to conduct a thorough evolutionary analysis. Recent examples, however, show remarkable consistency:

- Standard mid-peak of "W" slant at 120 degrees.
- No breaks except between names and "W" and "ilson."
- "i's " are often dotted with circles.
- Middle point in "W" is the signature's highest point.
- "A" and "W" drop subtly below the signature's horizontal plane.

Scarcity: Readily Available   **Price Range:** Less than $25

Signature from endorsed check, 1997   *Signature from player questionnaire, 1997*

Parnell Woods

Parnell Woods

Born: 1912, Birmingham, AL **Died:** 1977, Cleveland, OH

Career: 1933–49, Cleveland Buckeyes, Minor Leagues

A natural leader, Woods became the youngest Negro leagues manager ever when he took control of the Cincinnati (later Cleveland) Buckeyes in 1942. He earned the respect of his teammates and peers with his bat. Woods was a fairly consistent .300 hitter and a rabbit on the basepaths. From 1939 through 1942, he played for four different clubs and landed a spot on the all-star squad each year. He left the Negro leagues with a .275 lifetime batting average when the leagues began to fall asunder. While Woods was a solid all-around player, his effectiveness at third base was limited by a weak arm. With barnstorming in his blood, after retiring from baseball, he joined the Harlem Globetrotters basketball team as the traveling secretary and held the post for 27 years.

Woods presumably signed many documents in his capacity with the Globetrotters. Very few of these documents are circulating within the hobby. He died before there was significant collector interest in the Negro leagues. An insufficient database precludes a detailed analysis of his autograph.

Scarcity: Limited   **Price Range:** $100–250

Signature from the Bill Yancey Collection, 1938/39

Signature from Harlem Globetrotters document, early 1950s

"Wild Bill" Wright

Burnis Wright

Born: 1914, Milan, TN   **Died:** 1996, Aguascalientes, Mexico

Career: 1931–56, Baltimore Elite Giants, Mexican League

Wright had all of the tools of a great ballplayer—blazing speed, a strong arm, a sharp eye, and a drive to excel. An eight-time all-star whom historian James Riley compares to Dave Parker, the switch hitter annually punched in at .300-plus and registered a lifetime league mark of .336. He hit at a .371 clip in 27 exhibition games against white clubs. In 1943, he won the triple crown and missed leading the league in stolen bases by a mere one swipe. In the prime of his career, Wright left the Negro leagues to play baseball in Mexico. He ended up settling south of the border. He is a member of the Mexican Baseball Hall of Fame.

Signature Analysis

While Wright's name does not appear on the Hall of Fame Negro Leagues Committee's original roster of candidates, some Hall of Fame sources have indicated that he was considered a strong candidate for induction by the Veterans Committee in the mid-1990s. It's uncertain whether this support remains today. Wright was an obliging signer, but he made his home in Mexico and consequently did few public signings. Reports indicate that he returned to the United States only five times between 1945 and his death in 1996. Several autograph dealers maintained contact with him and thus his signature is available on the market, albeit in limited quantities for a star player who died recently. Wright single-signed baseballs are available with prices ranging from $100–300 for samples signed during the 1990s.

Like most of his counterparts who share his longevity, insufficient autograph samples predating the 1980s exist to conduct a thorough evolutionary analysis. Early samples tend to be quite graceful with large serifs. The vast majority of samples in the hobby are, however, from the later years of his life. As such these show characteristic signs of aging including a degree of variability that makes authentication more difficult. Some consistencies generally include:

- "B" is a single stroke and may or may not have a serif, but should have a horizontal loop at its base.

- "Wild" appears to be used only when signing autographs and generally in post-1980 samples.

- Breaks exist after "W" in his last name and after the "B" in his first name in later samples.

- There may also be a break between the "g" and "h." Loops on "l's," "d," "g," "h," and "t" may or may not be closed.

- Inconsistent "ll" slant of 115 degrees.

Scarcity: Limited   **Price Range:** $25–100

Signature from the Bill Yancey Collection, 1938/39

Signature from public autograph session, 1990s

Signature from public autograph session, 1990s

Signature from endorsed check, 1996

Laymon Yokely

Laymon Samuel Yokely

Born: 1906, Winston-Salem, NC   **Died:** 1976, Baltimore, MD

Career: 1926–44, Baltimore Black Sox

Baltimore baseball fans liked Yokely so much, they almost ruined his career. He was such a popular draw (as well as young Leon Day's idol) that the Baltimore club called on him to work far too frequently. The result was that the arm of one of black baseball's finest pitchers began to go dead after only five years. Before then, he led the Black Sox to the pennant in 1929 with 17 victories and was voted onto Cum Posey's all-star team by *Courier* readers. After going into a modest decline, Yokley revived his career in dramatic fashion by winning 40 games against all levels of competition (including 25 for the Philadelphia Stars) in 1939. He was named an honorable-mention *Courier* poll pitcher and is credited with six no-hitters against all levels of competition.

Although Yokely was an extremely popular player in his day, few of his autographs have surfaced. He died before the increased interest in Negro leagues autographs. An insufficient database precludes a detailed analysis of his autograph. The featured sample is the only one located in the preparation of this book.

Scarcity: Scarce   **Price Range:** $100–250

Signature from postal request, 1970s

Chapter 9
Negro Leagues Signature Gallery

Recent estimates place the number of players with Negro leagues experience between 1860 and 1961 at 5,000. In this chapter, we catalog signature samples from more than 350 Negro leagues players, executives, and associated figures. As Negro leagues player signatures were not widely collected until recent years, the majority of the autographs shown here are from living players or those deceased after 1980. Many of the autographs in this section are from the later years of the player's life and thus show typical characteristics of aging. This statement does not hold true for the "Executive Box" section, where most of the signatures were gathered from official Negro leagues correspondence. While the samples presented in this chapter may prove useful as a reference, please remember that people's handwriting varies significantly depending on circumstances. No single sample can provide an adequate basis for authentication.

We published the best quality signatures we could locate, but we are conscious of the fact that the reproduction quality of some samples is far from perfect. Today, collectors like to have autographed pictures, postcards, lithographs, baseballs and the like. While these are certainly fine mementos, signatures placed on such items are not always easy to reproduce. We did the best we could with what we had.

We have published as many signatures as we could locate during the collection period. We are cognizant of the fact that this list does not include all living players. We apologize in advance to those players who are not listed here. If your personal collection includes a player(s) not shown on this list, please send high-quality photocopies to the address listed at the beginning of Appendix D and we will include it in future editions.

Artie Wilson

The Executive Box: Umpires, Executives, & Luminaries

This section contains signature samples from more than two dozen figures who were not necessarily active players, but who were associated with black baseball. We note their affiliation with the game and, when possible, the years of their involvement.

Louis Armstrong (musician), owner, semiprofessional team: Armstrong's Secret Nine

Virgil F. Blueitt, player/umpire (1916–18, 1937–49)

Emmett Ashford, first African-American major-league umpire

Frank Forbes, player/umpire (1913–19, 1929–43)

Thomas Baird, owner/officer, Kansas City Monarchs (1920–50)

Rufus "Sonnyman" Jackson, owner, Homestead Grays (1934–49)

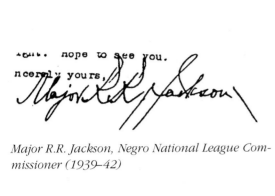

Major R.R. Jackson, Negro National League Commissioner (1939–42)

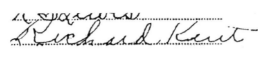

Richard Kent, owner, St. Louis Stars (1922–31)

Warner Jewell, owner, Indianapolis ABCs
(1917–25)

Robert S. Lewis, owner, Memphis Red Sox
(1923–28)

Jack Johnson (heavyweight boxing champion)
first base, Chicago American Giants (1903–04)

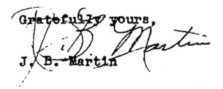

J.B. Martin, officer, Memphis Red Sox (1929–50)

Rev. John H. Johnson, president, Negro National
League (1947–48)

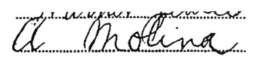

Augustin Molina, manager/officer, Cuban Stars
(1911–31)

Bob Motley, umpire

Ted Rasberry, promoter/owner, Detroit Stars,
Kansas City Monarchs (1953–65)

Jesse Owens (Olympic Gold Medalist) officer, Pittsburgh Crawfords (1940)

Bill Robinson (entertainer), a.k.a. "Mr. Bojan-
gles,"
owner New York Black Yankees (1931–50)

Steve Pierce, officer, Detroit Stars (1925–28)

Joe Rush, owner, Birmingham Black Barons,
and Negro Southern League president (1923–26)

Seward H. Posey, officer, Homestead Grays
(1911–48)

James Semler, owner, New York Black Yankees
(1932–48)

Roy Sparrow, officer, Washington Black Senators
(1938)

J.C. White, recording secretary, Philadelphia
Pythians (1860s)

Thomas T. Wilson.

Thomas T. Wilson, owner, Nashville Elite Giants,
Baltimore Elite Giants (1921–47)

The Roster: Negro Leagues Baseball Players, 1900–1960

This section features the signatures of more than 350 Negro leagues players. We note the player's name and the dates he/she played in the leagues. In some cases, the latter information was unavailable. The dates do not include non–Negro leagues professional or semiprofessional play. In the case of Hall of Famers Hank Aaron and Willie Mays, we provide signature samples from different periods in their lives.

Hank Aaron, 1954 sample

Ben Adams

Hank Aaron, 1988 sample

Tom Alston (1948)

Robert W. Abernathy (1945–48), uses rubber stamp

George Altman (1955)

Sandy Amoros (1950)

Russell Awkard (1940–41)

Andy Anderson (1951)

Willie Bacon

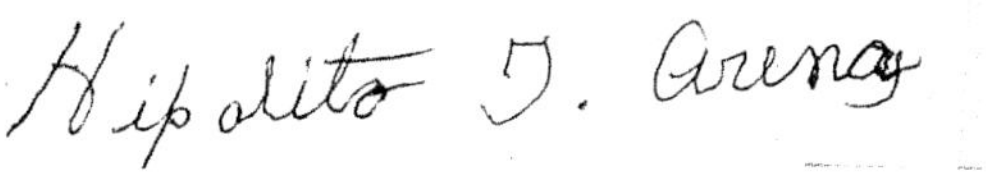

Hipolito Arenas (1932)

Otha Bailey (1950)

John S. Armstrong

Gene Baker (1948–50)

Hudson Baker (1942–48)

Frank Barnes (1947–50)

Ernie Banks (1950), Hall of Fame

Joe Barnes (1950–52)

Sam Barber (1943–50)

Herbert Barnhill (1938–46)

Bill Barnes (1937–47)

Ernest Barnwell (1937)

M.B. Beavers Jr. (1931–32)

Dennis Biddle (1953–54)

Jim Benton (1950)

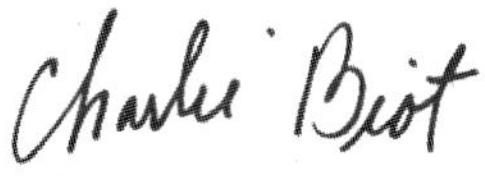

Charlie Biot (1939–41)

Bill Beverley

John Bissant (1934–48)

Charlie Beverly (1924–36)

Robert Bissant (1941–46)

Dan Black (1946–55)

Lyman Bostock Sr. (1940–49)

Joe Black (1943–50)

Bob Boyd (1946–50)

Garnett E. Blair (1942–48)

Bill Breda (1950–54)

William Blair Jr. (1946–50)

Leroy Breedlove (1950)

Sherwood Brewer (1946–50)

Allen "Lefty" Bryant (1937–47)

Sam Brison

Buddy Burbage (1929–43)

Ike Brown (1960)

Sidney Burch (1946–55)

J. Royal "Skink" Browning

Tex Burnett (1921–36)

Joe Caffie (1950)

Paul Casanova (1960)

Marlon "Sugar" Cain (1937–49)

Bill "Ready" Cash (1943–50)

Matthew Carlisle (1931–46)

Thadist Christopher (1935–45)

Marlin Carter (1932–50)

Louis Clarizio Jr. (1950)

A.B. Clay

Gene Collins (1947–51)

Zack Clayton (1932–44)

Jim Colzie (1937–47)

Cecil E. Cole (1946)

Daltie Cooper (1921–40)

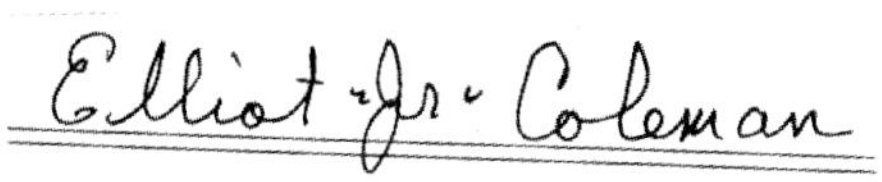

Elliott Coleman (1954–55)

Johnnie Cowan (1942–50)

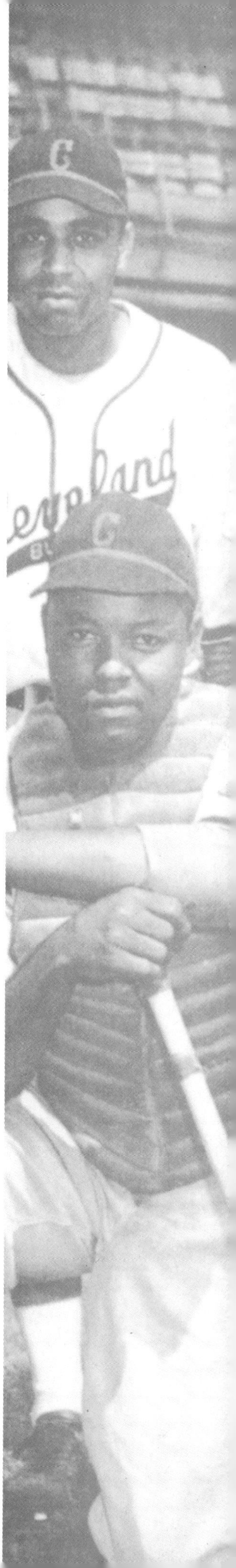

George Crowe (1947–49)

Ross "Satchel" Davis (1940–47)

Homer Curry (1928–55)

Saul Davis (1921–31)

Edward Dave

Felix Delgado

Charles Davis (1950–55)

Wesley "Doc" Dennis (1943–55)

Carl J. Dent (1950–52)

Mahlon Duckett (1940–50)

Edward "Lefty" Derrick (1944 & 1951)

Frank Duncan III (1940–47)

Joe Douse (1952–53)

Melvin Duncan (1949–55)

Joseph S. Doyle (1916–26)

Joe Dunham (1952)

Eddie Dwight (1924–37)

Frank Evans (1949–50)

James W. Earle Jr. (1954)

Lionel Ewelyn

Signed in duplicate this **9th**

Luke Easter (1947–48)

Thomas "Monk" Favors (1947)

IDORSE HERE

Felix Evans (1934–49)

Al "Cleffie" Fennar (1933–34)

Bernard Fernandez (1938–39/46–47)

Joe Fillmore (1941–52)

Rodolfo "Rudy" Fernandez (1932–43)

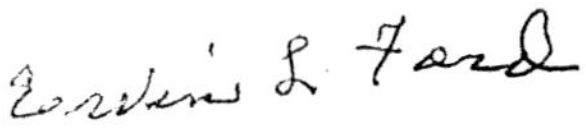

Erwin L. Ford (1951–54)

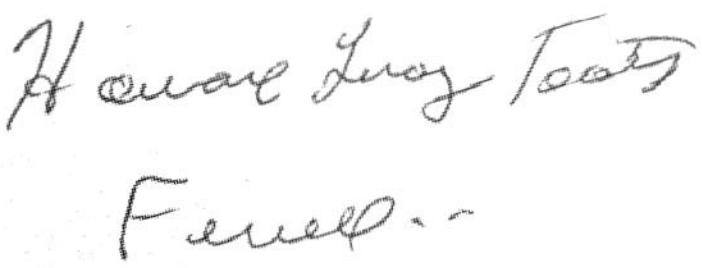

Leroy "Toots" Ferrell (1946–51)

William B. Foster (1956–58)

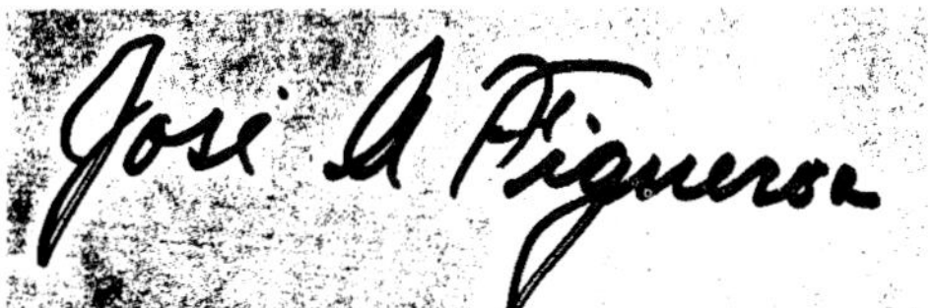

Jose Figueroa (1940–46)

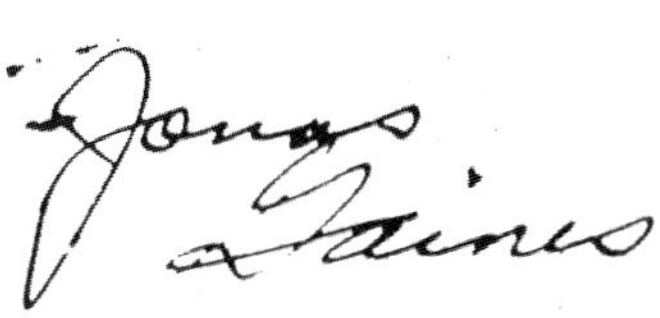

Jonas Gaines (1937–51)

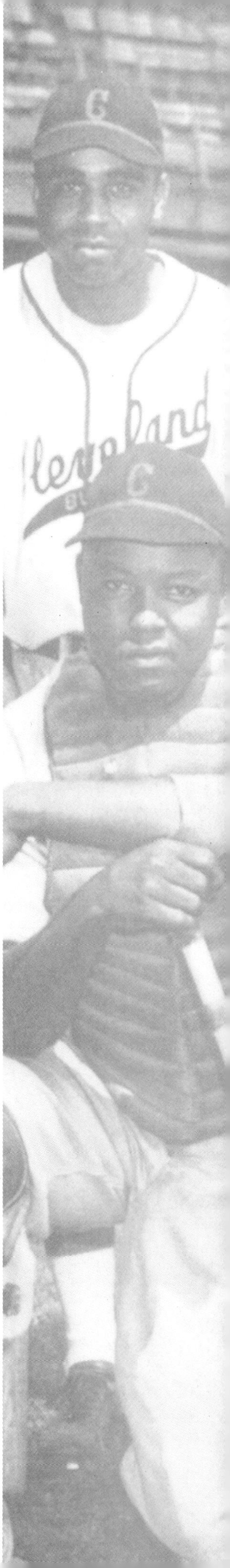

215

Horace Garner (1948–52)

Louis "Sea Boy" Gillis (1951)

Alphonso Gerald (1945–49)

Stanley Glenn (1944–50)

Josh Gibson Jr. (1949–50)

Harold Gould (1946–49)

Jim "Junior" Gilliam (1946–50), Major League star

Willie Grace (1942–50)

Whit Graves (1950–51)

Wiley Griggs (1948–50)

Chester Gray (1940–46)

Felix Guilbe (1946–47)

John W. Green

Nap Gulley (1941–49)

Acie "Skeet" Griggs (1951)

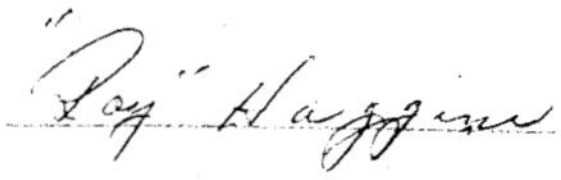

Roy Haggins (1949–58)

Harold O. Hair (1953)

Paul Hardy

Harold Hairston (1946–47)

Chuck Harmon (1947)

Sam Hairston (1945–50)

Robert M. Harness

Lowell Harden (1943–45)

David T. Harper (1943–46)

218

Barney Harris

Teenie Harris (1926)

Donald Harris

Wilmer Harris (1945–50)

Ernest "Oink" Harris

Bob Harvey (1943–50)

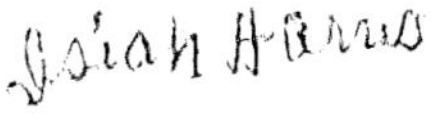

Isiah Harris (1949–55)

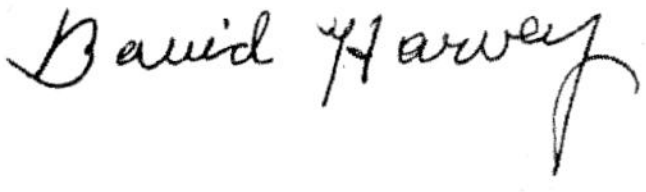

David Harvey (1932–45)

Harry Hatcher (1948)

"Prince" Joe Henry (1950–52)

Jehosie Heard (1945–50)

Jimmy Hill (1938–45)

Hayward Henderson (1954–55)

Ulysses Holliman (1950–54)

Neal Henderson (1949)

Gordon "Hoppy" Hopkins (1952–54)

Billy Horne (1938–40)

Henry Howell (1918–21)

Dave Hoskins (1942–49)

Jesse Hubbard (1919–34)

Carranza "Schoolboy" Howard (1940–50)

Preston Ingram (1934–37)

Reggie Howard

Clarence "Pint" Isreal (1940–47)

Elbert Isreal (1950)

Vernell Jackson (1950)

James "Sap" Ivory (1954–55)

George L. Jefferson (1942–50)

John W. Jackson Jr. (1950–53)

James "Pee Wee" Jenkins (1944–54)

Ralph Jackson (1950s)

Byron "Mex" Johnson (1937–40)

Charles Johnson (1949–50)

Jimmie Johnson (1937–43)

Connie Johnson (1940–52)

Josh Johnson (1934–42)

Don Johnson (1948–54)

Ralph Johnson (1950–52)

Ernest Johnson (1949–53)

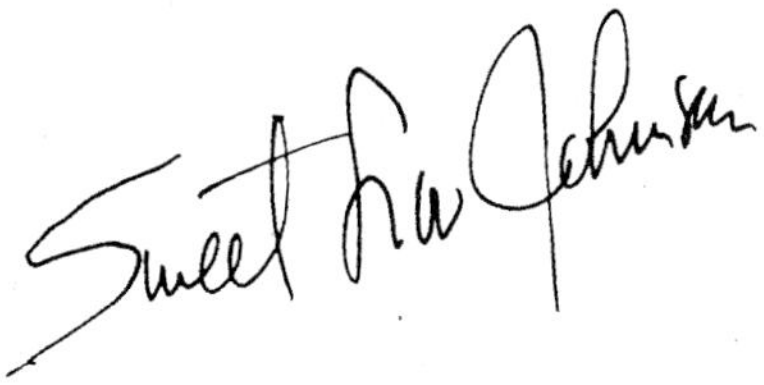

"Sweet Lou" Johnson

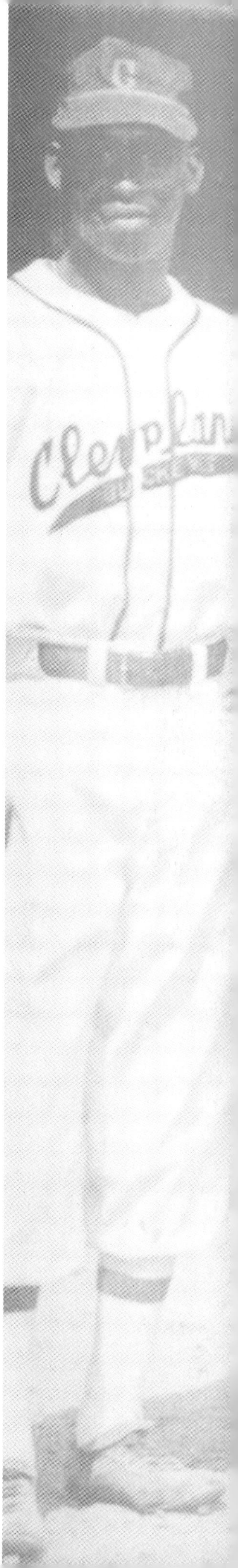

William H. Johnson (1923–29)

John Kennedy (1954–55)

Clinton "Casey" Jones (1940–55)

Larry Kimbrough (1941–50)

Rex Jones (1960)

Clarence "Pijo" King (1947–50)

Cecil Kaiser (1945–49)

Frank King

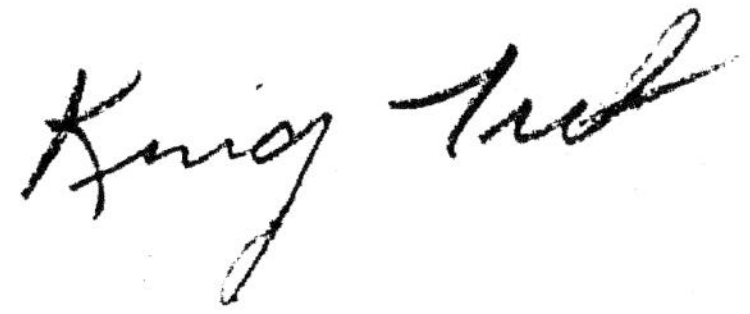

Richard King (1937–50), known as "King Tut"

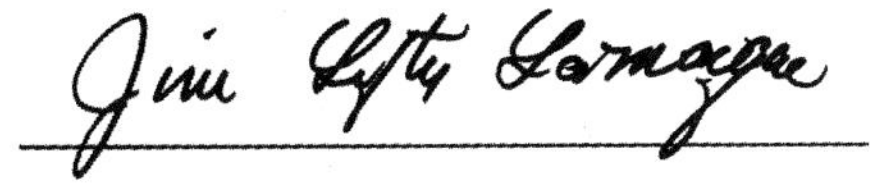

Jim "Lefty" LaMarque (1941–51)

Eddie Klep (1946) first white player in the Negro leagues

Bob Landers

Elmer Knox (1946–49)

Milfred (Rick) Laurent (1929–35)

Thurman Lacy (1954–56)

Brooks Lawrence

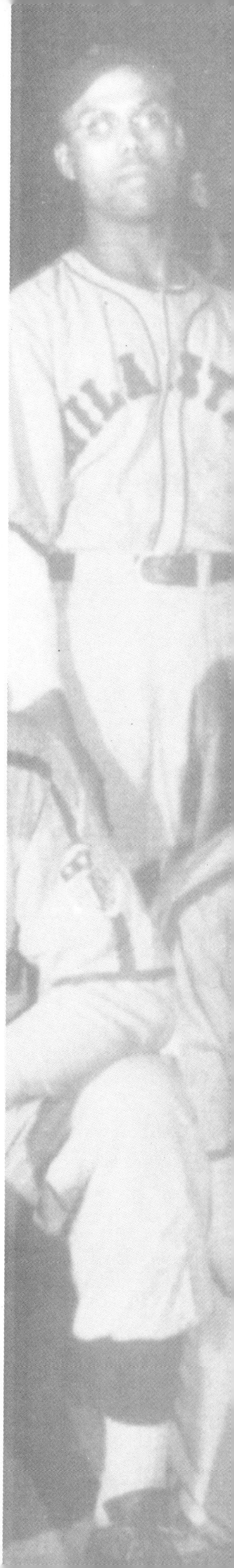

Vincent Lee (1936, 1941–42)

Maurie "Mo" Lisby (1934)

Willie Lee

Tony Lloyd (1959)

Rufus Lewis (1936–50)

Carl R. Long (1952–53)

William H. Lindsay (1934)

Ernest "The Kid" Long (1948–50)

Cando Lopez (1920–35)

Joseph Marbury

Norman Lumpkin (1946–47)

Ziggy Marcell (1939–48)

Chip MacAllister (1938–46)

Ed Martin (1951–52)

Robert Madison (1935–42)

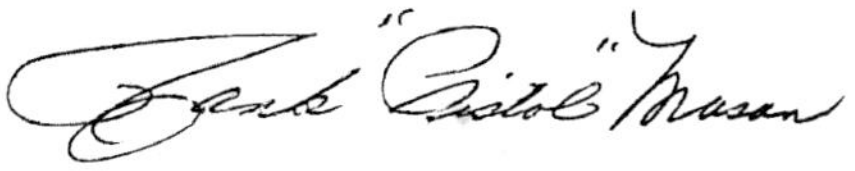

Hank "Pistol" Mason (1951–54)

Fran Matthews (1938–45)

Willie Mays, 1980s sample

Otis Matthews

Nathanial McClinic (1945–48)

Willie Mays, 1962 sample

Clinton "Butch" McCord (1947–50)

Willie Mays, 1970s sample

Walt McCoy (1945–48)

Jim McCurnie (1946–49)

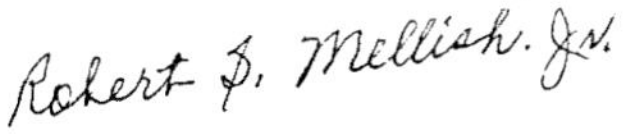

Robert S. Mellish Jr.

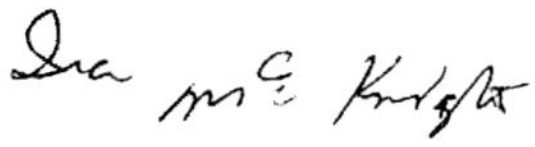

Ira McKnight (1952/1956–62)

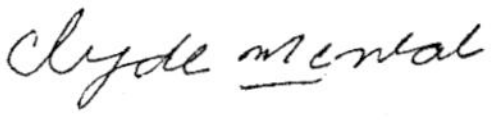

Clyde Mental

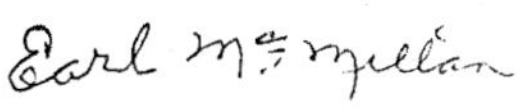

Earl McMillan (1923)

Purnell Mincy (1939–40)

Gib Meeks

Orestes "Minnie" Minoso (1945–48), 1990s Sample

John Mitchell (1956–60)

Grady Montgomery (1952)

Robert Mitchell (1954–57)

Lee Moody (1944–47)

Sylvester Mitchell

Herbert Moore

William Mitchell (1941–42)

James "Red" Moore (1936–40)

Connie Morgan (1954–55)

Emilio Navarro (1928–29)

Felton Morrison

Charlie Neal (1955)

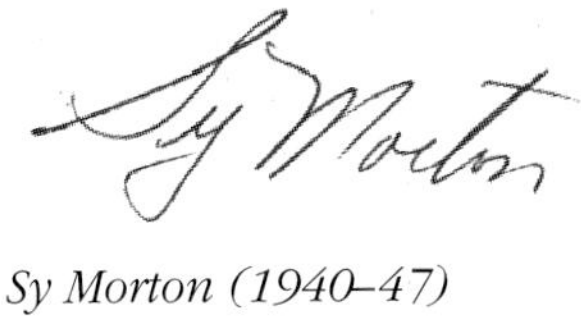

Sy Morton (1940–47)

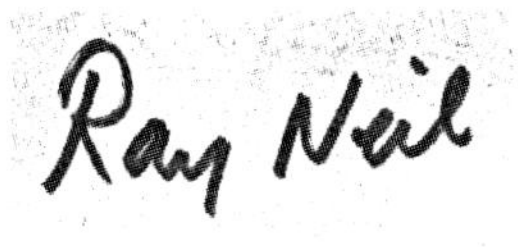

Ray Neil (1942–54)

Carroll Ray "Dink" Mothell (1924–34)

Don Newcombe (1944–45)

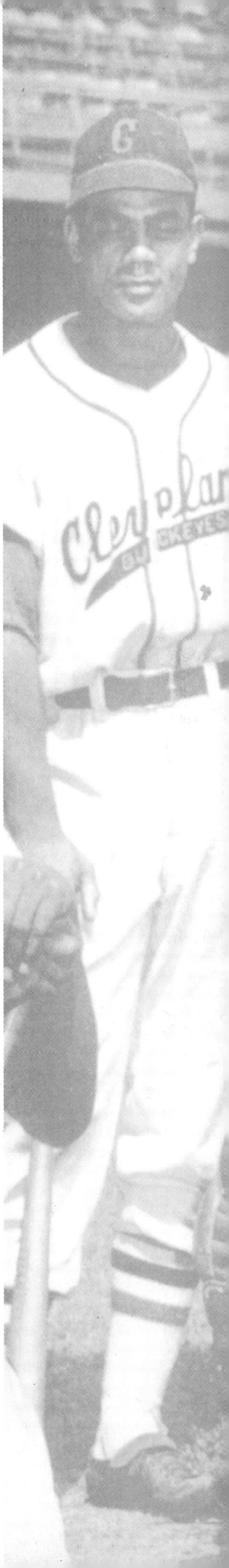

William Nichols (1936)

Raymond Owens (1939–42)

Ray Noble (1945–50)

Ralph Palmer

Orlando O'Farrell (1949–51)

James H. Parker

Warren "Dadd" O'Neil

Roy Partlow (1934–50)

Andrew L. "Pat" Patterson (1934–49)

Jim Pendleton (1948)

William Warren Peace (1945–48)

Art "Superman" Pennington (1940–51)

Frank Pearson

Howard Pernell (1950)

Maurice Peatross (1947)

Norris Phillips (1942–43)

Rogers Pierre (1939–41)

Dave Pope (1946)

Jose Piloto (1948–50)

Willie Pope (1945–48)

Nat Pollard (1943/1946–50)

Andy Porter (1932–50)

Milton Poole

Merle Porter (1949–50)

234

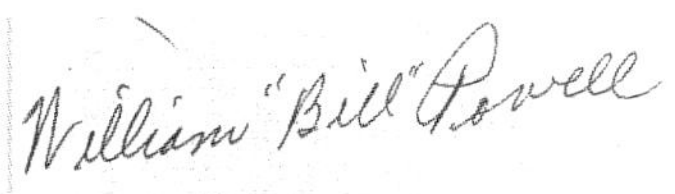

William Powell (1925–35)

Jim Proctor (1955)

Marvin Price (1950–52)

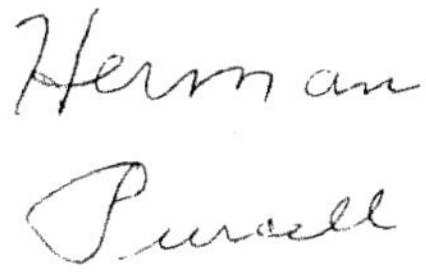

Herman Purcell (1944–47)

Roscoe Price (1945)

Ulysses Redd (1940–41/1951–52)

Charley Pride (1952–53), Musician

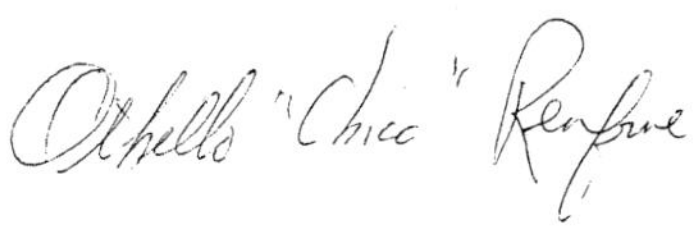

Othello "Chico" Renfroe (1945–50)

Johnny Reynolds (1958–60)

Charlie Rivera, 1933/1939–44

Harry "Lefty" Rhodes (1942–50)

Bobby Robinson

Ben Richardson (1952–55)

Booker T. Robinson (1945–46)

Normal E. Richardson (1947–53)

Frazier Robinson (1942–50)

Jim Robinson (1952–53/1956–58)

William "Nat" Rogers (1923–46)

Sammy Robinson (1954)

Bob Romby (1946–50)

Benny Rodriquez (1948)

Leon Ruffin (1935–50)

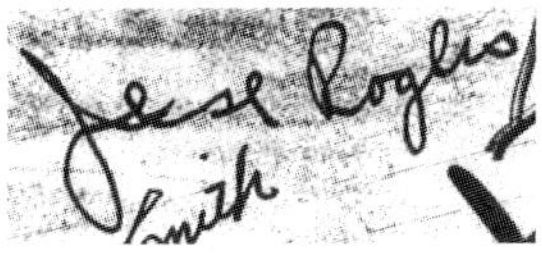

Jesse Rogers (1953–54)

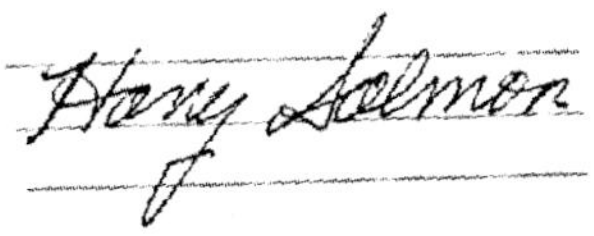

Harry Salmon (1923–35)

Bobby Sanders (1958–59)

Joe Burt Scott (1944–49)

1936-56

Jose Santiago (1947–48)

Robert Scott (1946–50)

Ed Scott

Eugene Scruggs (1956–59)

Joe Scott (1947–50)

Bonnie Serrell (1941–51)

238

Pedro Sierra

Woody Smallwood (1951–54)

Willie Simms (1936–43)

Al Smith (1944–48)

Harry Simpson (1946–48)

Ford Smith

Herb Simpson (1942–51)

Gene Smith (1938–51)

Qunicy Smith (1943–46)

Toni Stone (1951–54), first female player

Joseph B. Spencer (1942–48)

Sam Streeter (1920–36)

Riley E. Stewart Sr. (1946–50)

Mickey Stubbefield (1948)

Nathaniel Stone

Lonnie Summers (1938–51)

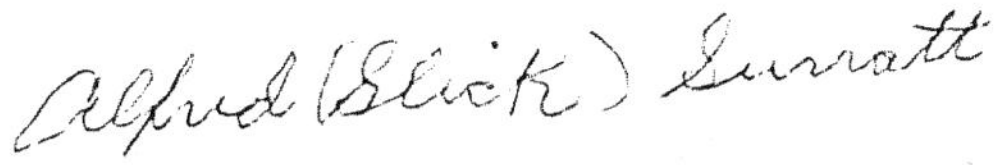

Alfred "Slick" Surratt (1949–51)

LeRoy Taylor (1925–36)

Earl Taborn (1946–50)

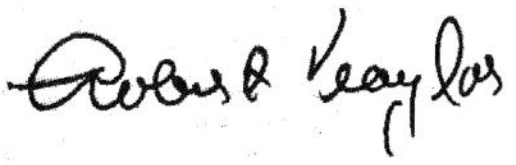

Robert Taylor (1938–42)

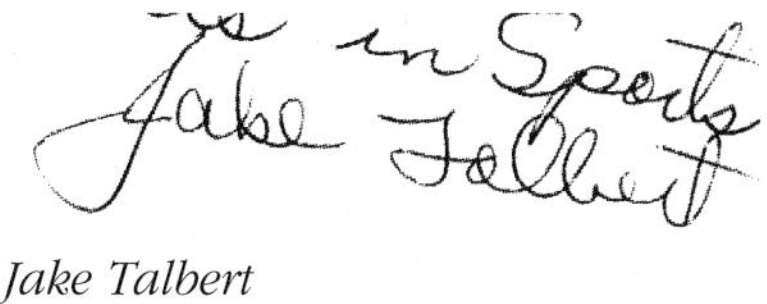

Jake Talbert

Sam Taylor (1953–54)

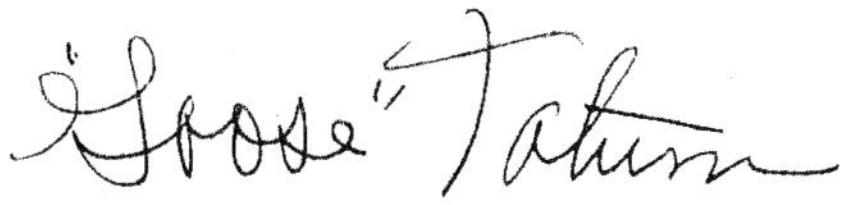

Goose Tatum (1941–49), famous Harlem
Globetrotter

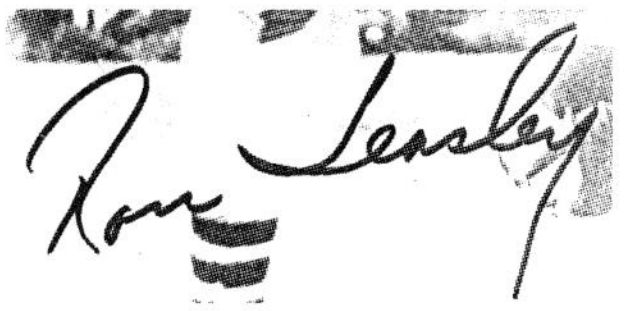

Ron Teasley (1948)

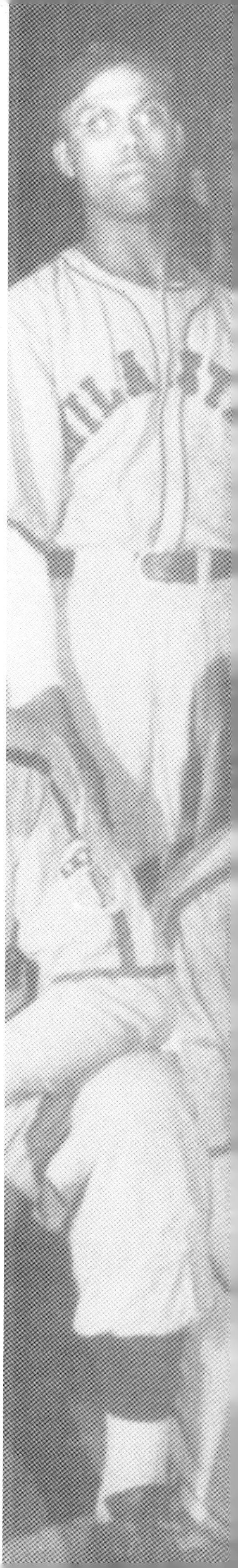

Allie Thompkins (1928–29)

Harold "Hooks" Tinker (1931)

Frank A. "Hoss" Thompson (1951–54)

Bill van Buren (1931)

Henry "Hank" Thompson (1943–48)

Clemente Varona (1948–55)

Bob Thurman (1946–49)

Armando Vasquez (1944–48)

Bo Wallace (1948–49)

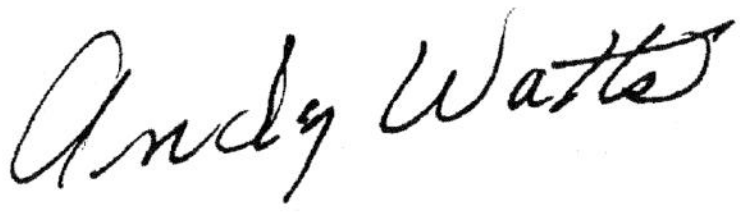

Andy Watts (1946–52)

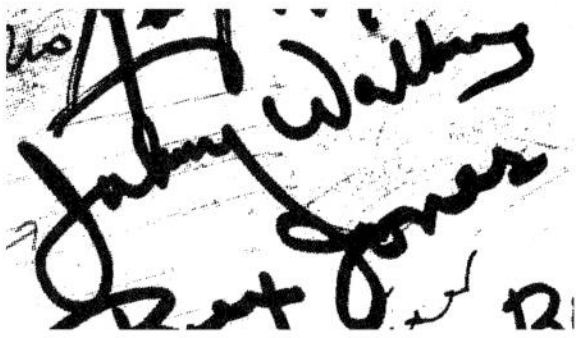

Johnny Watkins

Normal "Tweed" Webb (1926–31)

Murray "Skeeter" Watkins (1943–50)

Sonny Webb (1957–58)

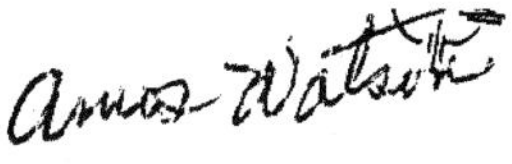

Amos Watson

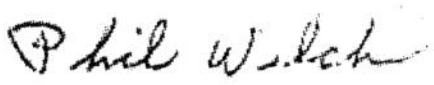

Phil Welch (1957–59)

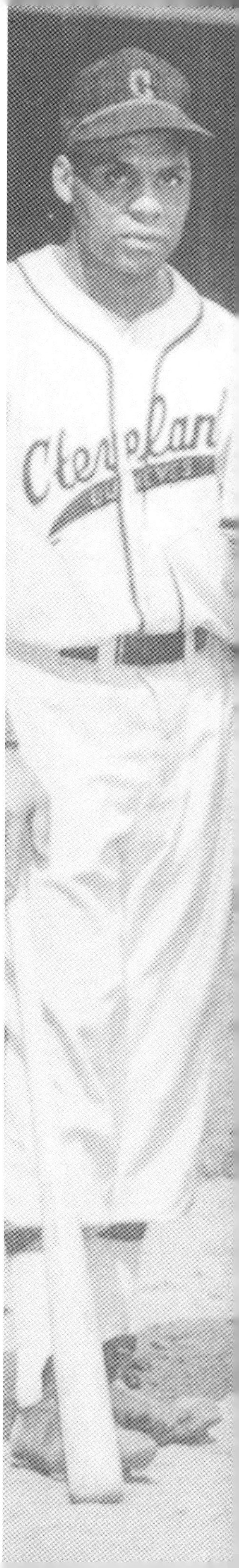

Price West (1955–58)

Eugene Williams (1958–60)

Eugene "Stink" White (1951–57)

Jesse Williams (1939–51)

Dave Whitney (1952–55)

Marvin Williams (1943–50)

Jimmy Wilkes (1945–52)

Robert "Cotton" Williams (1943–51)

Willie "Curley" Williams (1945–54)

Roy Winfrey (1947–51)

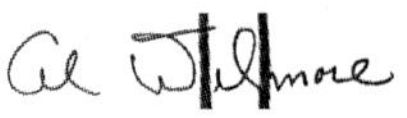

Al Wilmore (1946–50)

Ernest Wright (1941–49)

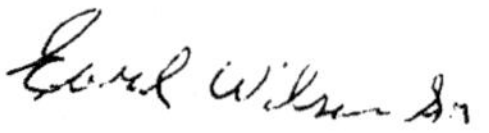

Earl Wilson Sr.

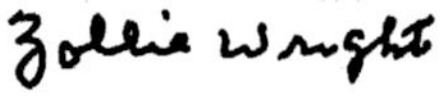

Zollie Wright (1931–43)

Emmett D. Wilson (1936–50)

John Wyatt (1953–55)

Archie Young (1946–55)

Willie C. Young (1945)

Jim Zapp (1948–54)

Verdell Lefty Mathis

Appendix A
Glossary of Sports Autograph Terms

Where is a 3x5 not in fact 3x5 inches? In the autograph-collecting hobby, that's where. Every field of endeavor has its own jargon, and autograph collecting has no shortage of words, symbols, and shorthand that may be confusing to the new collector. Here are some common words, phrases, and abbreviations with which all collectors should become familiar.

3x5: Collector shorthand for standard size index card, which is, in fact, 3 1/2 x 5 inches. It is a common medium for collecting autographs.

ALS: Autographed Letter Signed. Letter written in the hand of the signer.

Autopen: Signature generated by automatic writing device programmed to replicate a specific signature.

Book Price, a.k.a. Book Value: Value of an item as listed in a price guide. The phrase "books at $XXX" is commonly used.

Broadside: Cardboard or paper advertisement (usually large format) for a forthcoming event, such as a baseball game, circus, etc. Widely used by Negro leagues clubs to promote barnstorming contests.

Cabinet Photo: Nineteenth- or early 20th-century photograph generally mounted on cardboard backing.

CDV: *Carte de Visite,* or visitor's card. Photographic print attached to a card mount, similar to cabinet card but generally smaller. CDVs were in common use from the 1860s through the 1880s.

Ceiling Bid: Bid placed on an auction item indicating the highest price the perspective buyer is prepared to pay for an item (not including commission). Such bids instruct the auctioneer to bid on the perspective buyer's behalf up to this amount. Also known as an "Up To" bid.

Clubhouse Signature: Authorized but non-genuine player signature.

COA: Certificate of Authenticity. Guarantee of the authenticity of an item (also see LOA).

Cut or Cut Signature: Autograph removed (cut) from its original medium.

Device-Assisted Signature: Signature impression made with the assistance of a writing or gripping device. Commonly used by people with disabilities that hinder their ability to sign. Roy Campanella used a device to assist him in gripping the pen to sign autographs.

Document Examination Service: Service that attempts to determine if an autograph or document is genuine. Examiners are usually certified by trade associations.

First Day Cover, a.k.a. FDC: An envelope with a stamp canceled the first day it was issued. Usually produced to commemorate a special event or the introduction of a new stamp.

FMV: Fair Market Value. Phrase sometimes used by auctioneers to indicate the approximate value of an item if sold on the retail market.

Forgery: A non-genuine signature. In the autograph hobby, the term implies that the signature was produced in a conscious attempt to deceive the purchaser.

Foxing: Term used to describe brown spotting that appears on some leather baseballs and documents resulting from oxidation.

Ghost Signature: Authorized but non-genuine signature.

Hall of Fame Plaques, a.k.a. Plaks: Postcards depicting the plaques of Hall of Fame players. There are several varieties.

HOF: Hobby shorthand for the National Baseball Hall of Fame in Cooperstown, N.Y. Hall of Fame members are sometimes referred to as HOFers.

In-Person Signature: A collector-witnessed signature as opposed to a signature obtained/purchased through the mail, auction, or alternative means.

Inscribed, a.k.a. Personalized: Autograph signed for a specific individual or group. For example, "To John Smith, Best Wishes, Buck Leonard." Often times when listing multiple photos, dealers will add the footnote (P) or (I) to indicate that items were signed as such.

Letterpress: Process used to duplicate a document that involves "pressing" the wet ink from an original document into an absorbing (usually onion skin) paper. The process was used in the 19th century. Sometimes referred to as "ink impress."

LOA: Letter of Authenticity. Guarantee of the authenticity of an item.

LOP: Letter of Provenance. Statement describing the history, origin, and/or circumstances surrounding the acquisition of an item.

LS or TLS: Letter Signed or Typed Letter Signed. The body of letter is in a secretary's hand, typewritten, or press-printed, but bears the genuine signature of the "author" of the message.

LS: When used in conjunction with 3x5 index cards, denotes signature on the lined side. Sometimes noted simply as (L).

Mail Auction: Auction where potential buyers submit their bids by mail by a specified date.

MFA: Mentioned for Accuracy. Used by some auction houses and dealers to denote an insubstantial flaw or imperfection that does not affect the presentation of an item but is brought to the buyer's attention in the interest of full disclosure.

Minimum Bid: The minimum bid an auctioneer will accept on an item (excluding commission).

OAL: Official American League baseball.

Official Ball: Ball authorized for use by the baseball league in question and stamped accordingly.

ONL: Official National League baseball.

PC: Postcard.

Perez-Steele: Postcards produced by the Perez-Steele galleries in Pennsylvania featuring artistic renderings of sports figures.

Personalized, a.k.a. Inscribed: see Inscribed.

Private Signing: Signing session arranged between an athlete and a dealer to fill customer autograph requests.

Provenance: The history and/or origin of an item.

Secretarial Signature: Authorized but non-genuine signature.

Sepia Tone Photo: Photo with a brownish tone. Sepia processing began to be phased out in the 1920s.

Sharpie®: Brand of pen commonly used for signing photographs and occasionally baseballs. Not recommended for use on leather baseballs or other items of a porous nature due to its tendency to "bleed" over time. Registered trademark product of the Sanford Corporation of Bellwood, Ill.

Shellac: Protective coating applied to baseballs to preserve signatures. The practice was once quite common but over time the coating produces a brown or yellow toning of the ball. Collectors are advised not to apply shellac to baseballs.

SP: Signed Photo. Sometimes PS, for Photo Signed.

Sweet Spot: Area on a baseball where the seams come closest to meeting. Generally the preferred area for an autograph on a single-signed ball.

Third-Party Authentication: Opinion rendered by a neutral party regarding to authenticity of an item.

Tintype: Photographic image produced on a metal (tin) plate. The process was widely in use in the mid-19th century.

TLS: Typed letter signed. Refers to a typed letter with the signature of the writer at the bottom.

Toning: When used in conjunction with a baseball, the term refers to discoloration, usually yellowing or browning.

UAC: Universal Autograph Collectors' organization.

Unlined Side: Term used in conjunction with signed 3x5 index cards, denotes signature on the unlined side. Sometimes noted simply as UL.

Unofficial Ball: Ball not officially recognized or generally used in play by the league in question. Commonly store-bought baseballs.

Appendix B
Guide to Grading Signature Condition

Collectors learn quickly that the words used to grade the quality of signatures stretch the bounds of what Noah Webster had in mind when he crafted their definitions. To the layman, something in "Very Good" condition sounds just fine. To the autograph collector, it raises the question, "Can I even read it?" Listed below are working guidelines for what you should and should not expect to see when a dealer offers you an autograph in a certain condition.

Remember, grading is a purely subjective matter and dealer practices can vary significantly.

Mint (MT): A perfect signature. Pen strokes are bold, faultless and show no signs of wear or fading. Numerically categorized as a 9-10.

Near Mint (NM): A near-perfect condition signature. All strokes are bold and clear and show only minimal signs of wear and/or age. Numerically categorized as an 8-9. In other areas of the autograph hobby, the term Fine condition implies approximately the same grade.

Excellent to Mint (EX/MT): Sometimes referred to as EX+. A strong signature. All strokes are clear but show some faults and some signs of wear and/or age. Numerically categorized as a 6-7.

Excellent (EX): All letters are readable but show obvious signs of wear and/or age. All pen strokes are visible but are weak in some areas. Numerically categorized as a 5-6.

Very Good (VG): Overall signature is visible, letters are not easily readable. Portions of pen strokes are faded or partially eviscerated by other means. Obvious signs of wear and/or age. Numerically categorized as a 4-5.

Good (GD): Signature is difficult to read. Pen strokes are faded or damaged by scratching, scuffing or other means. Most letters are difficult to read. Dealers may also describe signatures in this category as "light but readable." Numerically categorized as a 3-4.

Fair (FR): Signature is difficult to read without magnification. Pen strokes are severely faded or otherwise eviscerated. Dealers may describe this category as "faded." Numerically categorized as a 1-2.

Poor (P): Virtually unreadable signature. May in fact be only the imprint left by the pen once the ink has faded entirely. Dealers may describe this category as "severely faded." Numerically categorized as a 1.

Appendix C
Namesakes and Ghosts

Namesakes

The following are signatures from three major-league players who share the same names or nicknames as players listed in the "Key Negro Leaguers" section of Chapter 8. Making a mistake in this area can be costly. Take the Rube Fosters for example. George "Rube" Foster of the Boston Red Sox played the same position during the same period as Negro leagues Hall of Famer Andrew "Rube" Foster. The difference in the price of their autographs? About $3,000. We note the player's name, the team with which he is most commonly associated, and the years he played.

Larry Brown, Cleveland Indians, 1963–74

George Rube Foster, Boston Red Sox, 1913–17

Vic Harris, Various Teams, 1972–80

Ghost Signers

A ghost or secretarial signature is an authorized but non-authentic autograph. Neither type is recognized as a legitimate autograph sample. The "ghosting" problem is particularly acute in instances where individuals were inundated with autograph requests or otherwise unable to sign. They may very well have authorized others to autograph material on their behalf.

Ghost signatures are not nearly as prevalent on Negro leagues items as on major-league ones, largely because players rarely received enough autograph requests to justify to the practice. There are, however, some notable exceptions to the rule.

Satchel Paige was swamped with requests in the aftermath of his Hall of Fame induction. His family reportedly signed many mail-request items on his behalf. Here we feature four distinct ghost-signed samples, all obtained through the mail. There are at least three other known varieties. Many of the Paige "forgeries" circulating on the market are indeed ghost signatures. Collectors acquired these in good faith through the mail, assumed them to be genuine and passed them into the market. Many Paige ghost signatures feature the "ll" spelling of his first name.

Ghost-signed Satchel Paige autographs, 1970s/80s

Roy Campanella's wife filled many of the mail autograph requests he received after his accident. These are not recognized by the hobby as genuine Campanella signatures, but there are many in circulation. The example shown here has attributes that clearly set it apart from an authentic pre-accident Campanella autograph. Specifically:

• Single-stroke "R" ends in a hook.

- "C" finishes with an extraneous loop at its base.

- "ll's" exhibit open loops.

- Final "a" ends with an extension that goes beyond the shadow of the final "l."

Roy Campanella's wife's signature

Newark Eagles owner **Effa Manley** frequently signed on behalf of her husband, **Abe Manley.** Several contracts suggest that she also signed on behalf of players; these contracts, however, merely may have been office copies.

Effa Manley's signature on behalf of Mule Suttles, 1937

Effa Manley's signature on behalf of her husband, Abraham, 1937

During the final years of **Jackie Robinson's** life, a ghost signer replied to many of the autograph requests he received in the mail. Unfortunately, Robinson's scribe did a good job producing a facsimile of his genuine signature. Unlike the Paige-ghosted signatures, which are easily recognizable as fake and are very slowly being worked out of the hobby, these signatures continue to be widely offered as the genuine item.

Jackie Robinson ghost signature, 1972

Rubber Stamps

Rubber stamping is a variation of ghosting usually prompted by an excessive volume of signature requests or due to an infirmity. As is the case with other ghost signatures, they are not recognized by the hobby as authentic autographs. We were able to document only three Negro leaguers who have used rubber stamps in lieu of authentic signatures, including Cum Posey's official stamp that went on the auction block in 1997. We also located a document from the 1950s stamped with Jackie Robinson's signature. The stamp seems to have been used almost exclusively for business purposes, as few of these stamped samples have been seen in the hobby. The most common rubber stamp sample collectors will run into is that of Robert Abernathy. The former player is no longer able to sign, yet he obliges requests using his stamp.

Appendix D
Collectors' Challenge:
The Ones That Got Away

You can't win 'em all —
or, in this case, find 'em all!

Despite our access to some of the largest private and public collections of Negro leagues documents and autographs, we were unable to locate irrefutable signature samples from a number of major Negro leagues stars, including some potential Hall of Famers. After reading the biographies of the 25 players and executives in this section, it will become obvious why the autographs of some of the key figures—Lefty Brown, George Stovey, and Bill Monroe, for example—proved elusive. But Clarence Jenkins and Bingo DeMoss? Surely autographs of these star players who died less than 50 years ago are out there somewhere. The question is, where?

The players featured in this appendix are either first-through-third-team *Courier* poll players, or players who had a historically important role in the development of black baseball. If you have document samples or team-signed sheets containing any of these players, we would like to include them in the next edition of this book. Please send high-quality photocopies to: Kevin Keating, Quality Autographs & Memorabilia of Virginia, P.O. Box 25274, Alexandria, VA 22314.

As with the "Key Negro Leaguers" section in Chapter 8, we list biographical information, team affiliation(s), career stats and highlights, and a photograph when available.

John Beckwith

John Beckwith

Born: 1902, Louisville, KY   **Died:** 1956, New York, NY

Career: 1916–38, Chicago Giants, Baltimore Black Sox

The immensely talented and powerful Beckwith compiled a .366 lifetime batting average. Historians say that on a good day, no one could hit the ball farther. The words "a good day" are important when discussing the temperamental Beckwith. The 6-foot-3, 220-pound shortstop's performance varied greatly depending on his mood. Beckwith was a pull-hitter, and opposing defenses usually employed severe shifts against him—*à la* Ted Williams. He led the Negro American League in home runs in 1930 and 1931. He was named a second-team utility player in the *Courier* poll.

David "Lefty" Brown

David Brown

Born: 1896, San Marcos, TX   **Died:** Denver, CO

Career: 1918–25, Chicago American Giants

Brown was considered by some to be the best Negro leagues pitcher of the late 1910s and early 1920s. He pitched Rube Foster's Chicago American Giants to the first three Negro National League titles. His Negro leagues record was 41-18. His life was as troubled as his pitching was brilliant. Brown had a hard time staying on the right side of the law. Foster paid a $20,000 bond to get him paroled from a highway robbery conviction so he could join the American Giants. In 1925, he allegedly killed a man in a bar fight and left baseball, on the run from the FBI. He reportedly died in Denver under mysterious circumstances. Brown is a second-team *Courier* poll pitcher.

Given his abbreviated career and his obvious need to keep a low profile—and perhaps to use an alias— it's safe to consider Brown's as one of the rarest important Negro leagues autographs.

Walter S. Brown

Walter S. Brown

Career: 1887, National League of Colored Baseball Clubs

Seeking to build on the popularity of the Cuban Giants in 1887, Brown pulled together six clubs to form the second all-black professional baseball organization, the National League of Colored Baseball Clubs, which was recognized by professional baseball as a minor league. While his intentions were admirable, the enterprise failed after a mere 13 games due to financial difficulties. If nothing else, his bold attempt to bring order to the black game would serve as a template for Foster's Negro National League more than 30 years later. Little biographical information is available on Brown, but historians know that he died before 1907.

Phil Cockrell

Phillip Williams

Born: 1898, Augusta, GA   **Died:** 1951, Philadelphia, PA
Career: 1917–46, Hilldale

Cockrell was the Negro leagues' answer to Burleigh Grimes. He had an excellent spitball that was made all the more effective because he paired it with a wicked fastball. This tandem of pitches kept batters off balance to the tune of 10-1 and 14-2 marks against Negro leagues competition in 1924 and 1925. He entered the second phase of his career in 1929 when he took the helm of the Hilldale club from Oscar Charleston. He managed and pitched with mixed effectiveness until 1935 when he changed hats again and became an umpire. Cockrell was selected for the third-team pitching rotation in the *Courier* poll. He was shot to death in a case of mistaken identity in 1951. Collectors should note that his legal name was Phillip Williams.

"Bingo" DeMoss

Elwood DeMoss

Born: 1889, Topeka, KS   **Died:** 1965, Chicago, IL

Career: 1910–45, Indianapolis ABCs, Chicago American Giants

Combining Gold Glove–caliber fielding, rabbit speed, and punchy hitting, DeMoss earned his place among the elite second basemen in Negro leagues history. He did not hit for high averages, nor did he wallop tape-measure home runs. His forte was his contact hitting. He was considered an outstanding bunter and hit-and-run specialist. DeMoss served as captain of the Chicago American Giants for six years. He was tapped as the second-team second baseman in the *Courier* poll.

"Rap" Dixon

Herbert Albert Dixon

Born: 1902, Kingston, GA   **Died:** 1944, Detroit, MI

Career: 1922–43, Baltimore Black Sox

Dixon's style of play has been likened to that of Tris Speaker. His fielding set the standard by which other outfielders of his era were judged. In 1929 he batted .382 and led the league in triples. The fact that he batted fourth behind Oscar Charleston with the Harrisburg Giants is testimony to his power and prowess at the plate. He finished with a lifetime batting average of .340 in Negro leagues play. He earned a third-team berth in the *Courier* poll. He died of a heart attack at the young age of 42.

Bud Fowler

John W. Jackson

Born: 1858, Fort Plain, NY   **Died:** 1913, Frankfurt, NY

Career: 1877–99, Various Teams

Fowler (John W. Jackson) was the first black professional baseball player. He began his career in 1878, one year after the formation of the first minor-league team. At that time there were no color barriers in baseball, and he played on mixed teams at the beginning of his career. In 1895, he moved to the all-black Page Fence Giants as a player/manager. A versatile player, Fowler played almost every position and reportedly was a solid hitter. He spent the latter days of his career organizing barnstorming clubs. No one knows why he adopted the name Bud Fowler.

Charlie Grant

Charles Grant

Born: 1879, Cincinnati, OH   **Died:** 1932, Cincinnati, OH

Career: 1896–1916, Various Teams

Grant was one of black baseball's early superstars. The hard-hitting, brilliant-fielding second baseman was one of the sparkplugs of the powerhouse Cuban X-Giants clubs of the early 1900s. In 1901, Baltimore Orioles manager John McGraw made an early attempt to break the color barrier by passing him off as Chief Tokahama, an Indian. McGraw's plan collapsed when baseball owners learned of the ruse. Grant resumed his successful career in the Negro leagues.

Pete Hill

J. Preston Hill

Born: 1880   **Died:** 1952, Buffalo, NY

Career: 1899–1926, Philadelphia Giants, Chicago American Giants

Hill was one of the finest all-around outfielders in the formative years of black baseball. In 1911, he hit safely in all but one of the 116 games he played in. He was considered by some to be the game's fastest player until "Cool Papa" Bell claimed the crown in the 1920s. Hill was an exceptional fielder who was gifted with an outstanding arm and pinpoint accuracy. He is credited with a .326 lifetime batting average and is a *Courier* poll second-team outfielder.

"Fats" Jenkins

Clarence Jenkins

Born: 1898, New York, NY   **Died:** 1968, Philadelphia, PA

Career: 1920–40, Harrisburg Giants, New York Black Yankees

Jenkins was a superb slap hitter, a rabbit on the bases, and an ideal leadoff man. He finished his 21-year Negro leagues career with a .334 average. A heady player who was widely praised for his hustle on the diamond, Jenkins earned berths in two East-West All-Star contests. While baseball paid the bills, the 5-foot-7 Jenkins was an outstanding basketball player. He was captain of the great Harlem Renaissance teams, also earning two all-star berths. Jenkins became a boxing referee after retiring.

Grant "Home Run" Johnson

Grant Johnson

Born: 1874, Findlay, OH   **Died:** 1964, Buffalo, NY

Career: 1895–1916, Page Fence Giants, Brooklyn Royal Giants, New York Lincoln Giants

Before there was John Henry Lloyd, Home Run Johnson ruled the roost as black baseball's premier short-stop. Playing for some of the finest clubs of the early era, Johnson consistently topped the .300 mark and provided strong defense up the middle. An intelligent, thoughtful man, Johnson was a fan favorite and remained involved in baseball in various capacities until 1932.

"Slim" Jones

Stuart Jones

Born: 1913, Baltimore, MD   **Died:** 1938, Baltimore, MD

Career: 1932–38, Philadelphia Stars

Buck Leonard thought Willie Foster was an excellent pitcher, "but not as good as 'Slim' Jones." The 6-foot-6 Jones didn't so much throw the ball as he did catapult it. Blessed with a Nolan Ryan–like fastball and an equally devastating curve, he mowed his way to the East's starting role in the 1934 and 1935 all-star games. By 1938, his arm began to falter and his excessive drinking caught up with him. He died of pneumonia at age 25. Despite the brevity of his career, he was named a third-team pitcher in the *Courier* poll.

Oliver "Ghost" Marcelle

Oliver H. Marcelle (Marcel, Marcell)

Born: 1890, Thibedeaux, LA   **Died:** 1949, Denver, CO

Career: 1918–34, Atlantic City Bacharach Giants

The *Pittsburgh Courier* poll cited Marcelle as the Negro leagues' greatest third baseman of all time, ranking him ahead of two Hall of Famers. "He was a ballplayer's ballplayer and the idol of fandom," the *Courier* said of the fiery Creole. The Ghost was a peerless fielder in his prime and particularly adept at quashing bunts. His lifetime batting average was .305. He died of ALS (Lou Gehrig's disease) in 1949. His son, Ziggy Marcelle, also played in the Negro leagues.

Danny McClellen

Dan McClellen

Born: Unknown   **Died:** 1931

Career: 1903–30, Cuban Giants, Philadelphia Giants

McClellen was one of the four great pitchers of the first decade of black baseball. He was a key hurler on the superb Cuban X-Giants clubs of 1903–04 and is credited with black baseball's first perfect game. What McClellen lacked in speed he made up for in savvy, mixing his pitches effectively to keep opposing batters off stride. After his playing days, McClellen embarked on a successful career as a manager. He is listed as the first-team coach and a fourth-team pitcher on the *Courier*'s all-star squad.

Jose Mendez

Jose de la Caridad Mendez

Born: 1887, Cuba   **Died:** 1928, Cuba

Career: 1908–28, Cuban Stars, Kansas City Monarchs, Cuban League

Major-league manager John McGraw characterized Mendez as "Walter Johnson and Grover Alexander rolled into one." The wiry fireballer was one of the dominant pitchers of the 1910s and '20s. He was at the top of his game between 1920 and 1926 when he led the Monarchs to three Negro National League pennants as a playing manager. Mendez died in Cuba of pneumonia in 1928. His death at a young age and the fact that he lived a good portion of the year in Cuba contribute to the scarcity of his autograph.

Bill Monroe

William Monroe

Born: 1876   **Died:** 1915

Career: 1896–1914, Chicago American Giants

Monroe was a central figure in the powerhouse Chicago American Giants lineups of the early 1910s. A fleet-footed runner and fierce batsman, Monroe was one of black baseball's first legitimate superstars. As cleanup hitter for Rube Foster's team, he was touted by Foster as "the most sensational player on the team." Remember, this club featured the likes of Pop Lloyd, Pete Hill, Bruce Petway, and Foster himself. As good as he was offensively, Monroe was arguably even better with the glove.

Bruce Petway

Bruce Petway

Born: 1883, Nashville, TN   **Died:** 1941, Chicago, IL

Career: 1906–25, Leland Giants, Chicago American Giants, Detroit Stars

Petway abandoned his medical school studies to pursue a career behind the plate. By all accounts, the medical world's loss was baseball's gain, as he quickly established himself as one of the sport's premier receivers. Petway, who caught on his knees, was known for his quickness and the pinpoint accuracy of his throws. He was one of the few catchers in the history of the game capable of capturing a stolen base title, as he did in the Cuban winter league in 1912. He was a good, albeit somewhat inconsistent, hitter. Petway is a second-team catcher in the *Courier* poll.

"Spot" Poles

Spottswood Poles

Born: 1889, Winchester, VA   **Died:** 1962, Harrisburg, PA

Career: 1909–23, New York Lincoln Giants

Poles was known as the black Ty Cobb because of his fierce competitive spirit and blazing speed. The speedster is credited with a .400 lifetime batting average in 15 years of play. In 10 exhibition games against major-league opposition he went 25-for-41, good for a .610 mark. If that's not enough, he was considered among the best in the league at fielding his position. He is a fourth-team outfielder in the *Courier* poll.

"Cannonball" Redding

Richard Redding

Born: 1891, Atlanta, GA   **Died:** 1948, Islip, NY

Career: 1911–38, New York Lincoln Giants, Brooklyn Royal Giants

"I would say Satchel Paige was our greatest pitcher," John Henry Lloyd once wrote, "but nobody threw harder than Dick Redding." A consummate power pitcher, Redding's repertoire consisted of two pitches: a fastball and an even-faster ball. He plowed his way to 17 consecutive wins as a rookie. On the Royal Giants, he teamed up with Smokey Joe Williams to form one of the hardest-throwing duos in baseball history. Redding is listed on the Hall of Fame Negro Leagues Committee's original candidates' list.

Sources indicate that Redding was illiterate. He died in a mental hospital under mysterious circumstances and there is still some uncertainty surrounding the exact year of his death. His autograph has been sought by many advanced collectors to no avail.

"Chino" Smith

Charles Smith

Born: 1903, Greenwood, SC   **Died:** 1932

Career: 1925–31, Brooklyn Royal Giants, New York Lincoln Giants

Smith's is black baseball's great "what if" story. During his seven-year career he compiled a phenomenal .423 batting average and similar stellar numbers in exhibitions against teams containing major leaguers. He has been likened to Rod Carew with Ken Griffey Jr.'s power. Satchel Paige called Smith one of the two best hitters he faced. Despite his short career, he was held in such esteem by his peers that he was named a second-team outfielder in the *Courier* poll. Smith's short career and death at age 30 contribute to the scarcity of his autograph.

Collectors should note that there have been several major-league players named Charlie or Charley Smith.

George Stovey

George Washington Stovey

Born: 1866, Williamsport, PA   **Died:** 1936, Williamsport, PA

Career: 1886–96, Cuban Giants, Various Teams

Stovey was the greatest African-American pitcher of the 19th century. He was the mound stalwart for several white semiprofessional clubs before the doors of segregation slammed shut in the late 1880s. The lefty held International League batters to a .167 average in 1886 and compiled a 34-14 record in 1887. That win total remains that league's high-water mark to this day. New York's National League club attempted to sign Stovey, but Cap Anson's objection to the signing of a black player killed the deal.

Collectors should not confuse George Stovey with Harry Stovey (real name: Harry Stowe), a star major-league outfielder who played in the same era. Harry Stovey's autograph is in high demand because he is considered a strong candidate for the Hall of Fame.

Cristobal Torriente

Cristobal (Cristobel/Christobel) Torriente

Born: 1895, Cuba   **Died:** 1938, New York, NY

Career: 1913–28, Chicago American Giants

A compact blend of power and speed, Torriente may be the greatest Cuban home-run hitter of all time. He was the RBI man for Rube Foster's Chicago American Giants clubs of the early 1920s. He led the Negro National League in hitting in 1920 and 1923, finishing his career at .333. He was selected as the first-team right fielder in the *Courier* poll. After his career, Torriente reportedly drank heavily and slipped into obscurity. He died of tuberculosis in New York City.

Two noted Cuban baseball-autograph collectors report that Torriente's autograph is extremely difficult to locate. He was not a prolific signer even in his homeland, where he was a national hero.

Sol White

Solomon White

Born: 1868, Bellaire, OH   **Died:** 1955, New York, NY

Career: 1887–1912 & 1920–26, Various Teams

In 1927, the *Courier* wrote that White "has been close to the game since its beginnings in 1885 and he hardly talks of anything else." Manager, executive, journalist, and great second basemen, White was all of these things and more. He is perhaps best remembered as the author of *Sol White's Official Base Ball Guide*, a 1907 volume that is the earliest major work on black baseball. Following his retirement from the Negro leagues, he coached at his alma mater, Wilberforce University, and continued to make his presence felt through his influential baseball column in the *Amsterdam News*.

George Wilson

George H. Wilson

No biographical information available

Career: 1895–1907, Page Fence Giants, Chicago Union Giants

As historians continue to uncover early black baseball statistics, Wilson is emerging as one of the truly dominating turn-of-the-century hurlers. The most well-documented year of his career was spent with an integrated semipro club in Adrian, Mich., where he posted a 29-4 record and batted .327. In 1907, author Sol White noted that Wilson "...is one of the most difficult to hit among colored pitchers. He is a bronzed 'Waddell' when right." And that's not the only comparison made between Wilson and Rube. The portsider joined the legendary Page Fence Giants (also of Adrian) and was eventually drawn to the Windy City just as that metropolis was establishing itself as the early hub of black baseball. He quickly proved himself as one of Chicago's finest hurlers. Wilson was one of the first Negro leaguers to head to Cuba to play winter ball.

Jud Wilson

Ernest Judson Wilson

Born: 1899, Remington, VA   **Died:** 1963, Washington, DC

Career: 1922–45, Baltimore Black Sox, Homestead Grays, Philadelphia Stars

An intense and powerful competitor, Wilson was among the most feared and respected players in Negro leagues history. He was feared as much for his power at the plate as he was for his hair-trigger temper. Satchel Paige considered him among the best players he ever pitched against. Wilson compiled a lifetime batting average of .345 and was named a third-team *Courier* poll player at both first and third base.

• • •

Other star players whose autographs we are searching for: Walter Ball, Emmett Bowman, Rev Cannady, George Carr, Pelayo Chacon, Morton Clark, Ed Douglas, Bunny Downs, Bill Francis, Nate Harris, Bill Jackman, Jimmy Lyons, Leroy Matlock, Dobie Moore, Jap Payne, Dick Wallace, Frank Warfield, Spec Webster, Frank Wickware, "Doc" Wiley, Gerard Williams, "Stringbean" Williams, Nip Winters, and George Wright.

Appendix E
Selected Reference Sources

The following books, magazines, periodicals, and World Wide Web sites were used as references or provided source or supporting material for this publication.

Books

Anderson, James B. *The Education of Blacks in the South, 1860–1935*. Raleigh, NC: University of North Carolina Press, 1988.

Ashe, Arthur Jr. *A Hard Road to Glory: The African-American Athlete in Baseball*. New York: Amistad, 1993.

Bak, Richard. *Turkey Stearnes and the Detroit Stars: The Negro Leagues in Detroit, 1919–1933*. Detroit: Wayne State University Press, 1994.

Baker, Mark Allen. *Baseball Autograph Handbook*. Iola, WI: Krause Publications Inc., 1991.

Baker, Mark Allen. *Team Baseballs*. Iola, WI: Krause Publications Inc., 1992.

Bankes, James. *The Pittsburgh Crawfords: The Lives & Times of Black Baseball's Most Exciting Team*. Dubuque, IA: William C. Brown Publishers, 1991.

The Baseball Encyclopedia. Ninth Edition. New York: Macmillan Publishing Company, 1993.

Baynes-Cope, A.D. *Caring for Books and Documents*. New York: New Amsterdam Books, 1981

Brashler, William E. *The Story of Negro League Baseball*. New York: Ticknor & Fields, 1994.

Bushing, David. *Sports Equipment Price Guide*. Iola, WI: Krause Publications Inc., 1995.

Chadwick, Bruce. *When the Game was Black and White*. New York: Abbeville Press, 1992.

Craft, David. *The Negro Leagues*. New York: Cresent Books, 1993.

Debono, Paul. *The Indianapolis ABCS*. Jefferson, NC, and London: McFarland Publishing, 1997.

Dixon, Phil with Patrick J. Hannigan. *The Negro Baseball Leagues: A Photographic History*. Mattituck, NY: Amereon House, 1992.

Gilbert, Tom. *Baseball and the Color Line*. New York: Franklin Watts Publishing, 1995.

Gitersonke, Don. *Baseball's Bearded Boys: A Historical Look at the Israelite House of David Baseball Club of Benton Harbor, Michigan*. Las Vegas: Self-published, 1996.

Hamilton, Charles. *Great Forgers and Famous Fakes*. Lakewood, CO: Glenbridge Publishing Ltd., 1996.

Holway, John B. *Black Diamonds: Life in the Negro Leagues from the Men who Lived it*. New York: Stadium Books, 1991.

Holway, John B. *Voices from the Great Black Baseball Leagues*. New York: DeCapo Press, 1992.

Holway, John B. *Blackball Stars, Negro League Pioneers*. New York: Carroll & Graf Publishers, 1992.

James, Bill. *The Politics of Glory: How Baseball's Hall of Fame Really Works*. New York: Macmillan Publishing, 1994.

Kahn, Roger. *The Boys of Summer*. New York: Harper & Collins, 1971.

Lanigan, Neale and Steven Raab. *The Educated Collector's Guide to Buying Autographs*. Self-published, 1995.

Leonard, Buck with James Riley. *Buck Leonard: The Black Lou Gehrig,*

McNeil, William F. *The King of Swat: An Analysis of Baseball's Home Run Hitters from the Major, Minor, Negro and Japanese Leagues*. Jefferson, NC: McFarland & Co. Inc., 1997.

Meyers, Robin and Michael Harris. *Fakes and Frauds: Varieties of Deception in Print and Manuscript.* New Castle, DE: Oak Knoll Press, 1996.

Moffit, Larry, and Jonathan Kronstadt. *Crossing the Line: Black Major Leaguers, 1947–1959.* Iowa City, IA: University of Iowa Press, 1994.

National Baseball Hall of Fame and Museum Yearbook. Cooperstown, NY: National Baseball Hall of Fame and Museum, 1996.

National Baseball Hall of Fame and Museum Yearbook. Cooperstown, NY: National Baseball Hall of Fame and Museum, 1997.

The Negro Leagues Book. Edited by Dick Clark, Larry Lester, and the Negro Leagues Committee of the Society for American Baseball Research (SABR). Cleveland: The Society for American Baseball Research, 1994.

Nickell, Joe. *Detecting Forgery: Forensic Investigation of Documents.* Lexington, KY: The University Press of Kentucky, 1996.

O'Neil, Buck, with Steve Wulf and David Conrads. *I Was Right on Time.* New York: Simon & Schuster, 1996.

Peterson, Robert. *Only the Ball was White.* New York: Prentice-Hall, McGraw Hill, 1984.

Rendell, Kenneth W. *Forging History: The Detection of Fake Letters and Documents.* Norman, OK: University of Oklahoma Press, 1994.

Rendell, Kenneth W. *History Comes to Life: Collecting Historical Letters and Documents.* Norman, OK: University of Oklahoma Press, 1995.

Ribowsky, Mark. *A Complete History of the Negro Leagues, 1884–1955.* New York: Carol Publishing Group, 1995.

Riley, James A. *The Biographical Encyclopedia of the Negro Baseball Leagues.* New York: Carroll & Graf Publishers, 1994.

Rogosin, Donn. *Invisible Men: Life in Baseball's Negro Leagues.* New York: Atheneum, 1983.

Sanders, George, Helen Sanders, and Ralph Roberts. *The Sanders Price Guide to Autographs, Fourth Edition.* Alexander, NC: Alexander Books, 1997.

Shatzkin, Mike, ed. *The Ballplayers.* New York: Arbor House, 1990.

Sullivan, Dean A. *Early Innings: A Documentary History of Baseball, 1825–1908.* Lincoln, NE: University of Nebraska Press, 1995.

Total Baseball. Edited by John Thorn and Pete Palmer. New York: Warner Books, 1991.

White, Sol. *Sol White's History of Colored Base Ball with Other Documents of the Early Black Game, 1886–1936.* Lincoln, NE: University of Nebraska Press, 1995.

Wills, Bret, and Gwen Aldridge. *Baseball Archaeology: Artifacts from the Great American Pastime.* San Francisco: Chronicle Books, 1993.

Zoss, Joel, and John Bowman. *Diamonds in the Rough: The Untold History of Baseball.* Chicago: Contemporary Books, 1996.

World Wide Web Sites and Multimedia Presentations

National Baseball Hall of Fame and Museum
http://www.baseballhalloffame.org

The Negro Leagues Collector's Site
http://ourworld.compuserve.com/homepages/mkolleth

Negro Baseball Leagues
http://www.blackbaseball.com

Negro Leagues Baseball Online Archives
http://www.infi.net/%7Emoxie/nlb/nlb.html

Shadowball: Remembering the Negro Leagues
http://www.negro-league.columbus.oh.us/

Skilton's Baseball Links: Negro Leagues Section
http://www.baseball-links.com/negro.shtml

CD-ROM: Complete Baseball, The Essential Major League Baseball Guide, Microsoft, 1995 Edition

Public Collections

The Burton Historical Collection,
Detroit Public Library, Detroit.

The Chicago Historical Society, Chicago.

The Effa Manley Collection,
Newark Public Library, Newark, NJ.

The National Baseball Hall of Fame and
Museum, Cooperstown, NY.

The Negro Leagues Baseball Museum,
Kansas City, MO.

The Pennsylvania Historical Society,
Philadelphia.

Oberlin College Archives, Oberlin, OH.

Sequin Public Library, TX.

About the Authors

Kevin Keating is the owner of Quality Autographs & Memorabilia of Virginia. A baseball autograph collector since the age of 10, he has amassed more than 100,000 signatures, some of which have been featured in newspapers such as *The Washington Post*. Part of the collection is currently on display at the National Sports Gallery in Washington, D.C. At the time of this writing, Keating owns at least one sample of all but one of the members of the national Baseball Hall of Fame.

Keating currently serves as a player memorabilia agent for such notables as New York Yankee legend Whitey Ford, with whom he founded the company "Whitey's" in 1998. Keating is also a frequent television and radio guest on topical autograph and hobby subjects, and he is considered to be a leading authority on autograph authentication. He has published multiple articles on various topics and currently co-authors "The Way It Was," a vintage-autographs column for *Tuff Stuff*, the national sports collectibles magazine. His work as an autograph authenticator includes major auction houses as well as The Topps Co., a baseball card manufacturer.

In 1982, Keating graduated from the United States Military Academy at West Point where he concentrated on Chinese Language and Far East Asian Studies. His Army training and qualifications also include Airborne and Ranger schools. He left the service in 1988 and moved to Alexandria, Va., where he currently resides.

Michael Kolleth is a lifelong baseball memorabilia and autograph collector who specializes in Hall of Fame and Negro leagues collectibles. Portions of his collection are on display at various museums around the United States, including the National Sports Gallery in Washington, D.C.

Kolleth is a contributing writer for The Vintage and Classic Baseball Collector magazine. He also co-authors, with Keating, "The Way It Was" column every month in *Tuff Stuff* magazine. He is a consultant to several sports autograph companies and auction houses on Internet-related issues.

Kolleth holds a bachelor's degree from Michigan State University and master's degree from the University of Cambridge, England. He lives and works in Switzerland.

Contact the Authors

Readers who have questions or comments about this book or Negro leagues autographs in general can contact the authors by e-mail at bookquestions@altavista.net.